Battered women as survivors

Violence against women knows no national, ethnic, or class boundaries. For every woman among the thousands sheltered, another is turned away. Many abused women are eventually killed by their mates.

Why do 'battered women' stay? Why are their violent partners allowed to stay? How do abused women transform themselves from victim to survivor? What is the connection between victimization, a society's values, and its social policies and practice?

Battered Women as Survivors addresses these and other questions in an urban (USA) field study of battered women and their social network members. In a life history perspective, using values and network analysis, it uncovers the social context of a 'secret' crime against women and reveals the relationship between personal crisis and traditional attitudes toward women, marriage, the family, and violence.

This book breaks new ground by redirecting our attention beyond victim-blaming and the medicalization of violence to understanding battered women as survivors who manage multiple crises despite public inattention to their plight. From analysis of the women's struggles with violence and its aftermath, Hoff proposes a new crisis paradigm, which underscores the sociocultural aspects of crisis originating from violence.

Through its multi-methods approach, this book bridges gaps between academics and activists, and between feminist and mainstream researchers. It illustrates a non-exploitative approach to research with disadvantaged groups by engaging battered women as 'collaborators' rather than mere 'informants'.

This highly researched book moves beyond the question, "Why do battered women stay?" and proposes that we ask instead "Why should victims – rather than their assailants – be expected to leave?" It underscores the need for change in attitudes, public policy, and professional practice to prevent violence, and to reduce its damaging effects on women, children, men, and all of society.

It will be of interest to those working in the social sciences, women's studies, social work, health and mental health professions, as well as to women's advocates and the general reader.

Battered women as survivors

Lee Ann Hoff

London and New York

First published 1990

Reprinted 1991 and 1993
by Routledge
11 New Fetter Lane, London EC4P 4EE

Simultaneously published in the USA and Canada by Routledge
29 West 35th Street, New York, NY 10001

Laser set by NWL Editorial Services
Langport, Somerset, TA10 9DG

Printed and bound in Great Britain by
Mackays of Chatham PLC, Chatham, Kent

British Library Cataloguing in Publication Data
Hoff, Lee Ann
  Battered Women as survivors
  1. United States. Battered women
  I. Title
  364.1'5553

Library of Congress Cataloging in Publication Data
Battered Women as survivors / by Lee Ann Hoff.
      p.   cm.
Includes bibliographical references.
1. Wife abuse–United States–Case studies. 2. Abused
women—United States–Case studies. I. Title.
HV6626.H63   1990   89–70148
362.82'92'0973–dc20   CIP

ISBN   0-415-04394-8 (hbk)
        0-415-04395-6 (pbk)

To victims, survivors and their advocates

Contents

Contents

Figures and tables

Preface

When I was deeply involved in the work this book describes, a colleague asked if I was embarrassed to be researching such a popular topic. The question carried the implicit stigma of problem-oriented research, in contrast to more strictly 'theoretical' issues. Although social scientists might be interested in this query for what it suggests about progress in social theory building, most battered women and their advocates would interpret it as belittling their concerns, or dismiss it as irrelevant to the issue of women's safety and equality.

This book documents the results of my collaborative study with battered women focusing particularly on their interaction with their mates and social network members. From the perspective of their life-histories, it reveals why the women stayed and eventually left their violent mates; what family members, friends, and professionals did or did not do for them and why; and what happened once they left the violent relationship and a shelter.

What emerges from these women's accounts is a view of them as survivors who struggled courageously with little network support to extract themselves and their children from the tragic results of their victimization. During the time spent with these women and their families, I observed their transformation from victims to survivors. And, because of their unique role in helping me complete the research, I concluded that they were much more than 'informants' or study participants; the women and their shelter advocates were research collaborators who made an unparalleled contribution to understanding their lives and the society that permitted their victimization. The women's experiences and their collaboration in the research process provided a dramatic perspective for the tension between academics and activists concerned with battered women. This research reveals why activists have been so suspicious of academics, but also demonstrates that such divisions between groups working on a common problem need not continue.

The book's four parts correspond to the phases in the women's life histories. The first part situates the study with background issues and the research approach, and details the periods before and during the violent episodes the women experienced, including the process of leaving violent relationships and moving from victim to survivor roles. Part II includes analysis of the social interaction and values of both the battered women and their social network members regarding women, marriage, the family, and violence.

Part III addresses the women's experience after leaving a violent mate. For most of the women, this period consisted of living in a shelter for several weeks. The problems of battered women and their children, including poverty and homelessness, are examined, as are the effects of violence against women beyond the crisis aspects of battering. Contemporary rites of passage to a violence-free life and to parenting roles arc also examined.

Part IV summarizes the research results and addresses theoretical and methodological, as well as public policy and human service practice implications of the study. The Epilogue reveals the women's lives through follow-up interviews five years later. An Appendix elaborates on theoretical and methodological facets of the study introduced in Chapter 1. Unlike most research reports, this material is placed at the end instead of the beginning, since it is of greatest interest to social scientists, whereas the book as a whole is intended for both professionals and lay-persons – academics, clinicians, and programme administrators, social activists, and any woman or man concerned about violence.

As I publicly thank all who helped with this work, I am reminded again of a pivotal message of this research: women need a chance to speak, to be heard, and to be acknowledged in the public domain. Yet, precisely because battering has been treated as a taboo topic, the chief collaborators in this study remain subject to stigmatization; thus, ironically, I cannot name them in this public statement. Though these women, their families, and other network members have chosen to remain anonymous, without them this work would never have been born.

Since the victims of violence cannot be publicly named, I acknowledge other collaborators only generally as well. These include the women of Woman House, whose dedicated work provides shelter and other life essentials to battered women and their children in spite of limited public support. Various academic colleagues made valuable contributions by their thoughtful response to my critique of the traditional knowledge system and approaches to researching value-laden topics. In this, they represent the truest understanding of academics' role in fostering the discovery of new knowledge about old problems.

Finally, my personal network of family and friends supported me in social, emotional, and material ways that represent the ideal of what social networks are all about. Since no public or private grant money was obtained to support this work, I am especially grateful to friends and colleagues who, because they believed in the study's importance, sustained me in numerous ways while I completed it with personal resources. Special thanks also go to those who read this lengthy manuscript and provided valuable feedback at various stages of its production. Each of you know who you are and how much you have helped. I thank you. In spite of all this help, I am, of course, responsible for any limitations of this work.

Lee Ann Hoff
January 1990

Acknowledgements

The author acknowledges permission from Addison-Wesley Publishing Company for figures 4.1 and 4.3 respectively which have been taken from *People in Crisis*, 3rd. edn. (1989) by Lee Ann Hoff.

Part I

Battered women: private struggles against a public problem

Chapter one

Reconciling the personal and political through collaborative research

Introduction

'Why do battered women stay?' has become the most frequently asked question in both academic and everyday circles, now that the topic of violence against women has emerged from hundreds of years of silence. Such silence signalled the belief that battering was a private matter between partners, a manifestation of the dichotomy between personal privacy and public interest that has dominated western thought regarding the family and sexual relations. Traditionally, man was in charge at home and abroad, while woman was to fulfil her 'natural' destiny as reproducer and nurturer of children and men. One consequence of this social arrangement is that women victimized by their mates have had to assume personal responsibility for a domestic problem that in reality extends well beyond the family, embracing all of society's institutions and values.

Traditional ideology supports oppressive social arrangements based on sex, race, and class. From such an ideology flows logically the tendency to blame a battered woman for her victimization by asking why *she* does not leave. Furthermore, the dominant ideology creates a climate that represses the probability of asking more appropriate questions about violence against women: 'Why are men violent? Why are women so easily victimized? Why are violent men *allowed* to stay?' And, after intensive socialization of women to think of their 'proper' place as the home, 'Why should they, the victims – rather than their assailants – be expected to leave?'

In such a climate millions of victimized women have learned survival tactics, largely through their personal effort and close ties with other women. Many others, though, continue to lose their lives or homes because of their husbands' or lovers' violence, partly because many still view this public issue as a 'private' spousal matter. For most women, violence or its threat continues to be a central issue of

3

physical, psychological, and social survival.

Academics and human service professionals have recently taken an interest in the topic of wife abuse. But professionals began to address the issue only when grassroots activists – many of them former battered women – had brought it to public attention, and demonstrated that wife abuse was one result of unequal power relations between women and men, rather than the assumed psychopathology of women who seek their own victimization.

Currently, diverse attitudes and agendas regarding wife abuse are revealed when battering is publicly discussed. Activists are primarily concerned with protecting women and changing the political and social conditions that contribute to wife abuse. Human service professionals, in contrast, ordinarily assume an apolitical posture when offering assistance to abused women. They may diagnose the problem in psychiatric terms, thereby avoiding the social ramifications of a woman's plight. Academics' major goal is to produce new knowledge through research, implying that the activists' political goals contradict the 'objective' pursuit of knowledge.

When examining the lives and interactions of particular women with their violent mates and social network members, the dichotomies and conflicts between activists, human service professionals, and academics become visible. This book reports on a field study with women who experienced violence from their mates, left them, and rebuilt their lives free of violence – usually with little formal assistance.

The central concern of this research is to trace the influence of values and social support on battered women, as expressed through a woman's social network. Several related issues, however, influenced the development and shape of this study.

Background issues

Researchers do not usually make contextual concerns explicit. But in this study several contextual issues were pivotal both to the problem of access and to the secondary effects of the research process described by the women in this study. These issues influenced the study's theoretical underpinnings, the collaborative multi-methods I chose, and the outcomes of the research.

Mainstream and feminist research

The first contextual question involved the polarization between mainstream and feminist researchers on the topic of violence against women. Broadly, mainstream researchers follow the positivist tradition in social science. They emphasize causal explanations of violence, and favour, but do not limit their analysis to, hypothesis testing through sophisticated quantitative techniques. Some traditional social scientists may express feminist sympathies, but nevertheless attempt to explain social behaviour 'objectively', without critiquing patriarchy (Yllo and Straus 1981). Feminist[1] researchers, on the other hand, are closer to the interpretive tradition and conflict theory. They focus on the socially constructed political, economic, and cultural *context* in which they believe violence against women flourishes with implicit social approval, and emphasize qualitative methods such as interactional, historical, and political analyses (e.g. Rapp 1978; Dobash and Dobash 1979; Stark, Flitcraft, and Frazier 1979; Elshtain 1981; Oakley 1981a; Smith 1987; Yllo and Bograd 1988).

Even in academic circles that are not polarized along feminist lines, theorists such as Giddens (1979: 234) note the 'disarray' that characterizes contemporary social theory. Social analysis can no longer be conducted according to a single grand theory such as structural-functionalism or general systems theory (Bernstein 1978; Giddens 1979; Berger and Kellner 1981; Knorr-Cetina and Cicourel 1981). The theoretical proliferation is evident in philosophical debates about the nature of social explanation, social action, and actors. Explanations of violence and victimization must be considered in the context of these debates (Winch 1958; Giddens 1979).

The nature of social explanation

The legacy of positivist social science has serious ramifications for constructing theories and researching violence. It is commonplace, for example, to look for 'causes' of domestic violence by asking questions such as: 'Why do some men beat their wives?' or, 'Why do battered women stay?' Lay and professional opinion often imply that drinking, unemployment, stress, or mental illness are the motivating 'causes' of domestic violence.[2] Yet, even if alcoholism, stress, mental illness, etc., are factors contributing to violence, to cite them as 'causes' is reductionist. It is therefore important to specify the sense in which 'cause' is being used.

One assumption in this research is that a cause-and-effect interpretation, paradigmatic of the natural sciences, is inadequate to explain a human, context-laden phenomenon such as violence. Therefore, in response to the question: 'Why do battered women stay?' this study looked for *reasons* that might clarify the *meaning* of some women's behaviour, rather than *causes* that *determine* it. Such an approach assumes that social science is different, not only in *degree* but in *kind*, from the natural sciences (Winch 1958).

The nature of social action and actors

Assumptions about the nature of social action and actors flow from assumptions about the nature of social explanation. If social phenomena cannot satisfactorily be explained in the causal framework of the natural sciences, then the nature of social action and human actors similarly defy causal explanations. Thus, a person who is physically attacked is not merely a helpless victim, and the attacker is not merely an irresponsible savage. Rather, human beings, who by nature are rational, capable, and governed by cultural rules, are engaging in social action whose sum is much more complex than individual behaviours. They are therefore responsible for their actions in various situational contexts, although consciousness may be clouded and responsibility mitigated by certain social, cultural, and/or personal factors, e.g. insanity or self-defence.

Theory and practice

A second issue which influenced this research concerns the gap between theoreticians and practitioners regarding violence against women. On the one hand, there are women scholars in various academic disciplines struggling to develop research-based feminist theory to answer questions and inform practice around women's issues (e.g. Chodorow 1978; Oakley 1981a; Wardell, Gillespie, and Leffler 1981; Gilligan 1982). On the other hand, feminist activists are concerned primarily with the political process and social-structural change to improve women's overall status and reduce their personal pain. Among these activists are women who establish and operate refuges for battered women (e.g. Warrior 1978; Schechter 1982).

Some activist women who are suspicious of academics, researchers, and professionals clearly illustrate the distance between these two groups. They are often indifferent about whether scholars are feminist, traditional, or anti-feminist, and some oppose research because they feel it unfairly 'uses' women, regardless of who is conducting it. This significant gap between academics and activists is dramatized by what I have called the 'problem of access' in studying violence in a naturalistic setting. The fundamental issue is whether researchers exploit disadvantaged or powerless groups, and how research methods may result in such exploitation.

As I considered this problem, three things became clear. First, I was caught in the middle of an historical struggle between theorists and practitioners over an issue of women's rights and how to interpret and correct violence against them, and related concerns. Second, what women in the practice field needed was not more theoretical rhetoric, but rather a *demonstration* of how research might be carried out so that the results would be useful without exploiting those being researched. Third, if I eventually succeeded in completing this study, it would probably yield new insights into the relationship between theory and practice and into methods of researching sensitive political issues. (See Appendix for further discussion of the access problem.)

Social network concepts and intervention

The third issue affecting this research was the disjunction between social network concepts and how they were applied to troubled people and members of their social networks. A vast body of social science and clinical research[3] underscores the need for support from natural and formal network members. Yet human service practitioners usually focus on the distressed *individual* rather than the group of which the troubled person is a member. Such an emphasis reflects the pervasive influence of the medical model in health and human service practice, which stresses the individual rather than social aspects of problems (Hoff 1989: Chapters 2 and 5).

This dominant individualized approach to clinical practice in western cultures is particularly significant for victims of violence, since the source of their victimization is predominantly family members, intimates, and other network members. Thus, while one's social network may be the most reliable source of support and aid during crisis, those network members are also the source of one's greatest risk of assault from cradle to grave (FBI 1982). The failure of human service practitioners to incorporate these social factors into clinical practice has contributed to the process of 'blaming the victim' (Ryan 1971).[4]

Interrelationship between person, problem, theory, and method

The fourth issue consisted of the relationship between the person of the researcher, the problem, the theory guiding the research, and methods of study. Basically, the topic of violence and theories about it, together with my critical perspective, led me to conclude that research methods, especially those claiming to be objective and value-free, may not only be part of the problem, but raise ethical questions as well. These interrelated factors also influenced my multiple-methods approach to the topic. Here I have extended Reinharz' (1979) notion of the relationship between the person, the problem, and the method. Reinharz and others (e.g. Watson-Franke 1980; Wallston 1981; Geigen 1982) urge researchers to examine the extent to which their values influence their choice of research topics and methods.

The person

As the person doing this research, I was prepared as a psychiatric nurse clinician with a crisis speciality, as well as a social scientist. The feminist perspective informing my clinical and academic work, moreover, produced a deep concern about the gaps between feminist theory and practice, and between mainstream and feminist research. To successfully bridge some of these gaps required close attention to defining the topic and choosing appropriate research methods.

The topic

Historically, researchers' approaches to the topic of violence have varied from 'selective inattention' (Dexter 1958; Gelles 1974), to medicalized definitions, to a political interpretation of the problem (Dobash and Dobash 1979; Stark, Flitcraft, and Frazier 1979; Schechter 1982: 215). My selection of this topic clearly arose from my activist concern for abused women. Accordingly, my theoretical approach to it accords with the feminist definition of the problem; that is, one of power relations between women and men. Implied, however, within this power disparity is the notion that women are not violent and that they are innocent victims and amoral beings. This view contrasts with research that suggests that men and women are equally violent (Straus, Gelles, and Steinmetz 1980).

Such 'evidence' seems to weaken the view of women as 'innocent victims'. But the issue is more complex than it appears. The so-called 'equality' between male and female violence in these data refers to 'incidence' of violent acts without specifying the *context* of the violence or the degree of resultant injury. These researchers add that in most instances women's violence is usually in self-defence; physical injury rarely results; women are in a weaker, more vulnerable position; and therefore first priority should be given to aiding beaten wives (Straus, Gelles, and Steinmetz 1980: 43–4).[5]

These contextual circumstances also suggest that, even though there is real power disparity between women and men (which calls for social action), women are not merely passive victims. And indeed, this research and other work (e.g. Dobash and Dobash 1979) reveals that, in spite of brutalization and lack of social support, battered women are long-term survivors in violent marriages, and many do eventually leave such relationships. Nevertheless, the customary tendency to report decontextualized statistical data is central to the antagonistic relationship between academics and activists that was uncovered in this study.

The theories

The polarization between feminist and mainstream researchers can be traced partly to differing theoretical orientations. Traditionally, explanations of violence against family members derived from general violence and aggression theories in non-family settings (Wolfgang 1958; Goode 1971: 624–36). In 1979, Gelles and Straus made the first attempt to develop a theoretical framework specific to the study of family violence. They reviewed three categories of theories: intra-individual, social-psychological, and social-cultural. From a feminist perspective, sociocultural and political factors are *central* to an interpretation of violence that does not imply the victim's collusion in the violence. To say that violence can be traced to the victim's psychological characteristics is simply to blame the victim.[6] These topical issues and theoretical arguments are considered further in relation to 'method'.

The method

Both the 'context' and 'incidence' of maltreatment suggest different definitions of violence and help to define appropriate research methods. Gelles and Straus (1979: 554–5) discuss the confusion of theoretical and ideological concerns around aggression and violence and attempt to solve the problem with a 'purely behavioral' definition: 'it [violence] is a physical act [of aggression]' which must be separated from its social meaning. In a medical framework, violence is often viewed as a 'symptom' of a personality or mental disorder or as a response to stress. Feminists, on the contrary, see these social meanings of violence as clear manifestations of the unequal power relations between men and women.

This research defines violence as a form of social action intended to inflict physical harm on another person. To understand this form of social action, the *meaning* of physical acts of aggression cannot be separated from the acts themselves, as is suggested in mainstream social science research. Since meanings are as variable as the number of human beings capable of violent behaviour, it is not sufficient merely to establish the incidence of violent acts women experience. Rather, it is crucial to understand the processes and *context-specific meanings* of violent social interaction, including the relationship between verbal and physical aggression.

Accordingly, it became evident that an interpretive understanding of violence against women demanded a research method other than a causal analysis of violent acts between family members (Cicourel 1964; Phillips 1973; Truzzi 1974; Reinharz 1979). Feminist critiques of mainstream social science research underscore this conclusion

Private struggles against a public problem

(e.g. Dobash and Dobash 1979: 25). Also, Oakley (1981a: 30–61), drawing on Miller's (1976: 6–8) discussion of the philosophical, moral, and scientific influences of dominant groups, describes traditional interviews with women as part of a methodological ideology which masks the superordinate/subordinate research situation under the guise of obtaining 'objective' scientific data. The paradigmatic interviewer-interviewee relationship in mainstream social science thus appears to complemnent the dominant/submissive theme of traditional male/female relationships. In contrast, feminist interviewing implies a *collaborative* relationship between interviewer and interviewee, and an openness to what develops from being 'inside the culture' of the person being interviewed.[7]

These issues revealed how the purposes, values, and politics of the society in which researchers and practitioners with victims and perpetrators of violence claim membership influence their research and practice. Whenever critics charge ideological bias, however, and propose other approaches, there is the tendency to claim that they are exempt from ideology. It is important to note that feminists do not *claim* to be value-free. They assert, rather, that the values informing research be made explicit, regardless of one's theoretical orientation. Feminists (and increasingly certain mainstream researchers) assert that values are inherent in *all* research, whether or not these values are made explicit by the researchers. For example, most researchers accept the relationship between violence against women and value-laden concepts such as 'sexism' and 'patriarchy'. What is most objectionable for critics of some mainstream theories is the *claim* of objectivity and the witting or unwitting use of theory to advance vested political interests, in this case male privilege and a 'naturally' subordinate position of women in the social structure.[8]

Accordingly, the ideological underpinning of *all* research was assumed, including scholarship claiming to be scientific and value-free. Even the scientific method itself is culturally and historically situated in the western tradition of rational discourse (Keller 1983, 1985). In this tradition, rationality has been associated predominantly with the public, male domain, while emotional life has been defined as the proper domain of women and domestic life (Cloward and Piven 1979; Gerhardt 1979; Elshtain 1981; Barrett and McIntosh 1982; Harding and Hintikka 1983). These arguments about values are central to this research where I have made explicit my assumptions through the research and reporting process. Basic to this research, then, is my clear recognition that the study of violence against women is not simply a matter of 'objective scientific analysis'.

Research focus

From the examination of these issues several research questions emerged:

What is the link between individual women's distress and crisis (micro factors) and broader social and cultural issues (macro factors), e.g. common values and beliefs about women?

What characteristics (structural and interactional) of a battered woman's social network might explain why violence occurs, why women often remain in violent relationships, and why they may or may not return to a violent relationship following relief from violence in an emergency shelter for battered women?

To what extent are social network members (family, friends, neighbours, health and human service workers, clergy, police) the practical avenues for expressing and reinforcing a society's values and beliefs about women, marriage, the family, and violence?

What part does the economic situation of particular battered women and their mates play in the continuation or disruption of violence between them?

My working hypothesis was that a woman's social network might constitute the link between the microcosm of an individually troubled woman and the macro-structure of social institutions that uphold values and norms about women, marriage, the family, and violence. Depending on what values a woman's network members held and their material resources, it seemed probable that the network would either be a source of aid and support, or a hindrance to a battered woman in distress. I was especially concerned to uncover the *processes* involved in a battered woman's decision to remain in a violent relationship, to return to such a relationship after relief from violence in a shelter, or to leave and begin anew.

A central concern of this research was a *context-specific* interpretive analysis, *not* hypothesis testing through statistical techniques. I looked for the meanings of the victim's experience from the women themselves, rather than seeking causal determinations about why battered women make the choices they do. I assumed that subjective accounts provide data as valid in an interpretive framework as survey designs where individuals are rendered invisible in aggregate statistics. Another assumption was that the complex factors influencing any battered woman's decisions and survival tactics cannot be carefully analysed apart from the larger contexts in which the violence and its aftermath have occurred.

I also wanted to examine the relationship between battering and the social concepts of sexism and patriarchy. In this study 'sexism' describes behavioural patterns complementing a social structure of male dominance in which individual men can behave violently against women with tacit social approval. Sexism and a patriarchal society are not seen as primary causes, but rather as *contexts* in which men may choose violence to resolve conflicts. Similar contextual factors, I thought, would influence what natural and formal network members did or did not do for a battered woman in crisis.

A collaborative research method

These questions were examined in a one-year naturalistic study with nine battered women and 131 social network members, plus three other battered women who acted as methodological consultants.[9] While the number of women participants is small, this limitation is offset by the understanding gained from an in-depth study of the women with their social networks over time. These women were from diverse ethnic and class backgrounds, most of them homeowners before being battered, and most in poverty afterwards. (See the Appendix for more details about the women and interaction with them throughout the study.) Qualitative data were obtained through participant-observation, in-depth interviewing of the women and social network members, as well as personal journals including poetry.

Contributing data and insights were obtained from the following sources: weekly staffing in a battered women's shelter and attendance of committee meetings and various special gatherings of shelter staff over a two-year period; participant-observation in police patrol units prior to formal initiation of the study. Additionally, eight staff members from the shelter were interviewed. Four of these were former battered women, four were unpaid volunteers.

Information from these sources, the women, and their social network members revealed the women's survival tactics, why the women stayed with and eventually left violent mates, and what their social network members did and did not do for them and why. What happened to them and their children over time was revealed through follow-up interviews five years after the initial study.

To understand the women demanded a research methodology which did not leave them feeling exploited. This issue is prominent among contemporary anthropologists and other researchers. But among feminist activists for battered women, understanding violence from the women's perspective is critical in explicating the relationship between the personal and political. Sensitivity to this issue led me not merely to 'use' battered women's stories to do 'my' research, but to engage them in a research partnership that departed from the usual hierarchical relationship between researcher and researched (Miller 1976; Oakley 1981a).

Nevertheless, research demands an empirical basis if its claims about the influence of sexism and patriarchy are to be distinguished from a journalistic account of battered women's biographies. Structured interviewing and systematic observation was therefore planned; it occurred mostly in the women's homes or the homes of relatives. Some interviews took place in my home, in coffee shops, and on two occasions, in the shelter. Participant-observation occurred in the women's homes during their interaction with children, family and/or friends; during ritual celebrations (e.g. baby showers, birthdays, divorce party); and at hearings in courts, welfare and housing offices, State legislative sessions, driving to and from outings in the park or at the ocean, coffee shops, or an occasional meal at my house. Besides a car, the telephone –local and long-distance – was a central means of keeping frequent and regular contact with the study participants.

The effort produced rich data and a depth of insight into the lives of those who were able to contribute to this research. The women's participation in this study varied in context, length, and extent. With a few of the women and their families the involvement was intense and extensive. Time constraints and privacy issues in a few instances prevented such involvement with all the study participants. A total of 367 direct contact hours (plus 20 hours for follow-up interviews) were spent with the women and their network members, and another 60 hours in direct interviewing of network members. The time span for contacts ranged between six and fifteen months. A combination of structured and unstructured approaches were used to explore mental health and stress, values, and social network factors.[10]

The use of formal tools may appear to contradict the naturalistic approach to this study. It is not merely the use of formal instruments, however, that results in exploitative, decontextualized research. For this study the research tools were demystified and developed in active collaboration with the project participants to ensure that the categories and questions were relevant to the women's experiences. While such an effort should be made in any good survey instrument, the instruments for this study were used primarily to guide in-depth interviewing. Since the tools were freely discussed between the researcher and those interviewed, they helped the women in their self-assessments. For example, one woman, after completing the Social Network Questionnaire, saw how many people in her family

network she could not turn to in crisis and realized anew the seriousness of her problem and her need for institutional assistance.

Interpreting the women's accounts

The collaborative approach also demanded that data analysis and interpretation of the women's accounts be presented in a way that
would illuminate their lives and the society in which they were victimized, while not compromising the activist goals of the women and
their advocates. Additionally, the participants and shelter advocates
were invited to read and provide feedback on the entire semi-final report. This approach recognizes the important relationship between
the women's own language and the language of theory, research reports, and human service practice concerning violence against
women. If scientific reports obscure the voices of those researched,
some of the study's value is also lost. I started with the assumption,
now common among social researchers, that knowledge from research should benefit those researched.

Unravelling the relationship between the personal and the political, and synthesizing the women's accounts with formal social
analysis, was a crucial challenge. Since the knowledge system is such
a powerful agent of domination (e.g. Ehrenreich and Ehrenreich
1970; Freidson 1970; Ehrenreich 1978; Elshtain 1981), it seemed
critical to bridge the gaps between feminist and mainstream social
science analysis of violence between the sexes. This task demanded
diverse theoretical sources. Just as the problem of violence crosses
class, race, and ethnic boundaries, so should interpreting it draw on
various theories.

Accordingly, the tragic results of violence and the courageous responses of these battered women were analysed using concepts from
several sources: critical theory and the sociology of knowledge, symbolic interaction and crisis theory, network concepts,
ethnomethodology, and feminist and anthropological analysis of kin-
ship, ritual, and belief systems. Overall, this study favours the
perspective of socialist and psychoanalytic feminism along with critical sociology and complementary theories (Berger and Luckmann
1967; Gergen 1982).[11] Those positivist theories based on mechanical,
natural science models that support views of battered women as psy-
chopathologically disturbed and therefore responsible for their
victimization are given little credence. The Appendix contains further detail about the theoretical framework of this research.

Unlike traditional research reports, this book shows how a collaborative approach to researching violence against women can
reconcile differences between activists and academics; can build brid-

ges providing new paths to service for battered women in crisis; and can reveal new, non-exploitative approaches to research on this poignant topic. It also provides a context for revealing how battered women and their advocates can make a unique contribution to the study of this topic if they are respected as research collaborators, not merely as 'subjects' to be analysed by an 'objective' outsider.

The engagement of the women as active collaborators in this study provides an important *context* for this study. The remaining chapters focus on the *content* of the study – the lives of the women and how their personal struggles and triumphs are connected to major social and political concerns today.

Chapter two

Battered women: what life experience reveals

Introduction

The women in this study resemble many other battered women who have shared with researchers the pain of the violence they experienced. Where they differ, though, is in their willingness to share their homes, their struggles with children, housing, money, work, and college after leaving a battering situation. Their own accounts of the struggles, pain, joy, hope, victories, and new beginnings that characterize their lives free of violence provide a broader perspective than could be achieved by focusing solely on the battering phase of their life cycle.

This chapter presents each woman's biographical sketch and evaluations of their life before, during, and after battering, including analysis of abuse during childhood, and the mother–daughter bond. The seventeen items of the Self Evaluation Guide (SEG) provide the framework for this analysis.[1]

Biographical sketches

Karen

Karen, now in her 20s, is the oldest girl in a family of several children. Throughout her childhood years Karen's family was troubled – not enough money, fighting between brothers and sisters, parental illness, poor housing, and general unhappiness. As a child Karen generally felt lonely, afraid, and unloved except by her mother. She cried a lot, always by herself. As a child she dreamed of being a teacher, a mother, and a housewife when she grew up. Since she was 'unsuccessful' as a substitute mother when her mother became ill, successful parenthood became an important goal during Karen's teen years. Karen's brothers were favoured over her. This was dramatized during her mother's lengthy hospitalization when her father chided her but not her brothers for not being responsible enough for the housework. The turmoil of Karen's stormy adolescence continued through her years of early dating and culminated in brutal, life-threatening beatings by her mate over a four-year period. During this time Karen became pregnant by the man who beat her and gave birth to two children. Because the problems and violence increased over time, she deliberately avoided marrying the man, while always hoping he would change.

Karen is now a single parent, a full-time college student, and a homemaker. She has been free of violence for over a year, feels healthy and happy, is succeeding with her triple job of parent, student, and homemaker, and is secure in her goal of becoming a CPA (Certified Public Accountant) and then a lawyer. On the way toward achieving these long-term goals, Karen is considering various approaches to improving her housing situation, including possible collaboration with one of her brothers who often babysits for her. Two other major concerns she has are building her relationship with her children and finding satisfying social relationships with men that avoid earlier pitfalls. Karen also takes part in television and other speak-outs about the plight of battered women.

Loreen

Loreen, now in late adolescence, is the oldest of several children. Her childhood was generally happy though punctuated by the effects of poverty and her father's illness. Loreen was close to her mother, less so to her father. She was aware of favouritism shown to her brothers and expectations of greater responsibility for herself as a girl. Her dream as a little girl was to be an actress. Through her teen years and early dating she was conscious of wanting a baby. Although Loreen's husband was violent with her before they were married, she married him anyway in her late teens, believing that the violence would stop after marriage. When the violence continued through her long-awaited pregnancy, Loreen returned to her parents' home and then to a shelter after less than two years with her husband. After pregnancy complications and the birth of her baby, Loreen considered reconciliation, but eventually decided on divorce when her husband failed to follow through on his various promises and she saw no serious changes in his life of irresponsibility, e.g. no stable job, trouble with the law, etc. Loreen is now a full-time parent and homemaker. She is considering returning to school to become a lawyer as soon as her young child is older. Her recent access to independent housing after living for several months with her parents, plus her successful

17

divorce, have stimulated her to think about additional accomplishments.

Sophia

Sophia is past 30 and is carrying on the strong tradition of her ethnic group by caring for her three children as her primary occupation. Throughout her basically happy childhood and adolescence as the only girl in her family, motherhood was her goal. To the present day she has not wavered from that goal as her destiny in life. What she did not bargain for, however, was that she would have to rear her children as a single parent. Although Sophia's husband had battered his previous wife, she romantically believed that the same thing would not happen to her. The brutal beatings and verbal abuse Sophia suffered over five years culminated in a near-fatal suicide attempt, hospitalization, and refuge in a shelter.

Because of technical legal problems in obtaining her marriage certificate from another country, Sophia's divorce proceedings have been unusually protracted in spite of extensive legal service obtained through a shelter advocate. This delay also complicated the sale of their jointly owned home, one result of which was to deprive her of basic furnishings necessary to care for her children. During this time Sophia's husband went to extraordinary lengths to attempt reconciliation. Cultural differences and Sophia's traditional reliance on family as her major source of support, make her present struggle to succeed as a mother free of violence all the more heroic, since her immediate family is far away. Sophia's success depends mainly on her single-minded determination to divorce her violent husband regardless of the many obstacles she has encountered. When the divorce is finalized, Sophia also expects her marginal housing situation to improve.

Jessica

Jessica, now in her 20s, describes herself as an idyllically happy youngest child, the favourite of her parents as well as of her older brothers and sisters. She and her mother were always very close. No responsibility was expected of her that was not expected of her brothers. In fact, she says that everyone in the family 'spoiled' her. Jessica's only ambition when she grew up was to be 'happy'. Unlike many women, Jessica had no desire to marry though she enjoyed intimate relationships with men. When the man she lived with became violent with her she was more than grateful that she had not married him. Jessica entertained some radical ideas about marriage and the importance of women's financial independence.

Nevertheless, by the time she ended her relationship with the man who beat her, she did not have sufficient financial resources to avoid using a shelter before reestablishing herself. She was unable to find permanent housing for herself and her child beyond 'slum' conditions for several months after leaving the shelter, and so returned to her mother's home temporarily. Jessica is firmly determined never to be financially dependent on a man again. Now that she is free of her violent partner, she maintains her lifelong spirit of independence working as a computer programmer by day and hostess during the evening. She also cares for her child and considers preparing herself for a career in public relations. Jessica's recent move toward housing independent of her mother is an important step in her goals of self-sufficiency.

Ruth

Ruth, now in her mid-20s, grew up in a troubled home. Drinking, violence, poverty, and abuse were observed and suffered by Ruth and others in the family. As the oldest girl, Ruth learned early to survive more or less on her own. Still, she had held onto her early desire to learn and eventually become successful in a professional career. Ruth's hopes lay dormant during the several years she suffered violence at the hands of her husband. Because of her husband's job, during most of the years she was beaten, she was far away from her family. When she finally freed herself from him she began work toward fulfilling her childhood dreams of education and a professional career, while caring for two young children alone. Ruth met serious obstacles, however, in her efforts to build a new life for herself free of violence. She had no permanent residence for several months after leaving the shelter and walked the streets in an advanced stage of pregnancy between short stays in shelters and with relatives. Ruth's family supported her in spite of their own hardship and trouble. Because Ruth was dependent on her family for housing for many months after leaving the shelter, independent housing is basic to Ruth's self-esteem and sense of accomplishment now that she is free of a violent husband.

Eileen

Eileen, the mother of three children, is approaching 30. She was the middle child among several brothers and sisters. Her childhood was marked by the combination of parental illness and devotion. As a 'child of the 1960s' Eileen felt simultaneous attraction to and rebel-

19

lion against the traditional middle-class values of her family. Marriage and children were like magnets drawing her after an interlude of anti-establishment attachments, including a two-year bout with drug addiction. After six years with a violent husband she gravitated back to the mainstay of her support through the years – her original family home. There she continued to suffer – now at the hands of her father and brothers. Her mother, however, was a central figure sustaining her in her career plans and struggles as a single parent. After living in owned housing with her husband, Eileen's forced dependence on her family and her inability to find permanent housing for many months was the source of her greatest concern after leaving the shelter. Following transfers between her parents' home, other relatives, and another shelter, she finally obtained a permanent residence. With that major goal accomplished, Eileen could finally concentrate on her other needs and those of her children after years of abuse and moving.

Naomi

Now in her mid-30s, Naomi was secure and happy as a child. She traces later vulnerability to the death of her mother during her early teens. This major loss was compounded by the expectations that fell on her as the oldest daughter. Naomi describes her parental home as rich in material resources but poor in emotional support and affection once her mother died. Various addictions, especially food, were Naomi's means of killing the pain of the losses and abuse she suffered, initially from her father and later from her husband. Marriage and motherhood seemed like both a natural destiny and an opportunity to leave her parental home.

Naomi's first stay in a shelter helped sensitize her to a new view of herself as a woman, even though she returned to her husband temporarily. When she divorced her violent husband after several years of attempting to make her marriage work, she also set the stage to conquer the addictions she used to deaden her feelings when she was being abused. After a second stay in a shelter, Naomi set out on a path to a new relationship with her several children. Far away from her original family, she created a new 'family' of friends through various peer support groups. She is also planning a career as a CPA and pursuing an artistic hobby.

Financial and housing problems are the major obstacles she has to overcome before these goals can be realized.

Gwen

Gwen, now in her mid-30s and childless, is the only daughter among several children of affluent parents. Her family history includes successful professionals extending over several generations. In spite of such a 'professional' heritage, Gwen was keen to fulfil what she envisioned as her 'destiny' as a mother, choosing a profession that would complement the mother role as much as possible. When Gwen married beneath her social status, it was not surprising, since she seemed to be acting on the subtle but definite message that less was expected of her than of her brothers. Gwen experienced violence remarkably similar to her much poorer sisters for several years at the hands of her husband. In addition to the physical abuse, her husband refused to cooperate in her ardent desire to have a child while he focused on his career development. Gwen's highly successful career was always secondary to motherhood. Yet now, as during the time she was abused, her career continues to sustain her sense of accomplishment, and is the means to financial independence and affluent housing. One of Gwen's current endeavours is to develop a new relationship with a man, free of violence, and enjoying the benefits of career success.

Yvonne

Yvonne, in her mid-30s, is the mother of two. She is one of several children in a family that placed high value on the traditional role of women. When Yvonne succeeded in a dual career as an artist and a health professional, she became something of an outcast in her affluent family that expected women to follow more traditional patterns. Yvonne's marriage to someone her father considered 'beneath' the family, together with her physical distance, eroded the support she might have received from her family when she was beaten for several years by her highly educated (at the doctoral level), professionally visible husband. While Yvonne was financially independent, other barriers – including a serious medical problem – influenced her extensive efforts to free her marriage of violence and avoid divorce. When she left her husband she also left the spacious, beautiful home she and her husband owned for a much smaller residence. Now that she is free of violence, her career success and financial independence are bonuses in her struggle to build a new life for herself in a small community where many people know her and her former husband.

These women reveal their common vision of fulfilling childhood dreams in socially expected roles of wife (or cohabiting companion of a man) and mother. They also have this in common: violence from a husband or lover dramatically and unexpectedly interrupted their normal transition through the life cycle. What they do not have in common are birth order, age, family stability, social class, ethnic identity, educational level, number of children, and psychological traits. How, then, can we explain the violence these women experienced? Central to this study is how the women themselves account for the violence in their lives.

The women's self evaluations

The Self Evaluation Guide (SEG) provides a social-cultural context for considering how the violence a woman experiences might affect her functioning through the life cycle. The women were asked to assess themselves on the seventeen items of the SEG during three phases of their life cycle: before, during, and after experiencing their mates' violence. On the item, Self-acceptance/Self-esteem, for example, the women were asked: 'How did you feel about yourself as a person during the period in your life *before* you were battered?' and then were asked to evaluate their lives in these seventeen topical areas *during* the years they were battered and *after* they were free of the violent relationship.

Comparing the impact of violence on a woman's self-esteem and emotional/mental health status before and after being battered is particularly relevant because it has been commonly assumed that women are battered because of their *own* psychopathology – a form of victim blaming. Such a comparison necessitates distinguishing stress, crisis, and burnout from related concepts of emotional or mental breakdown, or psychopathology (Hoff 1989: 46–51).[2] A particularly violent episode such as battering is usually very stressful, and may lead to emotional *crisis*, which may affect one's ability to cope emotionally, cognitively, or behaviourally. After several such violent episodes and the attendant problems, a woman's stress level may reach the point of chronicity and *burnout*. Burnout is distinguished from crisis by its chronic rather than acute character. If a woman reaches such a stage, the manifest symptoms are frequently feelings of cynicism, anger, and resentment, and poor social performance, making her incapable of coping with the demands of personal and public life. People suffering from burnout often are not aware of the connection between their feelings and behaviour, and the chronic stress they are under. These emotional states, however, though very distressing, should not be confused with emotional and/or mental breakdown, which is a psychopathological condition disrupting basic life functions and usually implying a psychiatric diagnosis.[3] Technically, this condition is referred to as 'psychosis' with accompanying psychiatric labels such as 'schizophrenia'. Analysis of the women's self-evaluations and stress levels before, during, and after battering was expected to situate the women along this spectrum of emotional states in relation to the traumatic event of violence.[4]

Comparative stress levels before, during, and after battering

Comparisons of the women's stress levels or adequacy of life functioning revealed significant differences before, during, and after their experience of violence. Before the battering phase, every woman's self-evaluation indicated low stress levels. During the battering phase, all their evaluations revealed moderate to high stress.[5] After experiencing violence, the women's stress scores again dropped to levels close to the pre-violence phase. Even a preliminary glimpse of the women's lives reveals the considerable stress they suffered from the trauma of battering and living with a violent man. But the data also reveal the women's general coping ability; that is, none experienced emotional breakdown as the term is commonly understood. These stress level evaluations, however, do not uncover the specific elements contributing to their increased stress during this period; nor do they tell us how the women coped.

Examining the women's concept of social support available during traumatic events provides a preliminary interpretation of their self-evaluations. A broad interpretation holds that social support is intrinsic to the human condition. Maslow (1970) speaks of a 'hierarchy of needs' which Hansell (1976) refers to as 'basic social attachments'. If our basic human needs are not met, or if social attachments are threatened or disrupted, a person manifests signals of distress and is vulnerable to emotional crisis (Caplan 1964, 1981; Hansell 1976; Hoff 1989). To be free of traumatic stress, one needs social support throughout the life span (Cobb 1976; Kaplan, Cassel, and Gore 1977; Berkman and Syme 1979). Value systems will largely influence whether and how such support is given and received (Antonovsky 1980).

It is the loss of such basic social attachments and the resultant signals of distress that the women's self-evaluations addressed. The increased stress levels experienced during the battering phase of their lives are related to the threatened or actual disruption of basic social attachments. To the extent that lower stress levels during the pre-battering phase demonstrate adequate functioning in areas considered essential for mental health, these women manifest none of the psychopathological characteristics too often associated with battered women.

This relationship, however, between disruption of basic life functions (physical, social, emotional, and cognitive) and signals of distress is not a simple cause-and-effect phenomenon. Rather, an interactional relationship is suggested. For example, losing a job or residence may result in high stress, which may trigger violence toward self or others, or substance abuse. These behaviours, in turn, may affect one's financial status, inhibit one's ability to perform another job, and/or disturb one's relationship with family. A person victimized by violence experiences a similar interactional relationship between threatened basic life attachments and signals of distress. Suffering another person's violence not only threatens basic survival necessities – physical health and safety, residential security, etc. – but also erodes self-esteem and fosters self-injury. For example, all the women in this study were suicidal after they had been abused by their mates.

If basic social attachments are intact (physical health, high self-esteem, satisfying social role, intimate bonds, mental health, housing and financial security), signals of distress are usually rare. This does not mean the absence of stress. Rather, it means the absence of impaired function through substance abuse, failure to use help, etc. When violence from one's mate is introduced, primary attachments or basic human needs are threatened or disrupted. Distress signals dramatically increase, reflecting a negative effect on the person's physical, social, emotional, and cognitive functioning. Later analysis of individual items on the SEG (e.g. violence experienced, family relationships) supports this interactional principle, as does the women's eventual resolution of crises around battering.

Abuse as children and the 'cycle of violence'

Increased stress levels after battering are more noteworthy when one realizes that seven of the nine women had experienced violence *before* they were battered by their mates. What is the comparative significance of this violence and abuse from someone other than one's spouse?

One popular interpretation of violence is the 'cycle of violence' concept, victimization and perpetration *of* violence which links to abuse as a child. Before these women were battered by a mate, their stress levels were low, even though four of the women were abused sexually as girls. This discrepancy suggests that the effects of childhood and adolescent experiences of violence need to be evaluated more specifically. When asked about 'violence experienced' the women included supposedly 'normal' forms of violence, like physical discipline and sibling fighting, along with sexual abuse.[6] The

women's self-evaluations and interview data about family relationships suggest that the *source* of violence and the *age* at which it
occurred create a significant difference in the relationship between
violence, self-acceptance, and functioning in significant social relationships.

The effects of victimization during childhood and adolescence can
be evaluated by examining three Life Function Areas on the SEG:
self-esteem, family relationships, intimacy; and two Signals of Distress: violence against self and violence against others. Three women
who were sexually abused by their fathers had moderate to high stress
scores on self-esteem, family relationships, and intimacy. The trauma
of such abuse assumes added meaning when compared with the family relations of the women who as children were not sexually abused
by their fathers, but nevertheless experienced some physical violence.
Of the seven women who experienced violence as children, three expressed satisfaction in their relationships with family. One received a
slap from her mother at age 14 for talking back and swearing at her.
Another was frequently assaulted by a violent sister who tore her
skin. Here is how these women describe themselves:

*How would you describe your relationship with your mother when
you were a child?* My mother and I were the best of friends. I talked
with her all the time. She raised me just like her sons. My mother
is fiercely independent. She's a 'take charge' person. My mother
had a very good sense of humour. When I'd threaten to run away
as a little girl she'd say 'I'll help you pack ... We're having roast
shoulder, apple sauce and chocolate cake for dinner.' And I'd say
'O.K. I'll go after dinner.' *Were your parents happy as a couple?*
They appeared to be happy. There probably was some unhappiness because my father moved out when I was five, but he came
back every Saturday and took me out. Whatever unhappiness
there was was kept from me. [This impression was confirmed on
interview with the mother.] *How was your relationship with your
father?* My father was very protective of me. I was his pet, 'his little
angel'. We talked about fun things to do. His friends gave me
money and candy ... I didn't even know there were heavy issues. My
father was an alcoholic but I didn't really know that until I was 20.
Describe a typical evening meal in your home. It was very pleasant.
We had dinner at 5 p.m. We'd giggle and argue about the day's
events. *A typical Sunday, holiday or birthday?* We'd have a big dinner at 3 p.m., watched movies, and talked. Birthdays were happy
occasions for big gatherings and many gifts. *Was there anyone you
felt really close to and could rely on?* Besides my mother I felt close
to my sister Lois who was like a second mother to me. We could

25

talk about anything and did things together. *How did you feel about yourself as a person?* Happy and loved ... I've always thought I was wonderful. *Was there any risk of suicide in your life as a child or adolescent?* Yes, when I was 14 I went through a fantasy with a cord. *What was happening?* It was when I was so unhappy in the boarding school, but my mother finally took me out of it.

Another woman said she felt closest to her mother, that family relationships were 'excellent', that she fell into disfavour only after meeting her future husband. Yet she said her self-esteem during the pre-battering phase was only 'fair', because 'my mother had a very poor self-image'. This woman was a very good performing artist but she got no support from her family. Her family's traditional values regarded her occupation as a human service professional and her performing as a 'dirty' hobby.

Another woman with a low stress level also described her social relationships and self-esteem as 'good to excellent' during her premarital years, despite the fact that her father teased her about 'not having to pay for college for her' because she was a girl.

Though one woman was raped by a stranger when she was 18, her stress scores suggest higher functioning than those who were beaten, raped, or molested by their *fathers* during adolescence. Though she reports that the experience was very traumatic, her description of that rape years later was much less emotionally charged than those of women who describe being molested and raped by their fathers. These accounts suggest that experiencing violence from someone close increases the significance of the event. Violence thus experienced turns one's expectations upside down. Instead of caring and support, one receives attack and exploitation, thus impairing one's self-confidence and sense of belonging in the family and social universe.

The importance of the source of violence is attested to by a woman whom a neighbour sexually assaulted at age 4 and a brother made sexual overtures to at age 10. Here, too, the degree of trauma seems related to the *source* of assault and closeness of the relationship. This woman, for example, recalled that her parents took serious action against the man who abused her, although her parents' failure to *discuss* the incident with her increased her trauma. Emotional trauma from such events is furthermore affected by age and meaning systems. That is, a 4-year-old cannot understand the full significance of adult sexual molestation, whatever the relationship. Often the child will construe the meaning of the events from the reactions of significant adults.

Among the nine women studied, three stand out in terms of age, type, and source of violence. These three women were raped, beaten, or sexually molested by their fathers between the ages of 13 and 16. They had the highest stress levels on three SEG items: self-esteem, family relationships, and intimacy. All their descriptions of their social relationships and self-esteem were much worse than the other women's evaluations. When asked what was the worst thing they could remember about this phase of their lives, these women cited the sexual abuse by their fathers. One woman, who was sexually molested by her father at ages 4, 8, and then again at 14, focused almost exclusively on the last incident. During her participation in this study she referred to this incident several times, suggesting the need to 'get it out', since she had never divulged it except to a close girlfriend. Until the sexual abuse she had always respected her father, even though he was always criticizing her. For example:

'What do you think, you're better than others?' He was always demanding things and yelling 'Why is this house like this? Why isn't supper cooked?' I feared him, though we could talk. My brothers were never pushed to do anything. They were supposed to do dishes but they hid them and got away with it. My father beat me until I was 15. One time he called me a fucking whore. That really hurt me.

After the incident she avoided her father whenever she could. Earlier this woman described her relationship with her mother as follows:

I was her first little girl ... My mother really loved me. We spent time talking. She didn't have any unreasonable expectations of me. She told my father he was too hard on me. My mother was not happy. She always put others before herself. It seemed like my mother was just an object to be poked at sexually.

Asked why she didn't tell her mother about her father's sexual advance, this woman replied that her mother had a nervous breakdown when she was 13 and again when she was 15. At this time the family broke up and all the children were placed in foster homes: 'We were all miserable. I felt I had to take care of the family but I hated it when people said "Oh, she's such a good girl helping her father and mother." ' When asked how she felt about herself as a person during childhood, she said: 'Lonely and afraid ... To an extent I liked myself, but I didn't have enough confidence in myself. I felt loved by my mother but felt less of a person around other people.' Questioned about how she felt about herself during adolescence, she responded: 'Guilty and responsible about my parents' breakup ... I thought all

27

I'm good for is to be used. I was too hard on myself for them not staying together.' At 15 she took an overdose of pills at her boy-friend's apartment. In this self-destructive act she stands alone among all the women in the study, though she resembles another woman who remembered trying to kill her pain as an adolescent by overeating. While sexual abuse appears related to her self-destruc-tiveness, other family problems most likely contributed to her unhappiness.

Since violence against children and adolescents usually originates in the immediate family, it is not unexpected to find impaired func-tioning in family and intimate relationships if a family member reverses expected roles and *attacks* rather than supports a child. Should the attack come from a parent (in contrast to a sibling) the child's ability to confide in both parents is threatened since the child generally perceives parents to be linked in some kind of alliance that excludes them. Self-blame is, therefore, a frequent outcome of paren-tal violence or abuse inflicted on children, and at times can be expressed in self-destructive acts.

With one exception, then, the women who were abused did not re-spond to these traumatic events either by suicide attempts (as many incest victims do) or by assaulting others. Indeed, no stress measures were higher than 2 on these items. The one suicide attempt noted above, though medically non-serious, signified overall distress, since it did not occur in direct response to the sexual abuse. This finding supports general clinical impressions that girls and women inter-nalize their stress and conflict, with subsequent display of distress in low self-esteem and depression (Brown and Harris 1978; Gove 1978; Cloward and Piven 1979; Gerhardt 1979). That these women were not seriously suicidal as girls, however, suggests the need for further study of the moral reasoning of girls and women around suicide (Gil-ligan 1982; Hoff 1985).

These findings have particular implications. They challenge the tendency to treat sexual abuse and rape by acquaintances and inti-mates less seriously than rapes by strangers. And they may alert us to look not only at serious physical damage but less evident damage as well (Holmstrom and Burgess 1978; Warshaw 1988). They also undermine the traditional tendency to blame mothers for the crime of incest against daughters (Howell 1978: 204–5; Herman 1981).[7]

The findings also suggest another line of analysis. It has been sug-gested that psychological problems and the propensity to accept put-downs and/or battering in later years can be traced to troubled family relationshipos, e.g. divorce, alcoholism, poverty, etc. But such social problems do not appear to be associated with the women's self-esteem at this early life phase. For example, one woman reported very high esteem though she described poverty, alcoholism, and divorce in the family. The two women who came from the most affluent families in the group also had no alcoholism, divorce, or similar social problems. Yet their evaluations of self-esteem were similar to those women whose families had one or more of these problems.

Several observations can be made about these possible associations. First, as a group, none of the nine women reported more than moderate stress (a score of 3) around self-esteem regardless of social/family problems or the violence they experienced as young girls and adolescents. In examining their evaluations of family relationships and intimacy, however, they all report higher levels of stress. What also stands out is that the three women who were abused by their fathers in their teen years reported the most distress during that period. These traumatic events alone might account for their self-evaluations in these Life Function Areas. However, another factor needs examination. As noted, social support acts to buffer the possibly damaging effects of traumatic events. Of the nine women studied, each had a positive relationship with her mother. Six of the nine had *very* positive relationships with their mothers.

The three women who reported sexual abuse by fathers and the worst self-evaluations on family relationships and intimacy before they were battered, 'lost' their mothers during early adolescence through death, mental illness, or battering. These young girls, therefore, not only suffered direct sexual and other abuse from their fathers, but also lost their major source of support, their mothers. This finding is especially significant in view of the tendency to blame mothers for colluding in their husbands' sexual abuse of daughters. These mothers did not collude with their husbands' sexual abuse of their daughters; rather, their absence, through death or mental illness, seemed to provide fathers with an excuse to abuse their daughters with impunity, much as alcohol is used as an excuse to avoid responsibility for battering. These same three women, not surprisingly, describe their relationship with their fathers as negative. The other woman with a negative relationship to her father was not sexually molested, but was 'whacked around' by him until age 16.

Another observation from these women's self-evaluations is that they were remarkably free of the standard distress signals such as substance abuse and self-destructiveness before they were battered. The one non-fatal suicide episode has already been noted. One woman ate excessively in response to stress, but not to the point of interference with her responsibilities. The same woman stole her father's car once after he beat her. Her stated reason was that 'after the death of my mother all that was good and unified fell apart.... I stole my father's car in order to be close to my aunt.' Significant in this description is her search for social support and use of the word 'stole'. Many a youngster engaging in the same behaviour might have accounted for it as 'using my father's car without his permission'.

What is the meaning of these women's accounts of their functioning during childhood and adolescence in relation to later battering? Several preliminary conclusions are suggested. The only thing they had in common before being battered later by their mates was that they felt close to and loved by their mothers. Six of the nine women felt very close. Their self-esteem and general freedom from major problems (Signals of Distress) common to many adolescents (e.g. substance abuse, suicide attempts) supports previous research (e.g. Hilberman 1980) which discounts women's *prior* psychopathology as an explanation for why women are eventually battered.

Even the three women who suffered abuse from their fathers might have weathered these childhood and adolescent traumas with less damage had they not lacked the support of their mothers for reasons not of their own or their mothers' making. These findings not only contradict psychological explanations of battering (e.g. a woman is weak, vulnerable, and masochistic) but point instead to an opposite conclusion: in spite of severe traumas and losses by some through their early years, these women appear generally strong and healthy by their own description using standard assessment criteria for emotional/mental health status. Since the only thing the women had in common prior to being battered by their mates was 'being loved by their mothers', the popular theory of 'mother love' and its importance seems evident in the lives of these nine women. There is a traditional stereotype of mothers saying to their battered daughters: 'I took it from your father ... You have to take it too ... It's a woman's lot.' Not only does this view not hold in regard to these mother–daughter relationships, but the women were remarkably positive in describing their mothers, including the two whose mothers had serious depressions.

Whether or not this 'mother love' carries through for these women when they are battered remains to be seen. This finding from the women's early years presages the question of whether the cultural norm of 'privacy' of trouble between a woman and her mate is perhaps stronger than the 'mother love' that might be mustered to support a battered adult daughter. Thus, rather than childhood traumas constituting an explanation for later battering, what they may suggest is the *resilience* and *strength* of women who experienced violence even before they were battered by their mates. Or, perhaps such long-standing abuse breeds such self-degradation and despair that a woman feels unworthy of her mother's love and unable to reach out for or accept the help available. Later analysis will shed some light on these questions.

Since six of the nine women did not experience such violence as girls, childhood and adult victimization should not be construed as a continuum *within the individual woman*. Nor does it support the concept of a 'cycle of violence' which postulates continuity of violence between generations for victims as well as perpetrators. On the other hand, the concept of a 'culture of violence' suggests the connectedness of different forms of violence. If this is true, it cannot be found only by examining the lives of women who experienced violence through all the phases of their life cycle. To analyse this issue further, we must look to the next phase of these women's lives, the period in which they were all battered by their mates.

Chapter three

Women in violent relationships: why they stayed

Introduction

To move from the pre-battering phase of the women's lives to their accounts of the violence they experienced reveals the relationship between violence and depression. The dynamic interplay between depression and violence is most acute when violence is treated as a private rather than public issue. Privatizing woman abuse illuminates the most frequently asked question around this issue: Why do battered women stay? One reason frequently offered for why battered women stay is their 'learned helplessness' which locks them into a chronic 'battering cycle' (Walker 1979). Another general systems interpretation suggests that victims may be 'unmotivated' (Rounsaville 1978), or may inadvertently reinforce the violent behaviour by playing out their respective roles in the family system (Straus 1973; Giles-Sims 1983).

In contrast, activists claim that women remain in a threatening situation because of economic factors, power disparity, fear, lack of support, and because there is nowhere else to go if shelters are unavailable or unknown (e.g. Martin 1976; Pizzey 1977). These explanations present two very distinct and conflicting views: *either* women are personally responsible for the violence; *or* they are helpless victims of men in a sexist patriarchal society.

Missing from these claims is an explanation that takes into account the possibility of dynamic interaction between four factors: (1) the woman's own reasoning process, i.e. how she makes sense out of her experience of violence; (2) the social-cultural roots of her reasoning process and self-concept; (3) the beliefs and first-hand accounts of persons in a battered woman's social network; (4) how these social-psychological factors might intersect with the political economy in the woman's social milieu.

My working hypothesis was that a woman's social network might constitute the intermediate structure between the subjective world of a troubled woman and the social, political, and economic institutions that uphold values and norms about women, marriage, the family, and violence. First, it was assumed that the women had probably absorbed the dominant cultural values about women, marriage, the family, and violence. Second, these values would probably influence how a woman responded when she was beaten the first time. Third, these interacting values and various material factors (e.g. money, proximity of family, etc.) would influence whether a woman escaped from or remained in the violent relationship.

The focal questions in this chapter are: Why did the women stay as long as they did? And if the battering cycle always includes reconciliation, how regular are these reconciliations, what constitutes a reconciliation, and then, why do women eventually leave?

The women's experience of violence

People may find it understandable why many women remain after the *first* occurrence of violence. There may be many positive aspects of the relationship the woman feels are worth preserving; she may lack economic independence; she may want a father for her children; she may believe the man when he promises he will never hit her again. If she *is* beaten again, however, many people are more inclined to believe that she must be masochistic, unmotivated, or just plain foolish. In exploring these issues I decided to examine in detail only selected examples of the violence experienced by these women. Dobash and Dobash (1979) analysed women's reports of the 'first, worst and last' episodes of violence. In the present study, particular attention was directed to examining what happened after the *first* beating and how, if at all, the *second* beating differed. Exploration of the first and second occurrences were expected to uncover possible processes leading to future chronic beatings. Besides exploring possible differences between the first and second beatings, the women were also asked about the most *typical*, the *worst*, and the *last* beatings.

My attempt to obtain an ordered sampling of the violence was only partially successful. The women found it extremely painful to describe the violence and wanted to 'forget it', although they often expressed relief after having talked about it.[1] For most of these women, the violence was frequent, extended over time, and included many similar incidents. Thus, they tended to blend the violence together as an ocean of overwhelming misery and pain. Some of the women, however, remembered very clearly the first and second incidents of violence.

The violent episodes

Excerpts from the accounts and their analysis encompass the remainder of this chapter.

1. The *first* beating happened one month after our marriage. He was drinking a lot and not paying the rent ... I told him that. He slapped me around and yelled. I left and went to another State for a month. I came back to my mother's house because I was pregnant. He called and promised to straighten out. Things were O.K. for a couple of years. I got a job as a computer programmer. I made more money than he. We had little arguments. After the baby was born he was jealous. I was exhausted and yelled at him to help me out.

The *second* beating was much worse than the first. He slapped me around and tried to strangle me. When I told him I wouldn't take it anymore he took an overdose and cut his wrists. He took drugs only when I threatened to leave. This left me feeling guilty, like it was all my fault.

The *worst* beating I got was when I picked up the plates and slapped him in the face. He got me down and started kicking me. I was 6 months pregnant with Alan. He kicked me three times in the head. He wanted me to abort Alan. That's when he started to abuse the kids. He grabbed Amy by the neck and broke Bobby's arm.

The most typical? He strangled me, slapped me around, punched, and kicked me.

The last beating? It was the same as the worst.

2. *The first beating?* He was going out alone ... I was always left alone, broke, no family or friends. I'd asked him to stay home or take us with him. I was four or five months pregnant – lonely. He wouldn't let me go anywhere ... he was jealous. He said no ... We argued. He pushed me down and then went nuts on me and kneed me in the abdomen. I panicked and screamed. No permanent injuries resulted, but I remember running out of the house, hiding, crying, confused. I didn't know where to go. I was ashamed, angry and scared, and alone. I wanted to hurt back but was afraid to and too shocked at the idea that he actually abused me. I couldn't believe it. It blew my mind ... I wanted to deny it. I was absolutely horrified at the whole thing ...

The *second* time was just before the delivery of my third child. He was having a party for his friends. He got drunk. His old girlfriend was there. I saw him kissing her in my heart. I got mad; (I'd already been mad and jealous) and said 'That's enough.' I told him to tell everyone to leave. He didn't like it ... he downed a bunch of booze, picked on one of the guys and went like a maniac through the house. I was protecting the kids in the bathroom. He picked on people he didn't like ... He was verbally abusive. Then he started in on me: 'Now everybody's gone ... It's all your fault.' I'd say: 'What kind of an idiot are you? I'm your wife ... You bring your old girlfriend to the party and make out with her ... If you don't want me, leave.' Then he belted me and called me all kinds of names ... I was pregnant and had no money. The next day I got some money from welfare and opened a bank account and then I told him about the money because of my stupid hangups about womanhood.

The second time he beat me was not as bad as the first. He was too drunk.

The worst beating? In some ways the first was the worst. The beatings increased with pregnancy because he had to give me more money. We had reconciled after a six-week separation. I'd do whatever he wanted so the kids wouldn't see ... We moved to another town. Six weeks later I started a part-time job working nights. He was jealous of me working. He threw my Thanksgiving turkey on the floor because I didn't make white potatoes. I went to work anyway and started hiding money. He came in at 3 a.m., yanked me out of bed (he was drinking) by my hair and started yelling 'You fucking gook' and started on me with his heavy fists on my back. I remember praying. I thought I was going to die ... It was so painful. I was pounded by this inhuman hulk, this beast. Finally he stopped. I crawled quietly up and sat for an hour afraid to move – afraid I was broken, afraid I would wake him. I prayed 'God, if you just help me get out with these kids.' I was thinking of how I could get the $40 my friend had (I had used my welfare money to buy a car) and start the car when the trash truck was moving so he wouldn't wake up. I had suitcases packed for days in case I could ever get away. I was like a thief in the night for fear he'd wake and beat me again. I got the kids ready and put everything in the car. I stole the keys out of his pocket. I got the $40 and drove 400 miles to my parents' house. That's when I found out how supportive my family were not. All they said was 'Oh, he did *that* to you?' He called incessantly with remorse. My father told me to go back and settle it. I stayed only three days with my family and then went back. *What about getting more help from welfare?* I grew up in a middle-class family, and whenever I told my sad story

35

to the people at welfare they didn't want to hear it.

The last incident? We were separated for three months and he wouldn't leave me alone. He said he wanted me back. I filed charges and the cops didn't do anything. [This woman had kept extensive records of the number of times she had taken legal action with unsatisfactory results.] I was locked out and went to him for help. *Why did you go to him for help?* I can't explain it ... I was crazy ... I was dependent ... I guess I went to manipulate and get my pictures back. The counsellors told me if you want him out of your life you can't even talk to him. But I got back into thinking that maybe he was rational. I wanted to talk him into not harassing me. So I said 'You want me to come and have coffee and talk? If I come will you let me leave?' He wouldn't let me out. I had an anxiety attack (when he said he had sexual ideas about our daughter) and he raped me. There was no drinking that time. After that there was no contact except in court.

3.   The *first* time he hit me we were at a friend's house. He stole some drugs and I confronted him. He slapped me in the face ... My brains just rattled. He ran off. I was a fool – I chased him to get him to come back. He said he was sorry and would never do it again ... that he didn't know what made him do it – it just happened.

The *second* time was one month later. I wouldn't go in a bar with him. He slapped and hit me, and gave me a black eye. *Was there anything different this time?* It was worse and he didn't promise not to do it again.

What was the worst beating? We had had an argument. I think it was his revenge for the time I hit him and gave him a black eye. He hit me in the eye ... I had to have five stitches. He cried. I lied to the doctor about what happened. After that he was real nice. We decided to get married.

The last beating? I was four or five months pregnant. He took my check, was drunk, and just kept beating me. He went to sleep and I just sat there for 20 minutes thinking about what to do ... 'My mother hates you, my father's gonna kill you.' I packed my bag and went to my parents' house while he was sleeping.

4.   *The first time?* We were talking and he slapped me. I didn't have any bruises or anything, but I was shocked. He apologized ... said he never meant to do it. I thought: 'People are human, they make mistakes.' We made love. I wasn't being honest with myself.

The second time? It happened a couple of weeks later. I nagged him about going to work and he slapped me about four times. It [the slap] was much harder than the first time ... I wanted to prove to him that he was worth loving and thought that maybe would stop him from being violent.

The *worst* and *last* time was when he beat me until I was black and blue over my face and arms. He choked me and kicked me in the stomach. Sometimes it seems unreal ... It's like I'd disown my body while talking about it. Sometimes I ask myself why didn't I crack up then, from battle fatigue ... Maybe I'm going through it now.

5. [The 'first' for this woman was not a beating but a threat.] We were wrestling, not in play. He had me on the floor and threw kerosene on and around me and threatened to light it. I cried and pleaded and he got up and left. Before the first time he beat me I'd gone out with the girls and got back at 2.30 a.m. He was mad and refused to speak. The next day I didn't cook dinner ... I just didn't feel like it. He got riled up ... We argued and he started punching me in the head and face. I had a possible skull fracture. He took me to the hospital. I told the doctor I got hit with a brick. He was in public service and I was afraid he would be disciplined and fired. I had no money for an apartment by myself. He said: 'I should have killed you . . . don't mess with me or I'll do it again.' I felt devastated ... I was afraid he'd kill me. [This woman could not remember anything special about the second beating except that it was three weeks later.]

The last time? It started over a holiday party ... He says out of the blue 'You have to get out.' I told him he had to wait. At 1.30 a.m. he woke me and said 'We're going for a walk.' He kept telling me how dumb and stupid I am, that he couldn't be bothered and that he'd had an affair. I felt forced to go with him. He started pushing me in front of cars and into the bushes and tried to strangle me. He said 'I'll take you to the police station and tell them how stupid you are.' The police said 'This is a family squabble ... Go home and get some sleep.' He threatened to kill me in front of the officers. The police told me to get a warrant the next day. We took a cab home. The next day he threatened me again: 'I want you out of here before I get back.' He called me every 10 minutes, threatening. I called the police and they gave me the shelter number. My girlfriend took me to the shelter.

In considering these accounts, it is important to move beyond shock, beyond asking 'But why did you stay?' to unravel meanings in a broader social context. This includes examining some of the *exceptions* to the general pattern. Five items on the Self-evaluation Guide guided the analysis: self-esteem; family relationships; intimacy; violence toward self; violence toward others. The intention was to focus the impact of the violence on the women's view of themselves, their social relationships, and their coping strategies. The results led to my understanding that these women are 'crisis managers', 'survivors' in the best sense of that term.

Self-esteem, violence, and power relationships

These accounts, as well as thousands of testimonials from other battered women, reveal that battering exacts an enormous toll on the woman's acceptance of herself. In their accounts of self-esteem while they were battered, seven of the women said that their image of themselves was 'poor' or 'very poor'. Even the woman who had said 'I always thought I was a wonderful person' thought less of herself after being battered. The woman with the highest reported self-esteem in the group, directly attributed this to her success as a professional person. Occupational success may provide a buffering effect against traumatic events that affect one's self-esteem negatively. Here are some of the women's statements about their acceptance of self:

'I felt totally disgusted with myself.'

'I thought of everyone else except myself ... I didn't *think*.'

'I started to believe his put-downs ... He never said these things [e.g. 'Other people will toss you away and use you if you leave me'] before he beat me.'

'I hated myself for living with him.'

'I still can't figure out what I did or said to make him hit me. Maybe that's just my way of blaming myself. He always said I started it ... He even said I liked being beaten.'

The respondents reported that the men made such attributions of blame several times. For example: 'Look what you made me do!' Add to this the verbal abuse and police direction to 'Go home and get some sleep' and their self-blame and low self-esteem become more understandable.

The question remains, though: Why did the women accept the blame and in turn blame themselves? To get at the answer I probed further into their reasons for staying. I assured them that I neither judged nor blamed them for what they had been through, but I also stressed the need to make public *their* reasons for staying, since some people refuse to believe that women cannot leave, especially after repeated beatings. Accordingly, the women were asked questions such as: Why did you stay after the first incidence of violence? Why did you marry him (especially after being beaten already)? What did you see in him?

> I believed I loved Jack. I had made a lifelong commitment. I knew that marriage wasn't easy – not made in heaven ... that it required work. I thought 'I won't leave after one negative incident.'

> After the kerosene incident I thought he'd change. When we met he was nice and understanding. We had common interests. I loved him ... I thought he was intelligent and I thought we'd go far together with family and school ... I was pregnant six months and said I wouldn't live with him without marriage.

> People are human ... They make mistakes. I made excuses for him, tried to make him change.

> I stayed probably for security reasons. I really loved him ... If I had left in the beginning maybe things would have changed ...

> Love makes you stupid and vulnerable. Men use your love against you: 'If you really loved me you wouldn't give up on me so easily.' I don't give up easily.

> I was 23, pregnant, I had no money and no place to go.

> I'd go to my friends' and mother's house. I just couldn't make ends meet. I still loved him ... I just wanted him to straighten out. I didn't think I could make it without him.

> I was one of the women who had the attitude: 'If you get hit you deserve it.' I was brought up to believe that women are less than human ... do as you're told. My father ordered everything. It was my duty to stand by my man. It's my cross to bear ... I did something to inflict this punishment on myself. I grew up seeing my mother cry all the time. I didn't know what to expect out of a relationship when I went into one.

In exploring these reasons further, I asked one woman: 'You have described your husband as something of a monster, "an inhumane hulk, this beast", yet, it seems, you were also attracted to him, e.g. you were mad and jealous about his old girlfriend; what did you see in him?'

> He was kind, generous and helpful, he saw money [in my family],

my father's house; he was a good lover when he wasn't drinking ... he was so good I became somewhat dependent on him sexually. But at the end even when he touched me, it turned me off. He'd beat me, make love and then laugh at me. He was good looking, macho ... he represented outwardly that strength I was told to rely on, he was charming. And I thought all he needed was for somebody to care for him and love him.

As we analyse the women's accounts of why they stayed after the first incident of violence, it is apparent that they loved their partners, tended to excuse the negative behaviour, and acted on their commitment to making marriage work. When pregnancy, child care responsibility, and their lack of confidence in their ability to 'make it' without a man – a point expressed by many women who are not battered – are included, why the women remained after a first violent incident becomes understandable. In addition to these reasons for staying, perceptions of power disparity between women and men influence a woman's decision to remain in a violent relationship. The women revealed that their conception of love includes friendship, and friendship implies mutuality rather than a paternalistic or superordinate/subordinate relationship between the sexes. These women, as do many others, associate violence with inequality between husband and wife or disparity in power within the couple unit. In fact, power disparity is central to the political attitudes of feminist activists working to stop violence against women. There is not much evidence, however, about how power operates in the daily interaction between women and men, nor what the differences are between power, influence, and authority in respect to battering.[2]

These distinctions are significant if violence against women is to be understood and ultimately stopped. For example, something like the following is often heard in response to the question, 'Why do battered women stay?:

After all, they are not chained to a bed or locked in a room, and are in fact free to go at least to the police station and take action against their assailants and the violence they protest. So why don't they do these things and leave?

Should the fact that they often do not do so for years be interpreted to mean that men have 'power' over women? Or, does power need to be distinguished from and interpreted in context with traditional authority and influence? We have seen that power, authority, and influence are often exercised to bring about conformity, e.g. forcing a woman out of her home under threat of death (see Chapter 10 for its use in denying access to public housing assistance). Since power disparity between the sexes is thought to be fundamental in explaining violence against women, the women were asked to define power:

The government has power. Individuals who have money have power. Some women, for example, the Queen of England, have power ... I had the strength to stand up to people and in this way I had power. Power is strength. God has power ... He has stood by me ... He answered all my prayers.

President of the United States, God ... Ruling the world. The doctors [at the hospital where she had worked] had power over nurses, the nurses over me. Men have special power over women, not mental ... Something that is abused. No one *has* power, people just think they do. Men believe we are put here to *do* for them. I never thought of this in terms of power ... The man's crazy! Why can he do these things and I can't?

A manipulative force over people, situations and circumstances so they come out in your favour ... Having someone under your thumb, convincing. It's absolutely worthless if you don't know how to use it.

Strength, authoritarian, dynamic.

Control over oneself and others.

It should be shared between husband and wife ... should be in equal terms. He kept me in when I came home from work ... 'Stay here while I go out and do this.' I couldn't go anywhere. He had the only key, where could I go? I usually did what he asked to keep it quiet.

Influence over a majority of people. Women have power over children. Men are supposed to be out there to protect us, but we have to protect against them.

I don't know, power gets to be really overwhelming if misused. For me, I felt very powerful to realize I could take charge of my own life.

These statements suggest that the women use the terms 'power', 'authority', and 'influence' interchangeably. Influence technically refers to the ability to affect a person or bring about a certain result, sometimes by the underhanded use of power; while authority implies the power one has from one's social status, public opinion, or esteem. Power, in addition to the authority and/or influence implied in it, includes the notion of force and strength, characteristics that enable a person to actually *exercise* power (Weber 1964: 152; Mousnier 1969). The women's statements display their commonsense knowledge that if they do not comply with a husband's wish, force lies behind the authority they see in their husbands and in representatives of the state.

The statements also suggest a certain acceptance of male authority and power, but not its abusive form of physical violence. They are thus in concert with women in traditional relationships with men who simply accept their subordinate position, who take it for granted that the last word (about discipline of children, or other issues) will be the man's. Dobash and Dobash (1979) link this view of male authority to traditional teachings of religion and other powerful social institutions. Pastoral practice has reinforced this view by advising battered wives to 'forgive' their violent husbands in the spirit of the Gospel, and do what they can to keep the family intact. This same tradition teaches a woman to project a positive image of the father to the children, regardless of his behaviour toward her, another powerful means of reinforcing respect for the father's authority.

Thus it does not seem necessary literally to imprison a battered woman for her to feel isolated and like a prisoner in her own home. The authority and influence vested in men at all levels of social life, plus the possibility of using physical force to exercise power, operate together to obtain a woman's compliance to a violent man's demands. Furthermore, when a woman herself uses force, more severe retaliatory violence usually results.[3] And, since the man's position in the family is publicly supported by police, and sometimes his violence condoned overtly or tacitly, the formula is complete for a woman's need to develop a master-plan for escape from her violent circumstances.

It is not, as popular belief often suggests, simply a matter of walking out of the door just because the man does not have her physically imprisoned. There are children to consider, money to get, alternative housing to arrange, and personal safety to think about. So long as these dilemmas persist and her situation is not immediately life-threatening, a battered woman may choose to stay.

Thus, a woman's decision to stay appears to follow logically from power disparity and the cultural rules she has learned about marriage, the family, and woman's role as traditionally defined. It is, after all, common cultural knowledge that women have been charged with and have largely accepted the emotional and social work of keeping families together in domestic tranquillity (Chodorow 1978; Smith 1987). Throughout history patriarchal societies have inculcated the notion of women as subordinates, not equal partners in the marriage relationship (Chapman and Gates 1977; Okin 1979; Harding and Hintikka 1983). Dobash and Dobash (1979: 31–47) and Davidson (1977: 2–23) provide overviews of religious, legal, and literary texts that explicitly urged or condoned wife beating through all the centuries of recorded western history. This misogynist legacy remains very much in evidence today.

Thus, a woman who is struck or beaten, even once, finds herself in a paradoxical situation: she is shocked and incredulous that the man she loves, the father of her children, would treat her so. But having internalized the cultural norm that women are largely responsible for the success or failure of human relationships, she interprets her mate's behaviour as somehow her own doing. When coupled with statements such as 'Look what you made me do', and the man's apparently genuine remorse, the woman's decision to stay and 'work on improving the relationship' follows logically. Should a woman seek outside help from marriage counsellors, this norm is implicitly reinforced by a focus on maintaining the functioning of the marital/family system, rather than on the socio-cultural roots and political implications of family dysfunction. (This idea is discussed further in later network analysis, p. 103–5).

The dynamic process in first incidents of violence is clarified further when the shame a woman feels at being thus treated by her mate is considered. Such shame encompasses both the woman and her husband. For the woman, the shame arises from her perceived failure. It moves her to keep the violence to herself, and presages the progressive and often extreme isolation in which battered women later find themselves. As for her mate, the woman's shame elicits protective feelings, the need to cover up and excuse what she (and sometimes he) sincerely believes will be a *single* occurrence of violence. The woman's reasoning here resembles that of other women who say that they most probably would *not* leave a relationship following a single incident of violence if many other important aspects of the relationship are intact.

This complex social-psychological dynamic of shame and protectiveness is confounded further by the social double standard concerning women in these situations. On the one hand, women are expected to be the nurturers and healers in conflicted family relationships; yet they have traditionally been regarded as the *source* of the conflict. For example, Loreen's counsellor said: 'Now let's see what you did to provoke him'; but when women attempt to heal a battered relationship, they are condemned for their 'stupidity' in failing to leave a violent mate.

The failure to leave after a first incident of violence, paradoxically, seems to contribute to an increasingly complex dynamic between the woman and her partner. This dynamic is unravelled in part by considering the difference between the first and second beatings among those women who could recall the details. Several of the women said that the ensuing beatings were not only more severe, but that their partners were less remorseful after the second time. What appears to evolve is the following scenario: man hits woman; she is shocked; he is remorseful and promises never to do it again; she believes him, acts on the basis of her commitment to make the marriage work, and stays with her partner. Although he is probably sincere in his promise not to hit her again, at an unconscious level the *fact* that she stays with him despite the violence, symbolizes for him a certain *licence* to repeat the violence. After the *second* incident of violence, the woman is even more condemned – including by her mate – for her 'stupidity' and 'weakness' in *accepting* the violence. Not only is the vicious circle closed, but there is little or no condemnation of the men for failing to keep their promises, and frequently indifference to the violence itself by police and other public officials. Thus, the stage is set for repeated, chronic violence.

In attempting to understand why some women stay despite repeated beatings, some people suspect that sexual attraction or 'female sexual slavery'[4] might be an influencing factor. It seemed important, therefore, to examine these issues in depth. Some of the women were willing to talk about why they stayed after repeated beatings:

My kids needed discipline. I didn't have a baby-sitter, money, or the strength – physical and mental – I was depressed about everything. This was not my idea of marriage. I don't know what I loved about him. When he wanted to be he could be kind, considerate, compassionate. My mother stuck it out for 40 years. I believed in marriage. *Did sexual attraction have a part to play in your staying?* He was not a good lover. Basically the reason was my religion and for financial support. I'd refuse sex and he'd force himself on me. A couple of times it could have passed for rape. I hated sex with him. When I told him about the brutal rape (when I was 18 and travelling in another State) he said 'You enjoyed every minute of it.'

I was just too afraid. The help wasn't strong, except my friend Jane ... She kept encouraging me to leave. *Why didn't you follow her advice?* I felt trapped with the kids, he had the money. He threatened to hurt the kids if I left. *Did sexual attraction play any part?* Sex was a strong contributing factor. I used sex to control ... to punish him, to prevent battering, and to prove my worthiness.

I stayed because divorce was unacceptable to me. And I was ashamed. I didn't have children ... Therefore I had 'failed' as a mother already ... Also, I stayed because of fear that he would wind up in jail, dead or in the gutter. Another reason was because my parents were living abroad for a while and I was afraid to leave because he might have destroyed the furniture ... He did $500 damage once to an antique painting. I kept hoping it would get better after the stressors were gone [i.e. after he got his degree and had a regular job]. *Did he seem threatened by your professional success?* Yes, clearly. But I said to myself, 'Well, men earn more usually and support the other, so why is it abnormal for me to earn more and support us?'

I kept believing he'd change. But I also felt protective of him and his reputation ... Everyone in this small community would have known. [This woman's husband held two doctoral degrees and was highly visible professionally. She said he was 'incredible' as a lover, but that when the battering got worse sexual enjoyment also changed for the worse.] She also said: 'I'm using you now so I can finish this graduate program and get out of here' ... That was the only reason I stayed.

I thought there hadn't been enough time for him to change. I don't like to hurt a person.

I wanted a baby for a long time and I kept making excuses ... And I loved him. I kept hoping he would stop.

I had my child and no money. I loved him for a long time. *Why did you hang on for so long?* It goes back to religion and Eve's implicating Adam. Men think we deserve it. They use original sin as an excuse. *Did sexual attraction have anything to do with your staying?* The sexual relationship wasn't as good as it might have been. I couldn't support my son ... We lived in a boarding house for a while. We had no place else to go. I couldn't stay with my mother. My sister didn't want me or at least she made me feel 'Don't ask.'

I was afraid that if I left he'd find me. I didn't know where to go, what to do, or who could help. I was hundreds of miles away from my family. I had never been out on my own. I was scared to be out on my own.

Several themes are evident in the women's accounts of why they stayed after repeated beatings. Economic dependence and child care responsibility are surely important factors, but four out of the nine women were earning more money than their husbands. The

45

economic factor must be considered in a dual context. Like the women Rubenstein (1982) studied, women who earned more than their husbands were a source of threat to the men. This placed the women in a no-win situation: either they could turn the money over to the men (which some did) and diminish their chances of escape, or they could assert themselves more authoritatively, a move often followed by more violence. One professional woman worked in the same agency as her husband. She received a promotion while her husband did not. To protect his ego and avoid more violence, she went to the agency administrator and asked that her promotion be divided equally between them. These findings support Yllo and Straus' (1981) research regarding increase of violence in states which have institutional indicators of equality for women, but where patriarchal, sexist values nevertheless prevail in certain male/female relationships.

Another contextual consideration of why some women remain relates to their values about marriage. Divorce may be seen as a failure in their commitment to marriage and the roles of wife and mother. These women extend their concept of a nurturing role to the men who brutalize them (Chodorow 1978). They are compassionate and loving with these men; they are sensitive about not exposing them; they excuse and cover for them; and they absorb the blame themselves. Ironically, their persistence over time in believing that their mates would change matched the persistence of the men's physical brutality, verbal criticisms, and broken promises.

Victim blaming and self-blame

Although economic factors figure significantly in some women's decision to stay, there still exists a popular notion that women who stay after repeated beatings are 'stupid', or provoke men into violence, or are 'too cowardly to leave', etc. When the women were asked if and under what circumstances they might have provoked the violence, they stated that not only did they *not* engage in such provocative behaviour, but also generally went out of their way to avoid any and all situations which they thought might lead to a violent episode. Such a pattern of trying to second guess the husband's wishes, of 'walking on eggshells' to prevent a beating, is reported by women in nearly all recent research on the topic, and was confirmed by the women in this study. If occasionally a woman says or does something which appears as the 'straw that breaks the camel's back' (Golan 1969) and a beating results, this should not be construed as the *cause* of the violence, but rather as one facet in the context of a complex interplay between the immediate circumstances of the violence and the cultural and socioeconomic factors noted above. Furthermore, considering such apparently random acts of violence as waking a woman at 3 a.m., demanding sex, or dragging her out of bed to fry bacon and eggs, necessitates a much broader framework than equilibrium in the dyadic or family system.

This issue evokes the dynamics of victim blaming (Ryan 1971). An ironic finding surfaces when the women's accounts of why they stayed as long as they did are examined. As noted, most women have been socialized into traditional nurturing roles, and have, in many cases, absorbed and acted on the culturally embedded belief that the most significant life task for a woman is to be a successful wife and mother. Yet when these women embrace this role and doggedly try to succeed in it against one of the greatest odds – violence – people repeatedly and naively ask 'Why don't they leave?'

Such a simplistic analysis of battered women's plight fails to take into account several factors: (1) cultural values regarding women, marriage, and the family, and how these values and beliefs influence the action of individual women entrapped in a violent relationship; (2) the social and economic realities women face when they leave a violent relationship and find themselves a single parent, homeless, and often forced to return to the parental home after carrying out the adult responsibilities of wife and mother; (3) the interaction of these factors with the reality of physical threat and danger faced by the woman who threatens or attempts to leave.

If, in addition, a woman is inexperienced working outside the home, then her dilemma is compounded. Even though a battered woman cannot predict whether the man will keep his promise not to beat her again, she is at least dealing with a known entity by staying, compared to the many unknowns she may face if she leaves.

Thus, battered women find themselves in a Catch-22 situation. They are caught between remaining in a violent relationship and venturing into the labyrinths of welfare, homelessness, unemployment, and single parenthood – all of which confer low social status. Battered women who remain in violent relationships face a situation analogous with that of political dissidents, disaster survivors, and certain occupational groups such as nurses.[5] Yet, traditionally, people appear to have greater difficulty remaining non-judgemental about battered women's decisions than the decisions of people like dissidents and disaster survivors. Why is it so easy to blame battered women for their victimization while only the most callous individuals would blame disaster survivors and political dissidents for their plights?

The reason is not necessarily that people are callous and inhumane when confronted with the crises of battered women. Rather, it appears to be rooted in the ideology of the family and gender roles and the way in which the problem of battering has been conceptualized, publicly defined, and commonly accepted. Violence toward women has traditionally been explained as women's lot. More recently medical or intrapsychic interpretations have explained violence as a result of stressed or psychiatrically disturbed men and masochistic women.

The medical or psychiatric interpretation of battering is clarified by examining concepts from the 'labelling perspective' (Becker 1963; Helm 1981), particularly the 'medicalization' of life and behaviour (Illich 1976; Freidson 1970). 'Medicalization' refers to the process of defining and regulating behaviour that was formerly regulated by religious and legal institutions, by medicine as an agent of social control (Ehrenreich 1978; Ehrenreich and English 1979). Thus, deviant behaviour that might have called for a moral decision from the body politic about a member's responsibility or excusability for action, now comes under the pseudo-scientific scrutiny of the psychiatric specialist. While esteemed by the criminal justice system and lay-persons alike as 'experts', one must remember that these experts nevertheless rely on the commonsense knowledge and social expectations of lay-persons for the scientific construction of what insanity is and its relationship to violence (Douglas 1970; Atkinson 1978; Daniels 1978; Melick, Steadman, and Cocozza 1979; Monahan 1981; Halleck 1987). Everyday conversation suggests the pervasiveness of the medicalized approach to deviance, e.g.: 'Only a sick or crazy person could strike his wife or child' (not guilty by virtue of insanity); 'I hit her because I was drunk and didn't know what I was doing' (avowal of deviance, plea to be excused).

Psychiatric labelling has had an impact on policy and practice regarding violent aggressors. But it also appears to have influenced human service workers' responses to victims of violence, even though behaviourist and psychiatric theories are now largely discredited (e.g. Hilberman 1980). A study by Stark, Flitcraft, and Frazier (1979) of 481 battered women who used a metropolitan hospital's emergency services showed that 'medicine's collective response' to abuse contributed to a 'pathological battering syndrome', actually a socially constructed product in the guise of treatment. The intervention strategy this research uncovered, treated medically such problems as alcoholism and depression and masked the problem of violence and its political and economic concomitants. Thus the abused woman is psychiatrically labelled, suggesting that she is personally responsible for her problems, and violent families are stabilized to foster family system maintenance (Bograd 1984).[6] Clearly, then, medical and psychiatric agencies appear to play a major role in reconstituting violence into a private event rather than relating it to the political and economic constraints of a patriarchal authority structure.

Even if traditional and medical interpretations of violence are rejected, there remains the need to explain why the women stay while preserving a view of them as knowledgeable, capable social beings, of acknowledging their victimization without blaming them for it. Thus, while battered women and rape victims have something in common with disaster survivors, they are often blamed while other victims are not.

Disaster victims and political dissidents appear (and generally are) innocent of participating in bringing on their own victimization. But women battered by their mates, one popular argument goes, are active participants in an on-going relationship. They are responsible social and moral agents, knowledgeable about their culture, and generally capable of solving life's problems. Thus it is that battered women are not seen merely as helpless victims, but as responsible moral agents whose very responsibility makes them colluders in the acts of violence. The problem with this reasoning is that it fails to take into account that men and women who are marriage partners still maintain their individual status. Battered women are responsible moral agents, but they are *not* responsible for the actions of their assailants.[7]

That these women are blamed rather than understood is related to the tendency to make violence a 'personal' problem. Aside from feminist analysis, the disastrous effects of violence on women generally has rarely been linked to commonly held social values and beliefs which implicitly and explicitly support such violence. Some analysts fall into the trap of 'reification'. They treat concepts like 'sexism' and 'patriarchy' as 'things' without demonstrating the connection between male-dominated institutions (including 'theories' about women and violence) and the subjective understanding and behaviour of individual violent men. In short, men *know* from experience that they can usually get away with violence against wives, and that their victims, not they, will be held accountable.

Self-destructiveness

The most extreme manifestation of the women's self-blame, recrimination, and internalizing the conflict is their tendency to self-destructiveness. As noted earlier, only one incident of medically non-serious self-destructiveness occurred during the earlier life phases of these women. In marked contrast, during the battering phase all nine women had self-destructive tendencies at varying levels of dangerousness.

When asked what kept them from killing themselves, three of the women referred to their children: 'My kids coughed in the middle of my hunt for a razor blade and when I thought of turning the gas on, I thought, My God! Who will they have? That saved my life.' This woman made the following journal entry and drawing of a broken heart (see Figure 3.1) during this desperate time:

Figure 3.1 A battered woman's drawing signifying her broken heart

Looking at yourself and hurting – Struggling to forgive yourself in spite of everyone else's lack of forgiveness, understanding. Aloneness is – having a broken heart and not knowing how to kill the pain long enough – wanting to feel and fighting not to feel – surviving is living through it. I must survive – and grow. It will pass! Believe it. God help me believe it!

Other women said: 'Only my responsibility for my children kept me from doing it.' 'I remembered that I had a baby inside me.' One woman, childless at the time, said her mother told her that she loved her. And another reflected: 'I really wanted to be alive but my whole life with him was very morbid, like living in a casket.' One woman who took a potentially lethal overdose, on waking and thinking of her children, cried and cried, 'Who will take care of them?'

The association between violence from one's spouse, low self-esteem, and suicidal tendencies is very strong, especially when observed in contrast to the women's pre-battering life phase.[8] Explanations of suicidal behaviour traditionally have favoured a psychological interpretation (Neuringer and Lettieri 1982). In this framework, depression, the most pervasive of diagnosable psychopathologies, and cognitive orientations are suggested as the predominant explanations of suicide. The poverty of such theories, however, lies in their failure to ask about the origins of depression, or the social foundations of women's self-concept development (Berger and Luckmann 1967; Chodorow 1978). Put another way, traditional psychological theory assumes that depression, especially the endogenous type, originates from inner psychic processes (e.g. Neuringer and Lettieri 1982) or physiologic imbalances.

Critiques of these reductionist theories, especially as applied to women, are now commonplace (see, for example, Millet 1970; Chesler 1972; Hoff 1985). Also, Gove (1978) in his argument against labelling theory (Becker 1963), asserts that women are not merely *labelled* psychiatrically; as a group they *are* in fact more depressed than men because they have more to be depressed about in view of their social inequality. Other researchers (e.g. Brown and Harris 1978; Turner and Avison 1987) also question intrapsychic interpretations of depression, stressing social factors such as poverty and women's unrelieved burdens of child care. However, psychodynamic interpretations of depression still form the basis of much clinical practice and assessment of suicidal danger (Neuringer and Lettieri 1982).[9]

This research supports an interpretation of depression which builds on concepts of male–female differences in the channelling of stress and anger (Cloward and Piven 1979; Gerhardt 1979). Men traditionally have been socialized to direct their anger toward others, to resist attack, to fight, on the assumption that the source of their stress is other than themselves. Women, on the other hand, assume, along with the rest of society, that their troubles and source of stress stem from themselves, their own inadequacies, failures, etc. (Sayers 1982).[10] They are thus more likely to direct their anger toward themselves. Therefore, if a woman does not perceive her trouble as *social* in origin rather than personal, she is unlikely to mobilize *social* resources on her behalf or attack 'outside' sources of her distress. (This interpretation is elaborated in later analysis of why women did not routinely call on social sources of available help, e.g. supportive family members, see pp. 94–5). Thus the women in this study directed more aggression toward themselves than toward others. This tendency of women to blame themselves is underscored by excerpts from a poem one woman wrote:

'Torture In Love'

As the shades of darkness are drawn
down about her, blocking out any possible
sign of life she once knew; ...

You can see the sorrow in her eyes,
once shining so brightly, now bloodshot
from all those terrifying, and sleepless nights ...

How could this man, she'd once loved
so deeply, hurt her so badly? She had
done everything he'd asked! Was it that
he'd just stopped loving her? Was he
jealous? She'd given him *no* cause to be! ...

When shall she be saved by peaceful death;
for this she feels, is the only answer, the only way
she'll escape this, 'torture in love', and find
her freedom from this terror, pain, and fear,
her once so-called, 'love', has brought into her fading life.

The accounts reveal the women's readiness to assume blame, to put themselves down as persons after being beaten. If, then, our society condones or readily excuses men's violent behaviour; if only the feminist community defines such behaviour as deviant; and if women's voices have no history of being heard in the public sector (Elshtain 1981), then we have a preliminary explanation of why these women were so ready to blame themselves, why their self-esteem was so low.

In general the women searched within themselves for the reasons they were beaten, or were questioned by counsellors regarding what *they* did to provoke the beatings.[11] Like millions of other battered women they modified their *own* behaviour in the hope of avoiding a beating. This implies a belief at some level that they were responsible for their victimization, a belief reinforced by the violent men and general mythology about battering. Lacking other explanations for why the men they loved and tried so hard to please beat them, they accepted the commonly held belief that the violence was due to something *they* had done.

Women's violence towards others

The fact that all of the women channelled at least *some* of their anger towards the *source* of their distress – the men who battered them – suggests that traditional images of women as passive and primarily self-blaming are not accurate. In spite of the striking contrast between the men's brutality and the women's self-blame and forgiveness, their accounts reveal that they, too, are capable of violence. Here is a sampling of how these women expressed violent impulses. One woman took a machete and states that she might have killed her mate had she not been stopped by a relative. Several of the women thought of poisoning their husbands or killing them in their sleep when they were powerless. They went as far as plotting to disguise the murder. One woman described how she surprised her husband with her violent fantasies:

> One day he was graphically describing how he would kill me and I commented that I had considered killing him in his sleep. This seemed to stop him short for a moment, as he realized at least momentarily that he was powerless against me, at least while sleeping.

When asked what kept them from carrying out their murderous fantasies, they replied: 'I decided not to spend life in jail for a crazy man'; 'I came this [she gestures with her hand] close to killing him with the machete ... He escaped to the bathroom ... I didn't kill him because I knew they would take me away and my kids wouldn't have anyone. And it scared me'; 'It wasn't worth it ... I would lower myself [by being violent].' In general, the women were inhibited by a combination of concern for their children and fear of the consequences for themselves.

Other forms of violence, however, were not beyond these women. In answer to the question 'Were you ever violent with your mate?' all nine of the women said 'Yes.' *Please describe*: 'Several times I fought back. I picked up dishes and hit him right across the face.'

> Once when I was high on drugs I grabbed him and said 'How do you like it?' I wouldn't have had the nerve to do it without drugs. I asked him 'Would you like it if I hit you?' and he said 'No, cut it out,' and I said 'I don't like what you do to me ... do you want me to do it back to you?' and he said 'No, cut it out, what's the matter with you?' I couldn't help it anymore, I started laughing 'cuz he was shaking in his boots ... I think I really blew his mind. *You said you were high. Did you know what you were doing?* The drugs definitely did do it ... *Would you explain that, for example, were you able to stop even though you were high on drugs?* Oh ya. *Were you in a sense driven and didn't know what you were doing?* I knew what I was doing, but at the same time it did make me have the strength to grab him and push him up against the wall and say 'Hey, pal, look what you're doing to me!' But I was able to stop it ... I don't know if I got so scared myself doing it anyway and maybe stopped because of that.

This woman persisted in not excusing her own violence on grounds of being high on drugs, in marked contrast to earlier statements excusing her husband's violence on grounds of alcohol or other drug influence. She also noted that the next beating was much worse than previous ones, and interpreted this as her husband's retaliation for her beating him. Another woman said: 'Once I hit him back – it only escalated the situation faster. I never tried that strategy again.' And another said: 'I did it only once, a long time ago ... I got so scared. He poured kerosene and said he was going to light a match. I never fought back again.'

These accounts suggest that battered women are not merely passive victims. They also reveal the futility of trying to stop violence with violence. While the usually self-defensive violence of the women only led to more brutal, retaliatory beatings, most people would recognize the self-defensive nature of their violence.[12] Yet when battered women retaliate in the form of murder, they generally face much harsher treatment by the criminal justice system than men do (Jones 1980; Browne 1987). This differential public treatment of men's and women's violence supports the general cultural norm of a nurturing rather than competitive, aggressive role for women.

Attention to the women's accounts reveals *their* reasons for staying, even though these reasons are not readily apparent to the superficial or indifferent observer. In large part, their reasons are embedded in traditional views about marriage and the family and the interpretation of violence as a private rather than public issue. Clearly, though, staying in violent marriages exacted an enormous toll on the women's self-esteem. We consider next the phases in these women's lives in which they move from victim states to a role as successful crisis managers and survivors, despite their personal burden of dealing with a public issue.

Chapter four

From victim to survivor: how they left

Introduction

The women's reasons for staying are embedded in social norms and beliefs about women, marriage, the family, and violence. But just how these values and structures affect the lives of individual women is less than clear. This chapter focuses on two major themes: (1) how the women made sense of their victimization and how their mates' violence affected sexual intimacy needs; (2) how and why they finally left violent relationships, accounts that reveal them as crisis managers rather than helpless victims.

Beating during pregnancy

The beatings these women suffered destroyed their hopes for marriage and a family. But some of them were also attacked while pregnant, because the husband was upset over his wife's pregnancy. Those women who were beaten while pregnant were asked how they explained it to themselves:

> It's the worst thing he could have done. I was afraid of losing the baby. I thought 'The guy really has got gall.' It's the lowest thing he could have done. He didn't really resent the baby, but there's nothing he could have done worse.

> I always thought when you're pregnant it's really special and so I wanted to be treated special ... I got the exact opposite. He was having an affair with someone. I made excuses and tried to make him change.

> He beat me during all three pregnancies. I was scared to death ... in absolute shock. I couldn't understand why he did that. I couldn't explain it and just kept thinking 'What did I do?' I remember dur-

ing my first pregnancy ... I'll never forget it. It was in the summer. I was itching so bad from the heat and the pregnancy. I kept throwing water on my face during a picnic to cool off. Then during the night I woke up itching and asked him to scratch my back. He scratched me so that I bled and I got an infection from it. During the second pregnancy I think he wanted me to have a miscarriage. I wanted kids and didn't believe in abortion. I didn't want an only child. After the second one he had a vasectomy. It was alright with me because I was satisfied I had two healthy children. The third one was accidental. During the third one he demanded I get an abortion. He's very selfish. All he wanted was sex, sex, sex and it just made me sick.

I thought it was horrible. It launched me on a crusade to get him admitted [to a mental hospital]. Anyone who'd beat a pregnant woman is nuts. They discharged him the next day from the State hospital.

It was not any more terrible, but I felt I had to do something about it.

To many, beating a pregnant woman is so contemptible that it is dismissed as a barbaric act of a 'few sick men'. The limits of such medicalizing of violent behaviour have already been discussed. A more plausible interpretation would link male violence against a pregnant wife to child rearing practices in a patriarchal capitalistic society. Chodorow (1978: 199) writes:

Men both look for and fear exclusivity. Throughout their development, they have tended to repress their affective relational needs, and to develop ties based more on categorical and abstract role expectations, particularly with other males. They are likely to participate in an intimate heterosexual relationship with the ambivalence created by an intensity which one both wants and fears – demanding from women what men are at the same time afraid of receiving ... Men grow up rejecting their own needs for love, and therefore find it difficult and threatening to meet women's emotional needs.

This explanatory framework suggests why many pregnant women may not receive the emotional support they expect from their husbands while pregnant. Battering a pregnant woman may present a more extreme response of jealousy toward the unborn baby and anger at the threatened displacement from the centre of the woman's attention. Another psychoanalytic interpretation stresses men's deep-seated fear and envy of women's reproductive power ('womb envy'), a fear which contradicts the Freudian concept of women's 'penis envy' (Fromm-Reichmann and Gunst 1973: 77–80). Frequently men deal with these emotions by asserting physical power over women. The women's discussion of intimacy supports this notion.

Sexual intimacy in a violent relationship

The women's sex life after being battered reveals another aspect of intimacy and family relations. Their accounts of violence reveal that the men often forced themselves sexually on the women. Only occasionally, though, did the women refer to such sex under duress as rape, even when specifically asked 'Did he rape you?' Generally, the women espoused several traditional values regarding the wife's role, including the notion that sex is a duty a wife owes to her husband. It is not surprising that these women rarely interpreted coerced sex by their husbands as rape. After all, rape in marriage has only very recently been discussed as even a legal possibility, so strong is the tradition of a man's unconditional sexual access to his wife (Russell 1982; Frieze 1983).

We have observed that the women's sexual attraction to their mates may have influenced their decision to remain in the relationship, at least temporarily. Popular folklore about marital conflict situations suggests that women want to achieve reconciliation by 'talking about the trouble', while men want to resolve conflict by 'making love'. These complexities of the sexual relationship were explored for their intersection with the social/political (Dobash and Dobash 1979) aspects of the problem.

Several of the women were able to talk about how sexual intimacy was affected by the battering. One woman spoke of becoming

> somewhat dependent on him sexually because he was such a good lover when he wasn't drinking. But at the end even when he touched me it turned me off ... And I thought all he needed was for somebody to care for him and love him.

In a similar vein another woman said:

> I can't believe I stayed with him. He didn't want me to love him. I saw something in him. He could be very kind and sensitive. Violence is just his defence, I guess I'm guilty of using someone [sexually]. *Do you mean because of having sex after violence?* Yes, I did it 'cuz I was afraid to say no. I'd block out what was happening before and concentrate on what was happening then. I lied to my-

self, made like it didn't happen, or it wasn't that bad – I would find excuses ... There were times when sex was good, but often it was not, though it was all we had in common. What makes the difference is what happens *before* you go to bed. I used to hate myself for not saying no.

One woman, who readily acknowledged her husband's sexual attractiveness, said she did not feel like having sex after he beat her: 'I'd refuse and he persisted and would say "What's the matter?" Maybe this was his way of making up, but he never apologized verbally.' This same woman said that after the first beating sex was 'still good, maybe because I believed he wouldn't hit me again. *How about after repeated beatings?* It was not as good. He got very demanding.' By the end of the study this woman was still trying to answer the question I had put to her earlier about what she continued to love about this man – he drank, took drugs, stole from her, was in trouble with the law, did not work steadily. After she was separated for several months, had had no sexual intimacy with her husband or anyone else, and had decided on a divorce, she said:

I know he's a jerk but I still love him. *Do you think, then, that you might eventually go back?* No, I do want the divorce but he still has a hold on me. *You said earlier that he was a good lover. Do you perhaps miss having sex with him?* No. *How do you explain that?* I don't know ... I still haven't figured out why I liked him that way. My daughter's more important to me now. We were still fighting when we tried to put it back together again, but I just don't want her [the daughter] in that – no way, no way. I've seen what happens upstairs [with the neighbours] ... The kids are crying 'Mommie, Mommie, look what Daddy's doing.'

This woman's response is better understood in the context of her having recently given birth to her first child. It seems quite clear that she transferred her need for intimate attachment from her husband to her child. Thus, this woman's strong commitment to the traditional value of motherhood helped her make the break from a violent relationship with a man she found very attractive sexually. This interpretation is supported by Chodorow's (1978: 197–9) claim that while women often romanticize and idealize their relationships with men, they are nevertheless more sensible and rational in their love relationships with men than men are with women, as illustrated by the frequent irrational jealousy of men. Thus, a woman's richer inner world constitutes a resource for placing a husband in a role secondary to mothering (Chodorow 1978: 198). Ironically, the success of women in the 'reproduction of mothering' in male dominated capitalist society apparently leaves men – as well as women and children – at a disadvantage *vis-à-vis* emotional resources and the ability to sever themselves from mother-like attention even in marriage. This psychodynamic process in male–female personality development supports the above analysis of battering pregnant women. Immersed in traditional mothering roles, the women tried also to mother the men who beat them.

These accounts are remarkable for the way they reveal complexities surrounding intimacy. That the women can extend love, nurturance, and forgiveness to their violent mates and blame themselves for having sex in spite of the beatings they had suffered is a variation of victim blaming. The attitude resembles Victorian ideology about women and sexuality: women should be readily available to provide sexual service to their partners. But if a woman happens to enjoy sex with a violent partner it is subtly implied that she is 'addicted' to sex. What these simplistic judgements of battered women miss is the complex interplay of several factors: a woman's acceptance of wifely duty, fear of reprisal if she refuses, desire of a man with *some* positive qualities, and strategizing through sex to change the man and avoid further beatings. In short, sex was used sometimes as a bargaining point – to punish or reward, to persuade him to change, or as a symbol of worthiness and lovability in spite of having been beaten.

To compound an already complicated scenario, some of these women described cruel humiliation from their mates in the sexual relationship. One woman said that her mate, very conscious of his sexual prowess and ability as a lover, persuaded her to make love after a beating. After arousing her, he deliberately backed out and 'sat there laughing at me'. Another man, when his wife threatened to leave him, told her how undesirable she was and said 'If you get rid of me no one else will want you – they'll just use you and throw you away.'

These testimonies add to those of thousands of others about how they begin to believe their husband's verbal put-downs. If the women's forgiving and nurturing behaviour toward their mates is contrasted to the men's cruelty, the women's self-accusations of worthlessness and undesirability can only be understood in cultural context: i.e. the widespread cultural devaluation of women which individual women absorb as part of their self-concept. Thus, if psychological abuse is added to their fear of reprisal for saying no to sex, their social isolation, and economic dependency, little foundation exists to judge battered women as 'sexual addicts' if they continue to have sex with violent mates.[1] Nor are they unlike millions of married women who, for centuries, have often provided sexual services to insensitive husbands simply to fulfil their wifely duty. Widows and women writing to popular advice columns have frequently noted that widowhood has freed them from a slavery of sorts rather than deprived them of an addicting habit.[2]

Without exception these women acknowledged positive qualities in their mates even after leaving them. They forgave them and believed the men when they promised to change. They excused their violence because of stress or 'illness', and kept hoping for change. They focused on making the marriage work in spite of enormous obstacles. These behaviours arise in part from deeply inculcated values about how women should carry out their roles as wives and mothers.

Though nurturing, forgiving behaviours would be positively interpreted in most other contexts, battered women are still often blamed rather than understood. The tendency to blame women and the women's own tendencies to blame themselves can best be understood in the perspective of theory as ideology: that is, the theories themselves are part of the problem.[3] Central to women's emancipation is their awareness of widespread sexual oppression, and the necessity of perceiving themselves as autonomous beings possessing capabilities and dignity equal to men. A new definition of their personhood must replace entrenched definitions of their functional roles, primarily as reproducers and nurturers (Chodorow 1978; Okin 1979; Elshtain 1981). The traditional concepts these women held reveal how their beliefs about womanhood affected their sexual relations and were, in turn, affected by the violence they experienced. Battering produces a crisis in which either the woman accepts that she is always vulnerable to violence, or she resolves it by leaving the situation and redefining her self-concept. How, then, might a woman's personal values influence whether she remains in a violent relationship or leaves it?

How and why the women left

To address this question the women were asked why they came to the shelter, or (if they did not go to a shelter) why they left the violent relationship.

> I was contemplating suicide ... I was willing to do it [suicide] but couldn't go through with it on account of the kids.

> I had nowhere else to go. I felt I had to get out.

> The turning point was when he said if he had to go to jail for killing me it would be worth it. He actually said 'When you're with me you have no rights.' I was deprived of my rights as a person.

I was washing dishes and he touched the pipes to see if I was using hot water. He shut the faucet off and told me to wash dishes with cold water. I told him I wouldn't. He said 'Shut up.' I answered back 'Don't tell me to shut up ... I'm not a baby.' Then he hit me and shook me. I was pregnant seven months. I tried to protect the baby. I went to the basement ... I wanted to kill myself. Then he grabbed the broom and pressed it against my throat and said 'I'll kill you ... I don't care if you're pregnant.' He hit me really hard on my face and back. I bit his finger and pushed him down the stairs. He said 'You're gonna get it.' ... I thought: 'O.K. If you treat me like that I'll kill myself.' Then I took bufferin, almost a bottle full. Eileen [her daughter, age 5] saw me and said 'What's the matter?' I said 'I don't feel good.' She [Eileen] told him 'Mama don't feel good.' He grabbed me and pushed me in bed. I said 'You treat me like a dog, not like a wife.' I took some more pills. I thought: 'I'll kill myself, the baby and everyone.' He put me in bed. I got up and took some more pills. Carol [her cousin] called ... My aunt and cousin came ... They swore at him. I felt terrible. They took me to the hospital and I had my stomach pumped. The psychiatrist and social worker came. I wasn't crazy ... I wanted to die. When I woke up and thought of my kids I cried 'Who will take care of them?' Then I went to the shelter.

I thought 'Women get divorced for drunkenness, abuse, unemployment, adultery.' I realized that I had *all* of these reasons. And I started to think about my life and that it wasn't going anywhere, plus I saw how good it felt to go to bed and sleep through the night without waking up from his choking me and demanding sex in the middle of the night. [This woman had been away to attend graduate school.]

After I became pregnant I was fearful for my baby. I said to myself: 'What are you making excuses for? He isn't going to stop.' That's when I started to get out.

When he started to make threats to my family I needed to get totally away and get myself together and get my mind organized. I left to keep abuse from my family.

I became ... well, that's when I started talking back, saying no. I just couldn't stand it anymore. I was afraid I would kill myself ... He was finishing up his dissertation for his second PhD. I was desperately ill ... I almost died ... And I can remember him standing at the front of my bed saying 'I'm supposed to take my comps today', and he was so angry ... I was absolutely helpless, lying there looking at this man. I didn't know what to say, I felt so guilty for getting sick

... I was eight months pregnant and had a blood clotting problem and he knocks me to the ground. I wanted my mother to come and he said: 'Tell her not to come.' And there was something in me that particular day, it just snapped. I wanted to leave him and the house and everything. And I left and stayed in the gatehouse down the street until it got dark. And that night I went back to the hospital. He didn't even ask me where I was. And then the baby was born ... they were afraid I would bleed to death ... He used to call me 'birdbrain' and 'mushroom brain' right from the beginning. I was dumb to stick around. [This woman had earned a graduate degree and was also a successful artistic performer.] I was furious ... I made up my mind that day that I was leaving him. It took me nine years to finally make up my mind ... I said I'm leaving and that was it. And the marriage got worse from that day on. I didn't try anymore.

These accounts illustrate the complex process involved in deciding finally to leave. For each woman the circumstances and events leading to that decision were unique to her situation: fear that he would kill her; that she would kill herself; fear for her children or family; recognition that there is no hope for change; the shock of a particular beating; the horror of being beaten while pregnant.

But their decision-making also varies according to their social circumstances and to their own resources, and reveals that human beings do not behave according to invariant, fixed patterns or laws. They make decisions, change their minds, etc., on the basis of social and material circumstances (e.g. need to support children, availability of alternative housing) and values (e.g. belief in responsibility for making a marriage work) that vary for each woman. As battered women consider these dilemmas, their experience with their spouses begins to appear as diametrically opposed to their views of what love, marriage, and friendship should be. Trudy Mills (1982) refers to such an insight as a 'moment of truth', which may be followed by a plan to leave. Their new vision reveals that their actual marriage relationship is characterized by the abuse of traditional male power. Despite the women's traditional values regarding love and marriage, the ideal of mutuality they believe to be part of love and friendship becomes irreconcilable with the notion of male authority in marriage. Mutuality implies consensus, while authority implies hierarchy. To eliminate violence in the marriage, then, the balance of power must either be equalized, or the woman must leave to escape further violence.

Some of the women appeared to be in acute emotional crisis when they decided to leave. Others appeared not to be. Are there common themes or reasons to explain why women finally leave? Does leaving a violent relationship represent the resolution of an emotional crisis around a particular battering episode? Or is the decision to leave perhaps the end-point of a longer problem-solving process? These questions led me to examine how helpless the women felt, and in what aspects of their lives they may have felt helpless. If women perceive themselves as essentially helpless, passive recipients rather than active agents capable of effective planning and doing, how do we account for the fact that they finally broke the vicious 'cycle of battering'?[4]

In their accounts the women sometimes spontaneously used the term 'helpless' to describe their feelings about the battering situation. If 'helpless' is understood in the literal sense of 'destitute of help', then these women often felt 'helpless'. Indeed, a frequently heard expression was 'Where was the help?' To examine this issue more closely the women were asked: 'During the years you were being battered, did you feel or think of yourself as "helpless", and if so, in what sense?' Here are some of their responses:

Yes, I thought he would kill me.

Yes, because I wasn't physically strong enough, and there was no help out there, and that maybe the only way I could free myself of him was to kill him.

In the sense I was unable to have him understand, his behaviour was inappropriate ... I had no power over him to prevent it.

Absolutely. I had no one to go to for help. It wasn't until the final years that I was able to confide in friends ... It was also more difficult to hide because of my bruises.

The women's accounts partially support the concept of 'learned helplessness' (Walker 1979), which is often posited as a reason why women stay, why they cannot escape the 'cycle of battering'. But factors such as physical strength and social resources also affect helplessness or self-sufficiency. Despite their desperate situations and the difficulty in identifying sources of aid, the women were hardly helpless. Generally, they were always scheming about how to stop the battering, e.g. by examining their own behaviour or ways of escaping the situation, by considering how they could get and keep some money. They took steps to please their mates and to satisfy their demands; they protected and took care of their children. Often they were the primary wage-earners in the household. Their accounts also reveal that they actively defended themselves and that when they did not, it was not necessarily because they felt helpless; rather, they had learned that a worse beating or other negative consequences would ensue.

A primary problem with the concept of learned helplessness is that it relies on women's psychological characteristics to explain their victimization. The model, therefore, can be misinterpreted to support traditional notions of women as passive, helpless victims, instead of stressing the social origins of women's learned helplessness. It is important that the language of 'helplessness' be used with caution, as it decries a view of women as capable, responsible agents.[5]

The women's experience suggests that if a 'battering cycle' exists, the factors involved are far more complex than merely the psychological elements. First of all, their experience was not as patterned as the 'cycle of battering' concept suggests. Some beatings occurred in the middle of the night when totally unanticipated. After the first beating there were no routine pleas for forgiveness, but rather diminishing remorse by the man. Also, some incidents were not remembered by the man because he was drunk, or they were denied outright. Only one woman said 'He always apologized afterwards.' But even her account contradicts this pattern in respect to the last beating when she spent the night at the gatehouse: 'He didn't even ask me where I was.'

If the battering cycle attempts to explain why women stay, then it could be construed that if this cycle is interrupted, the woman leaves, e.g. when the man fails to apologize. But even in the above instance when an apparent pattern of apology (in stage three of the cycle) is interrupted, it was not the man's indifference or failure to apologize that mattered. Rather, the woman cited the pressure she felt to tell her mother not to come even though she badly needed her during delivery. As she put it: 'Something snapped ... I made up my mind that day that I was leaving him.' The last beating and his failure to apologize occurred *after* her decision to leave.

To examine the propositions that victims do not define themselves as victims at first and 'the family system tends not to deal with the violence as a serious problem' (Giles-Sims 1983) the women were asked: 'During the years you were being battered, did you feel like or think of yourself as a victim? If so, in what sense was this so?' Their responses varied:

Yes, but I did not feel that I had to take someone beating on me.

I did not think of myself as a victim *then*. I assumed most marriages were similar

> Not initially ... probably not until the last one to two years and then I felt trapped and depressed, but I never thought of myself as the 'victim' per se.

> In the sense that my rights were being infringed upon as a human being, even to the point of my sanity being tested.

There is also a problem with the issue of judgements about the seriousness of violence. In spite of the widespread cultural acceptance of violence, the women in this study *did* regard the violence at first as serious. Typical of their response were expressions such as: 'I was shocked ... I couldn't believe he would do that to me.' Not only the women, but the men as well were often reported as shocked at what they had done. In fact, their shock at their behaviour can be seen at least partially as a reason for the men's remorse and promises not to do it again.

This typical response to first violence does not necessarily imply that the people involved judged it either as serious or non-serious. Certainly many women do not judge it as a serious enough reason to terminate a relationship. Some unmarried women who are beaten marry the man afterwards. But do these behaviours mean that violence is not seen as serious? The seriousness of an initial incident of violence is a highly subjective judgement, one that should not be generalized to battering situations as a whole. The men's elaborate promises not to do it again suggest that they more often regard it as serious. The very idea of 'promise' connotes seriousness and the expectation that the behaviour will not happen again. The women *believed* the men when they said they wouldn't do it again: e.g. 'I absolutely thought it would never happen again ... I never thought it would happen again after the 60th time.' Statements like this raise serious questions about whether there is an increased expectation of further violence once the rules against violence are broken. The women in this study did not *expect* to be beaten. They expected the men to keep their promises and *not* beat them again.

Antonovsky's (1980: 99–100) research on concentration camp survivors illuminates the women's reasoning process. He stresses the role of 'coherence' (the person's *interpretation* of stressful events) and 'resistance resources' (including especially social network support) as buffers against traumatic stress. A sense of coherence, writes Antonovsky,

> is a global orientation that expresses the extent to which one has a pervasive, enduring though dynamic feeling of confidence that one's internal and external environment are predictable and that

there is a high probability that things will work out as well as can reasonably be expected.

(Antonovsky 1980: 123).

He states that when he discusses the concept people often take it to mean 'I am in control'. Supporting this concept, I propose that instead of focusing on pathogenesis (i.e. what makes people sick, as implied in learned helplessness and systems concepts) we should ask what keeps people healthy (salutogenesis). Antonovsky proposes that social support and the *meaning* a person attaches to stressful events can influence their outcomes in the direction of pathogenesis or salutogenesis.[6]

It has been assumed that women's reasons for leaving a battering situation cannot be neatly categorized or explained by a single concept. In its broadest sense, leaving a violent relationship can easily be interpreted as a commonsense, healthy, positive thing to do. But if a woman does not permanently leave a relationship after one or two incidents of violence, a judgement of unhealthiness or masochism is not necessarily warranted. Antonovsky's concept of salutogenesis can be expanded by examining crisis theory and other research for its relevance to battering.

Stress, crisis, and illness

As noted briefly in Chapter 1, stress has long figured in explanations of why men batter their wives. Here the question is how the woman herself copes with a stressful life event such as battering; how her coping with battering while *in* the relationship might differ from the coping involved when she finally leaves. Concepts of coping with stressful life events often focus on the relationship between stress and illness (e.g. Berkman and Syme 1979). Here the stress/illness relationship is expanded to include the concept of crisis.

Research on the relationships between stress, crisis, and illness often fails to integrate clinical and social science insights (Pearlin and Schooler 1978: 2; Gerhardt 1979: 196; Brim and Ryff 1980: 376–7). Historically, it has been mainly anthropologists and clinicians who have addressed the concept of crisis.

Anthropologists and psychoanalysts for years have referred to human developmental transition states as 'life crises' (Chapple and Coon 1942; Freud 1950; Kimball 1960; Erikson 1963; Giovannini 1983). In anthropological terms, 'life crisis' refers to a highly significant, expected event or phase in the life cycle, marking one's passage to a new social status, with accompanying changes in rights and duties. Traditionally, such status changes are accompanied by ritual

67

(such as puberty and marriage rites) designed to assist the individual in fulfilling new role expectations, and to buffer the stress associated with these critical – though normal – life events. In traditional societies, families and the entire community are intensely involved in the life passages of individual community members. 'Crisis' in its clinical meaning refers to the sudden onset and brief duration of acute emotional upsets in response to identifiable traumatic life events with accompanying difficulty in problem-solving (Caplan 1964; Hoff 1989).

Battered women's experiences often encompass both meanings of crisis: violence from one's mate is a traumatic event, and if the violence occurs chronically as 'battering', it often necessitates a change in social status from married to divorced, usually accompanied by single parenthood. Such violence, and its attendant problems, fulfil the classic definition of crisis as a period of both danger and opportunity. It also highlights the importance of social, cultural, and material supports (Caplan 1964, 1974) individuals require to avoid acute emotional upset.[7] People in crisis are also influenced by social expectations of how to behave and by values guiding their interpretation of expected and unexpected life events (Geertz 1973: 3–30). Such factors influence whether a crisis will be resolved positively or negatively, i.e. characterized by growth and development, or self-destructiveness and emotional/mental disturbance.

How the event of battering is treated reveals certain disparities between clinical and social analysis of coping with stressful life events. Does the man who beats his wife do so because he is under severe stress? Is the victimized woman in emotional crisis or merely under stress? Are either of the two or both emotionally or mentally ill? If so, is the illness the 'cause' or the 'effect' of the battering?

In systems and behaviourist models, battering can readily be interpreted as a response to stress. These models present battering as an unplanned reaction to triggering events rather than a planned coping device. The overall picture is one of mechanical, *impulsive* responses rather than *purposive* human behaviour. Behaviourist models are coming under increasing scrutiny (Gergen 1982). The nature of the human life cycle involves response to the physical, social, and emotional tasks associated with growth and development and the various events one encounters in that process. Coping with developmental tasks and life crises demands a repertoire of skills and resources. The women's accounts in this research support the conclusion that there is nothing inevitable about human response to traumatic events.

Moreover, acute crisis states may *distort* an individual's cognitive functioning (e.g. memory and decision-making) due to interference by intense emotion, but not usually one's mental competence if mental faculties were intact before the crisis (Caplan 1964; Hansell 1976; Hoff 1989).[8] Thus, a person's decision to hit or kill their spouse during the high tension state accompanying a marital fight may not be wise, but can it be *excused* on the basis of mental incompetence? Should this behaviour be regarded as the action of a responsible social agent, or is it merely a behavioural event as behavioural analysts suggest? Are temporary insanity claims really insanity, or are they 'excuses' (Gelles 1974) used to evade responsibility for one's behaviour?

Some recent jury acquittals of women who killed their husbands suggest that these women were not mentally ill, nor were they merely passive victims, but rather that the stress and danger of their circumstances after years of abuse were sufficient grounds for excuse.[9] Similarly, many men are excused for their battering, while some are convicted. When women are convicted of murdering their husbands, however, historical and other research (Jones 1980; Browne 1987) suggests gross discriminatory practice. One explanation for such discrimination may be society's greater disapproval of female deviance, an attitude deeply rooted in customary notions of 'ideal' feminine behaviour. Even in radical feminist circles the willingness to examine female violence in relation to concepts of 'victim blaming', 'learned helplessness', and women as moral agents is just emerging.[10]

This study indicates that stress does not constitute a plausible causal factor in violence. Instead, evidence suggests an interactional relationship between stress and violence involving several factors: (1) violence is one of many possible responses to stress; therefore it is not determined (caused) by stress; (2) violence may, and usually does, result in stress and crisis for its victims: physical damage, psychological upset, change in social situation (e.g. marriage disruption, residential and/or economic change); (3) the extent of this stress, however, is probably influenced by individual 'definition of the situation' (Thomas 1931) and social support from network members. This interactional relationship is illustrated in Figure 4.1.

Developmental vs medical paradigms

Let us consider this interactional relationship further. In the last chapter it was noted that psychiatric labelling has been used to explain why women stay and to excuse their assailants. Here the medicalization of violence and its victims is examined from two perspectives: (1) How did the victims interpret their status *vis-à-vis* illness and health while they were battered? (2) Can a medical paradigm explain the *process* by which these women finally ended their violent relationships?

Figure 4.1 Interactive relationship between *stress* and *crisis* and possible *illness* in a battering situation. The arrows suggest the interactional relationship between stress, crisis, and illness. Trouble and stressors in a marriage can lead to positive or negative outcomes through several different routes, depending on personal, social, and economic circumstances.

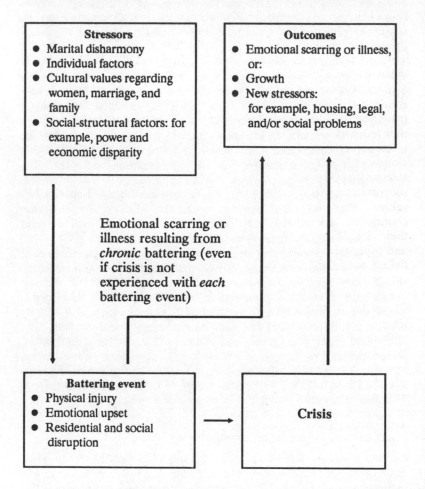

The women's self-evaluations revealed physical and psychological abuse to varying degrees over a two to twelve-year period. What is not clear is the extent to which these women were in 'crisis' in the clinical sense: an acute emotional upset in which one's usual problem solving ability fails. Whether these women could be termed in crisis is important not only theoretically, but also clinically since it has implications for social and clinical responses to battered women. Clinical definitions of crisis confine it to acute upsets lasting between one and six weeks (Caplan 1964; Hoff 1989). If this definition is followed, then each battering *episode* could retrospectively be viewed as a crisis, but not the entire battering period of several years. Application of the term 'crisis' depends on objective observations as well as subjective interpretations supplied by the upset person. Accordingly, these women cannot be assessed retrospectively for whether they were or were not in emotional crisis during each battering episode. What we do know, however, is that they somehow coped with the trauma of battering by various means, some of which were constructive (e.g. seeking help) and some destructive (e.g. suicide attempts or overeating). What needs to be examined further is the adequacy of their coping.

In earlier analysis (p. 46–50), the women's self-destructive behaviour was linked to women's traditional socialization to channel their stress responses and deviant tendencies inward, since they have been socialized to perceive their troubles as originating from within themselves rather than from external sources. But these women also channelled their stress responses outward, in fantasies about killing their violent mates. The combination of the women's self-destructive and other-destructive responses to stress can be better understood if linked to the concepts of 'resistance resources' and the women's values about women, marriage, the family, and violence.

It has been noted that some of these women felt socially isolated. They coped essentially alone for many years with the trauma of battering. Whether they were in emotional crisis with each battering episode or not, the fact that they survived and no longer live in terror demonstrates that they managed highly traumatic situations to the best of their ability. Significantly, no matter how they *felt* emotionally, they nevertheless carried out their social roles as wives, mothers, and/or wage-earners over many years of repeated trauma. This picture of competence, strength, and ability to cope starkly contrasts with the one of helpless victim or one haplessly driven by 'forces' inside and outside the 'family system'. It also suggests that 'survivor' is a more appropriate term for them than 'victim'.

Phases of crisis development

Two concepts from crisis theory reveal the continuity between the women's coping with the trauma over the years and their final decision to leave: (1) phases of crisis development (Caplan 1964); (2) natural and formal crisis management. These concepts also elucidate the relationship between stressful events and crisis.

Crises do not occur instantaneously but develop incrementally, in phases, highlighting the importance of coping to prevent acute emotional crisis and its potential for destructive outcomes (Caplan 1964). The phases of crisis development are:

1. *traumatic event causes an initial rise in anxiety level* (the woman's mate strikes her, she is shocked and wonders why, worries about what she can do to prevent it from happening again);

2. *one's usual problem-solving ability fails* (she tries to talk to him, he refuses to talk, she tries to be nice and second-guess his desires, he ignores her or hits her again);

3. *one's anxiety level rises even further following failure of coping strategy* (in response, new and unusual coping devices are tried, e.g. seeking help from a relative, calling the police);

4. *state of active crisis* (social support and internal strength fail, problem continues, anxiety rises to an unbearable state, e.g. a suicide or homicide attempt is made).

If a battering episode is seen in the context of developmental phases rising toward acute emotional crisis, then each battering event may be understood contextually: e.g. coping resources, personal interpretation of the event, severity of injury, etc. Each event of battering has the potential to become an emotional crisis (acute emotional upset accompanied by failure of usual coping devices), but does not necessarily constitute a full-blown crisis. Thus the conflict tactics a couple employ during a fight do not necessarily proceed in a neat hierarchical order from simple to complex. In the last fight described by Sophia, for example, conflict began with verbal arguments, followed by the man's attempt to choke her. Sophia hit him and pushed him down the stairs, and he verbally threatened her. She left and asked for help from relatives and then returned and tried to talk. He refused, threatened to kill her, and shoved her into bed. This battering episode illustrates all the phases of crisis development, culminating in a full-blown, acute crisis which Sophia resolved by taking a lethal overdose of pain tablets.

The women as crisis managers

Sophia's crisis leads to consideration of the concept of 'natural and formal crisis management'.[11] Sophia's behaviour during this battering episode can be seen as 'natural crisis management', a process that is an organic part of the human response to traumatic life events. Sophia was not a helpless victim; she actively resisted her husband's violent treatment. Recognizing her limits in dealing with the event, she sought outside help. She considered the advice received, decided to follow it, tried some further tactics of talking and 'being nice' to resolve the conflict, was met with resistance, interpreted what was happening as being 'treated like a dog', and finally decided on suicide as the only means left for ending her pain. In Antonovsky's perspective, her 'sense of coherence' was shaken, the social support she sought was ineffective, she was no longer in control except for her power to kill herself. Therefore, she resolved her crisis self-destructively.

Another woman said that her usual way of coping with the trauma of battering was by overeating, a device she also used before she was ever battered. The terms 'illness', 'unhealthy', or 'destructive' can certainly be used to denote addictions and assaults on oneself and others in response to the stress of being battered. Regardless of how such negative coping devices are labelled, however, the women's accounts in this chapter support the earlier suggestion that stress, crisis, and illness (physical, emotional, mental) are *interactionally*, not causally related (see Figure 4.1, p. 70). Figure 4.1 suggests that stress not only precedes but also follows a battering episode, and that emotional crisis may or may not be part of the total episode. These findings also support the work of Hilberman (1980) in which mental and emotional disturbances of battered women were found to *follow* rather than precede battering.

Analysis thus far reveals not so much a *failure* of coping by individuals as it does the limitations and misdirection of personal coping responses (natural crisis management) to certain traumatic life events. That is, suicide, assault, addictions, and emotional disturbance *are* forms of coping, though most people would regard them as unhealthy or ineffective (Caplan and Grunebaum 1967; Hoff 1989: 60–2). Put another way, 'natural crisis management' needs to be supplemented by 'formal crisis management', assistance from sources beyond the individual and immediate family.

The need for both *personal* coping strategies *and* social support (discussed in detail in Chapter 5) has profound implications for the successful resolution of crises around battering. In Sophia's case the initial support she received from her family was misdirected, e.g. 'You go back ... he won't do it anymore ... Welfare won't support you ... Here's $10, go buy a pizza and forget everything.' Only after a near-fatal suicide attempt were institutional networks mobilized, and these only for emergency rescue purposes. Prior to this destructive crisis outcome, however, crisis management did not go beyond the 'natural' level. The suicidal outcome of the crisis suggests that 'for-

Stage 1   Natural crisis management

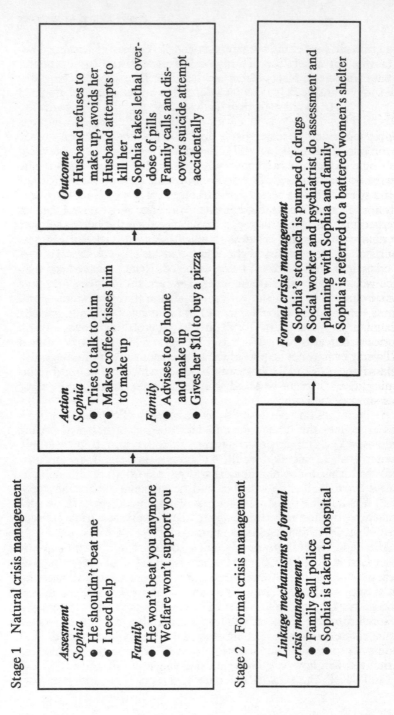

Assesment

Sophia
● He shouldn't beat me
● I need help

Family
● He won't beat you anymore
● Welfare won't support you

Action

Sophia
● Tries to talk to him
● Makes coffee, kisses him to make up

Family
● Advises to go home and make up
● Gives her $10 to buy a pizza

Outcome
● Husband refuses to make her up, avoids her
● Husband attempts to kill her
● Sophia takes lethal over-dose of pills
● Family calls and dis-covers suicide attempt accidentally

Stage 2   Formal crisis management

Linkage mechanisms to formal crisis management
● Family call police
● Sophia is taken to hospital

Formal crisis management
● Sophia's stomach is pumped of drugs
● Social worker and psychiatrist do assessment and planning with Sophia and family
● Sophia is referred to a battered women's shelter

Figure 4.2   Natural and formal crisis management during a battering episode

From victim to survivor

mal crisis management' was needed as well. The distinctions and relationship between natural and formal crisis management as applied to battering are illustrated in Figure 4.2.

The influence of crisis origins on crisis resolution

Sophia's suicidal response to the battering trauma is even clearer if the origins of stress are considered. Gerhardt (1979) proposes that if the origin of particular stresses can be traced to *individual* sources, *personal* coping strategies will be appropriate. If, however, the origin of the stress is social, a strictly individual coping response will probably not succeed. What this means is that stress is poised in a complex interactional relation with differential origins, on the one hand, and the nature of the crisis, the strategies for crisis management, and the results of the resolution, on the other. The traditional classification of crisis into situational and developmental types mirrors the theories and practice traditionally posited to explain battering and why women stay: e.g. personality traits, intergenerational cycles of violence, marital stress factors. Just as domestic violence was presumed a 'private' matter, so crisis theories have omitted categories designating the *public* aspect of this problem.

To compensate for this omission in explanatory models, this study reclassified emotional crises according to the *origins* of the events leading to crisis. Thus, crisis origins fall into three categories: situational, transitional state, cultural/social-structural.

Situational origins. Crises identified as situational originate from three sources: (1) material or environmental (such as fire or natural disasters); (2) personal or physical (heart attack, diagnosis of fatal illness, loss of limb or other bodily disfigurement from accidents or disease); and (3) interpersonal or social (death of a loved one or divorce). Crisis counselling and grief work (Parkes 1975) will usually result in a positive outcome (unless psychopathology was present before the crisis) from crises originating in such unanticipated traumatic events.

Transition state origins. Crises originating from transition states consist of two types: (1) universal life cycle transitions consist of normal human development phases from conception to death; (2) non-universal transitions are true passages signalling a shift in social status, such as migration, retirement, the change from worker (including homemaker) to student, from a violent to non-violent marital relationship, or from married to single parent.[12]

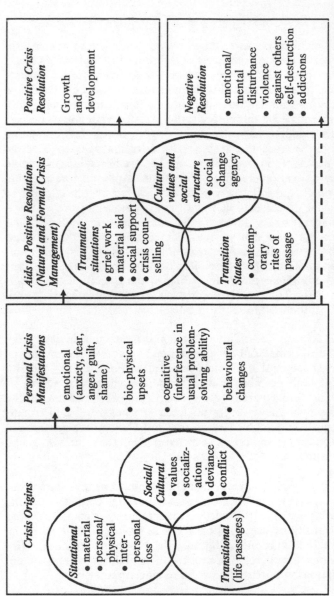

Figure 4.3 Crisis paradigm. Crisis origins, manifestations, and outcomes, and the respective functions of crisis management have an inter-actional relationship. The intertwined circles represent the distinct yet interrelated 'origins' of crisis and 'aids to positive resolution', even though personal manifestations are often similar. The solid line from 'origins' to positive resolution illustrates the *opportunity* for growth and development through crisis; the broken line depicts the potential *danger* of crisis in the absence of appropriate aids.

Cultural/social-structural origins. The third source of crisis is cultural values and the social structure. Crises arising from social/cultural origins include job loss stemming from discriminatory practice based on deeply rooted cultural values about race, age, and sex (as opposed to job loss from illness or poor personal performance, which can be viewed as a result of a prior crisis of illness). Also in this category are crises resulting from deviant acts of others, behaviour which violates accepted social norms: robbery, rape, incest, and physical abuse. Crises from these sources are never truly expected; there is something shocking and catastrophic about them, as seen from the accounts in this study. In crises originating from complex social/cultural or interrelated sources the implications for intervention are also more complex than in crises arising from universal transition states or other unexpected events. It is most important, then, that social and cultural factors not be misconstrued as individual, *personal* liabilities producing crises (Gerhardt 1979). To do so is to contribute to the process of victim blaming.

The relationship between the origin of a crisis and its positive or negative resolution is depicted in Figure 4.3.[13] This model of the crisis process encompasses both the personal and sociocultural factors involved in a woman's coping with battering. It suggests that if a crisis is to be resolved positively, the aids to positive resolution (or 'resistance resources' against traumatic stress) need to correspond to the distinctive *origins* of the stress. Battering in this model can be defined as a traumatic event originating from the deviant behaviour of one's mate, which in turn expresses certain values about women, marriage, the family, and violence. This is not to say that 'situational' factors such as stress related to job loss or interpersonal conflict around marital infidelity, for example, are not also involved. Since a battered woman usually undergoes a change in marital status, the model depicts that the triple origins of crisis are often intertwined. However, if crisis resolution strategies around an event like battering are not tailored to its complex origins, positive outcomes of the crisis are less probable.

To return to Sophia's situation, all the initial strategies used were confined to the top circle, which includes interpersonal situations. The conflict was defined by the family as only between the couple; formal network members not only were not involved, but they were written off, e.g. 'Welfare won't support you.' (Analysis in Chapters 5 and 6 shows that when formal networks are involved, the definition is still largely a personal or interpersonal one.) Accepting this interpersonal definition of the problem, Sophia returned to her husband as her brother-in-law advised, having been assured that she would obtain no public support if she left. She then tried everything at her 'personal' disposal to resolve the conflict and prevent more battering – talking, 'being nice', fixing coffee, etc. All to no avail. Finally the only recourse she saw was suicide.

Sophia could also be viewed as in the process of passage from a violent to a non-violent marriage relationship. In so far as she had insufficient social support for a successful passage, Sophia could be said to have remained in a 'liminal' state, with resulting personal insecurity and an ambiguous status in the community (van Gennep 1960) for which 'rites of passage' are indicated, as discussed in Chapter 9.

This interpretation of battering episodes and the emotional crises that may follow from them views the victim as actively involved in the process of crisis resolution. Nevertheless it also reveals that the victim is necessarily limited in producing positive outcomes if *social* strategies are not joined to her personal efforts. In other words, *individual* strategies applied to *social* problems will probably be ineffective. Social problems demand *social* solutions by collectivities of individuals united in the political pursuit of social change. Inattention to crisis origins with consequent mismatching of strategies toward resolution can result in negative crisis outcomes such as suicide and addictions, or constitute the basis for development of chronic episodes of battering.

Thus a woman may be beaten again and again *not* because she likes it, has learned to be helpless, or fails to follow through when pressing charges, etc. Rather, she is acting in a pattern that logically follows from a definition of battering as primarily an interpersonal, private matter between intimates. For example, the legal obstacles a woman faces if she presses charges are one manifestation of the predominant interpretation of battering as a *private* matter. Clearly, then, *definitions* of the problem can contribute to its perpetuation, as Sophia's case illustrates.[14] Static definitions of the problem and consequent masking of its sociocultural origins also explain the frequent failure of institutional sources of support available to battered women, apart from recently developed refuges.

Even if such services were sensitive to the sociocultural and political aspects of the problem, many battered women either do not know of them, or, since they accept the problem as personal, something *they* are responsible for alone, would not think to use them. For a woman, then, to leave a violent relationship and avoid killing either herself or her mate, requires external social resources, a 'definition of the situation' that no longer targets *her* as the source of the problem, and her ability to combine these external and internal resources in an action plan that preserves her own and others' lives.

Part II

Battered women and their social networks

Chapter five

Social network members' responses to battered women

Introduction

Since personal efforts are usually not sufficient to enable an abused woman to escape her mate's violence, formal assistance, corresponding to the public nature of the problem, is necessary. Yet most network contacts consisted of family and friends to whom the women themselves turned. The negative response of agency personnel to battered women who seek help is well known. We know less, though, about the dynamics of the negative interaction between battered women and formal network members. Thus, in spite of the scarcity of data from institutional network members, the women's accounts are analysed to indicate what does and does not count as help when in crisis. The women expressed complaints as well as understanding of people they turned to for help. In spite of their desperate need of assistance, they often gave people the benefit of the doubt, even when deeply disappointed in the responses they received to their appeals for help. This and the following chapter examine and compare the limits of support these women received both from natural network members and from formal network members. Chapter 7 analyses the values that influenced social network interaction. A brief overview of network analysis and how it is used in this research provides background for all three chapters.

Overview of social network analysis

Network analysis asks who is linked to whom, assesses the quality of the linkage, and explores how the linkage affects social interaction and individual behaviour (Boissevain 1979). In this case, network analysis examines the process of asking for, giving, receiving, or withholding help during a crisis around battering. *Social network* in this study draws on both theoretical and clinical usage of the term. Kepferer (1969: 84) describes network as a 'set of points (individuals) defined in relation to an initial point of focus (ego) and linked by lines (relationships) either directly or indirectly to this initial point of focus'. Clinicians define social network as the sum of human relationships that have a lasting impact on a person's life (Speck and Attneave 1973). Clinicians often refer to network contacts as 'significant others' (Hoff 1989). For this study network includes family, friends, clergy, employers, self-help groups, and anyone else significant to the woman – as Stack (1974: 90) states: 'Those you count on.' *Social support* here includes the gratification of emotional needs such as approval from significant others (Kaplan, Cassel, and Gore 1977: 50), as well as the material, social, and cultural requisites for avoiding crisis. I draw here on Caplan's (1964) concept of 'supplies' for mental health and Hansell's (1976: 31–49) expansion of Caplan's work in his description of 'essential attachments', the disruption of which results in 'signals of distress' and possible crisis, as discussed earlier.

My approach to networks in this study weaves together three strands in the development of the field: (1) network analysis in social anthropology (e.g. Bott 1957; Mitchell 1969; Barnes 1972); (2) network intervention strategies in clinical practice with people in crisis (e.g. Polak 1971; Garrison 1974; Hansell 1976; Tolsdorf 1976; Hoff 1989); (3) interdisciplinary research on the role of social support as a buffer against stress in individuals experiencing traumatic life events.[1] As noted in Chapter 1, a vast body of research points overwhelmingly to the role of social network members in an individual's susceptibility to disease, the process of becoming ill and seeking help, the treatment process, and the outcomes of illness – either rehabilitation and recovery, or death.[2] Clinical literature reveals that many practitioners are skilled in recognizing some social network members' destructiveness toward their own, as, for example, in child abuse cases. Much less is known, however, about two important aspects of network interaction.

The first paradox concerns social network members being both the most natural source of support yet the source of the greatest risk of assault. Usually, this paradox has been explained in terms of the emotional investment we have in persons close to us. As Simmel wrote many decades ago,

> The more we have in common with another as a *whole person*, however, the more easily will our totality be involved in every single relation to him. Hence the wholly disproportionate violence to which normally well-controlled people can be moved within their relations to those closest to them.
>
> (Quoted in Levine 1971: 91–2)

Although the necessity of social support from others is well established, as is the fact that the highest risk of violence comes from intimates and family members, we know less about the *process* whereby relationships become destructive rather than supportive among social network members. When it is clear that individuals can no longer expect support but rather fear assault and destructiveness from certain social network members, there is little knowledge and experience about how to create *substitute* sources of social support.

Several sources of data were used to examine these questions about social networks: (1) the women's general reports of their satisfaction with family relationships using the Self-evaluation Guide; (2) structured interviews with 25 (14 female and 11 male) network members of seven of the women, focusing on values regarding women, marriage, the family, and violence (the focus of Chapter 7); (3) a formal network analysis of 137 network members of five of the women using a detailed Social Network Questionnaire;[3] (4) participant-observation data from the women and some of their network members, plus results of one group discussion with four of the women.

Time and physical distance were barriers that prevented interviewing all network members identified by the women. Privacy was another barrier to obtaining information about network interaction. For the most part, violence between couples is directly observed only by their children. Even adult natural network members rarely witness the violence these women described. With more time, further direct observation of the women's interaction with social network members might have been possible.

In this research 'network members' are categorized as 'natural' and 'formal'. The 'natural' network includes family, friends, neighbours, and peer group members. This category is analogous to what most writers refer to as a 'personal' or 'effective' network (Barnes 1972: 11). The 'formal' network includes representatives from various social institutions the woman may have called on for assistance. This category resembles roughly what is referred to as one's 'extended network', i.e. those with whom one has less intense and less frequent relations (Barnes 1972: 14). Because of the history of research on violence against women and public debate on the topic, and because battered women seek support from both natural and institutional sources, here a social network member refers to anyone the woman was significantly related to and who could actually or potentially be called on for help.

The context, source of access, and extent of network member interviews varied. Access to network members was gained after initial interviews with the women and later discussion with them. Consistent with the collaborative approach to the study, in no instance did I seek interviews with the women's network members without their consent. For example, one woman, who lived with her parents for several months after leaving the shelter, stated explicitly that her parents would have nothing to do with the research. This is the same woman who said her father was very unsympathetic toward her both during and after her experience of violence, and whose mother reportedly abhorred people like social workers or other representatives of the 'establishment'. Another woman said her family relationships were highly unsatisfactory and they were hundreds of miles away. She deliberately created a new 'family' for herself through peer support groups from OA (Overeaters Anonymous), AA (Alcoholics Anonymous), and Al-Anon.

I also followed the women's judgement about the most appropriate way to gain network members' co-operation. Among the 25 network members interviewed formally, 16 were also contacted informally through participant-observation over several months. An additional 40 network members were contacted informally through participant-observation, but did not take part in formal interviews.

Time limitations prevented including all the women in the detailed network analysis (the Social Network Questionnaire), since it took three or more hours to complete, depending on size of network. For one woman there was a language barrier which, for a formal interview format, presented validity issues beyond those already inherent in questionnaire techniques. To compensate for this barrier, many additional hours of participant-observation were spent with her, and her two cousins (fluently bi-lingual) assisted at all phases of the research.

General evaluations of social support

The women's general evaluations of the help they received from network members are summarized from their responses to two items on the Self Evaluation Guide: family relationships (natural support), and agency help (formal assistance and support). Responding to the question: 'How was your relationship with your family during the time you were battered?' one woman said her family relationships were 'excellent'. She was the youngest in the study – in her late teens – and close to her parents before and after the battering. Another woman said she felt emotionally close to her parents though they lived thousands of miles apart while she was battered. This woman deliberately kept the 'secret' of her battering from her parents partly because her husband threatened her if she told, and partly out of shame that she had not lived up to her mother's ideal of a wife's right to respect and protection from her husband. This response suggests that the reasons women have for staying in a violent relationship or for not seeking help are more complex than is implied by the popular statement: 'I put up with it from your father ... You have to put up with it too.'

Eight of the nine women reported that their relationship with their families remained the same or improved after separation from a violent mate. Only for one woman did it get worse. And even in this instance, the woman lived with her parents and received emotional support from her mother, though her father – a former police officer – said, in effect: 'You made your bed, so lie in it.' The only woman with a high stress rating was the one who felt forced to return to her husband after driving 500 miles to seek refuge with her family. Significantly, this is also the woman whose mother had died when she was 15. These evaluations suggest that the women's relationships with family members are generally less negative than is popularly supposed.

Introducing the women to evaluation of formal network assistance, I asked: 'How successful were you in getting help from agencies (or doctors) when you needed it?' Responses reveal that before battering all but two of the women reported no problems here or said that the question did not apply to them. During battering only one was successful, although the picture generally improves after battering. These self-evaluations assume more meaning when considered in context and the exception to the general trend is examined. First of all, three of the women even *before* they were battered stated that the item did not apply to them, and one said she was seldom successful. Their responses revealed either that the women's problems at that time did not *warrant* seeking agency help, or their attitude toward the agencies was so negative and their expectation of a favourable response so low that they would not even ask. One woman said: 'I would never go (to get help). I didn't trust them. They'd look at you so accusingly I was afraid they'd send me to a sanatorium or something. I never went before I was battered either. I didn't trust them.' Two of the women with very negative perceptions of agencies were non-white. The women's reluctance to seek help in the first place raises serious questions about the *general* image of an agency's accessibility. The problem of unequal access to health and social services for people of colour and the poor has long been the concern of social activists. Findings from this research underscore the even greater urgency of this issue when women are in crisis around a value-laden problem like violence from one's mate.

In spite of these problems, however, all but one of the women (a black woman who would *never* have asked for help aside from physical refuge in a shelter) appealed to various formal sources of help.

85

Battered women and their social networks

Only one woman said she was always successful in obtaining help when she needed it. All the other women stated that they were 'seldom' or 'never' successful in getting help from agencies. With one exception the women's network contacts (natural and formal) were unsatisfactory, and their evaluations of agency help are usually worse than their evaluations of family relationships. This is noteworthy since an agency's publicly stated purpose is to help people whose needs extend beyond personal or family resources.

Social network characteristics

When social support issues were examined through the Social Network Questionnaire the picture is somewhat more positive than in general evaluations. One reason for this is that analysis of network characteristics did not distinguish in this instrument between natural and formal network members except in answers to individual items. Interview data compensate somewhat for this limitation. Although analysis of data from the entire Social Network Questionnaire was done with only five of the women, the other four women were asked questions 23 and 24 about the 'most helpful' and 'most disappointing' aspects of network interaction. Information from participant-observation supplements formal analysis of data from the Social Network Questionnaire. The women's networks were analysed according to interactional and structural/morphological characteristics. Interactional elements include content, directedness, intensity, frequency, and durability. Structural characteristics include reachability, density, and range (Mitchell 1969). (See the original work, Hoff 1984b, Appendix A for the complete Questionnaire.)

Interactional characteristics

The *content* of network interaction was examined for two elements: (1) emotional support; (2) information and material aid. The content characteristics of networks were examined separately for each element because of the crisis aspect of the battering situation. That is, a network member may be very supportive of a battered woman *emotionally*, but lack the *material* means of assisting her. Thus it was important to ask if a person *could* assist with money, a ride, etc., to distinguish their *willingness* to do so which is more likely to be influenced by values regarding the issue of battering. The following questions addressed emotional support, information, and material aid:

How much does this person make you feel liked or loved?

86

How much does this person make you feel respected or admired?

How much can you confide in this person?

How much does this person agree with or support your actions or thoughts?

When this person learned from you or someone else that you were beaten, what was his/her emotional response to your situation?

For each of your network members, note what is the *typical* kind of interaction you have with him/her; e.g. entertainment such as going to a movie or outing, talking over general problems, baby-sitting, family gathering, professional advice seeking.

For each of your network members, indicate what is a *typical* topic of conversation he/she might have with you; e.g. asking advice about kids, superficial discussion of things like the weather, sharing general trouble with husband, asking advice about partner's violence and what to do about it.

When you were beaten and/or your life was threatened by your mate, what was the *most* helpful thing a member(s) of your personal network did for you?

When you were beaten and/or your life was threatened by your mate, what was the *most* frustrating or disappointing to you in your effort to get help from members of your personal network? E.g. was there something you needed or wanted very badly that no one would or could give you?

If you were confined to bed for several weeks, how much could this person help you?

For each of your network members, indicate what is the *typical* kind of help you receive; e.g. borrowing money, a place to stay in emergency, a ride to the hospital, etc.

Directedness of network interaction was examined in the following questions to ascertain whether the relationship was one-way or reciprocal; i.e. would the woman ask and would the network member respond?

When you had non-violent trouble with your mate, how likely were you to *call on* this person for help?

If you asked this person for help about *general* conflict with your mate, how likely would this person *respond* in a helpful manner?

What is the probability of your *asking* for help in a family or marital emergency (other than a strictly *medical* emergency)?

What is the probability of this person *providing* you with help in a family or marital emergency (other than a strictly medical emergency)?

Intensity of network interaction was examined in the following questions:

When you were beaten by your partner and/or your life was in danger, how much help was this person?

When you were beaten and/or your life was threatened by your mate, what was the *most* helpful thing a member(s) of your personal network did for you?

When you were beaten and/or your life was threatened by your mate, what was most frustrating or disappointing to you in your effort to get help from members of your personal network? E.g. was there something you needed or wanted very badly that no one would or could give you?

Frequency of interaction was evaluated by this question: How frequently do you actually have contact with this person (phone calls, visits, or letters)?

Durability was examined by asking: During the past year, have you lost any important relations with persons you listed?

Morphological/structural characteristics

Reachability was assessed as follows:

What is the physical distance between you and this person?

In case of emergency, what are the physical possibilities of this person coming to your assistance in person (i.e. has a transportation vehicle or money for same)?

This structural aspect of social networks is closely linked to the Content element identifying members' material ability to offer information and assistance.

Density refers to whether the woman's network is close or loose-knit (Bott 1957). It was assessed in the following four questions:

How long have you known this person?

How many other members of your personal network does this person know?

How many other members of your personal network is this person on friendly or co-operative terms with? E.g. would two or more of them come to your assistance together in a marital emergency, or would they take opposite sides?

In an emergency situation, how many of the members of your personal network would possibly be available to you at the same time? E.g. if one person's phone were busy, how many others could you call on?

Range of network refers to the total number and types of relationships included in the network. Besides the natural and formal categories already defined for this research, the Range of network members was further categorized here: (a) family; (b) friends and neighbours (a and b coincide with the natural category); (c) institutional representatives (coincides with the formal category). Among family, the violent mate's family members were noted separately; among friends and neighbours, shelter *residents* were noted separately, while shelter *staff* were noted separately among institutional representatives. Except for questions which referred to the original battering situation, the women were asked to differentiate network characteristics *during* the violent phase and *after* separating from their mates.

Analysis of network characteristics

Data from the Social Network Questionnaire were analysed quantitatively and qualitatively. For quantitative analysis, responses to seventeen of the questions addressing the interactional and structural characteristics were organized on an interval rating scale from one to five. For example, in a question evaluating the structural characteristic of reachability, the women were asked: In case of emergency, what are the physical possibilities of this person coming to your assistance in person (i.e. has transportation vehicle or money for same)? Each network identified was then evaluated on this scale:

5 = definitely could not come in an emergency
4 = probably could not come in an emergency
3 = could come by private or public means within one hour
2 = could come by car or taxi within 15 to 20 minutes
1 = could walk or come by car or taxi within 5 to 10 minutes

The scores on questions constructed for quantitative analysis were standardized. Thus, a score of 100 per cent in each category would represent a social network with these characteristics: the network would be very *dense* or close-knit; it would include an extended *range* of members who are easily *reachable* and with whom the woman (*ego*) is in *frequent* contact in reciprocal or two-way interaction (*directedness*). The interaction would be *intense* or emotionally satisfying because network members that can be counted on over time (*durability*) would provide *emotional support*, *information*, and *material aid* during the crisis around battering. The scores representing network characteristics of the five women sugest that the maximum *potential* of social network support was not realized by any of the women; on the other hand, they were by no means without *any* social network resources.

Content and quality of interaction

First, then, let us consider questions which probed the *content* and *intensity* of network interaction. The women's descriptions here focus on natural network members, though some institutional representatives (discussed in detail in Chapter 6) are included as well. Typically, with family members, interaction varied according to the nature and intensity of the relationship; their interaction and conversation seemed quite normal, focusing on family news, children, and items of general interest, an observation the more striking in view of the personal pain these women were suffering. Predictably, those women who included counsellors and social workers as significant network members, stated that battering was the typical topic of conversation. With highly supportive friends the women could talk about 'anything and everything'. Questions about 'typical help' received revealed a similar pattern. Friends and family members offered emotional support, guidance, shelter and protection, money, rides, car use, baby care, and more. This was also true for a woman who was 1,500 miles away from her family. Two brothers made special trips to help her escape. One mother-in-law confronted her son with his violence. One woman's neighbour initiated court proceedings against the violent husband. Friends also helped by providing shelter, transportation to a women's refuge, and as importantly, by not withdrawing emotional support during the months – and sometimes years – it often took for a woman to leave. Those police officers who helped did so by providing rides and information about women's shelters.

To obtain a fuller picture of the positive and negative aspects of social network interaction, all the women were asked what was the 'most helpful' and the 'most frustrating or disappointing' in their efforts to get help from members of their personal networks. Here are some responses:

> *Most helpful?* My mother and sister got me out of that environment. They came to my rescue. *Most disappointing?* My father didn't want me back in the house. This was really depressing and frustrating. And my sister now is rubbing it in: 'Why did you marry that bum?'

> *Most helpful?* My friend took me to the shelter. Moving my furniture from point A to B helped a lot, too.

This woman said that 'emotional support' was what she needed most and didn't get. She also said that one friend helped but it was 'not the right kind' because she influenced her to drink when she was upset. Another woman said that the most helpful thing was that her two sisters listened to her. What she needed and wanted most, but no one could give, was 'the return of my old self-respect and self-love', but she received 'everything I needed that they could provide'. A man friend of this woman helped her regain confidence.

Another woman highlighted the role of her one loyal friend: 'She encouraged me to get a lot of help, to find out what my rights were. She assured me that I had rights. She gave me hope and information.' This woman said she was most disappointed in not getting from her family what she got from this loyal friend:

> that it wasn't my fault ... They said things that were victimizing. They told me to go back and settle it – 'It's your problem, go take care of it.' No one had the nerve to say 'Who the hell are you – she's got a 12 inch bruise on her back.' No one confronted him. Other than my friend, my network was mentally unhealthy.

She tempers this, though – in effect, excuses it – with the following explanation:

> They waited until everything was calmed down. They said 'Are you crazy? I'm not going to get into the middle of that.' They wouldn't help, they were afraid. I would go in with a knife and risk it with a batterer. The pain keeps the person isolated, but people get into psychological indifference out of fear. The responsibility was on me in the middle of being beaten, but I was powerless. People were so mind-blown about it.

> *Most helpful?* My parents let me come home for a couple of days. Then we all decided it was for my sake I go to the shelter, and after

going there, to return home and have my baby and live there with them until I could get an apartment. *Most disappointing?* Some relatives were talking badly about him and I knew that he needed help and needed to change, but no one could give that but himself. I was both frustrated and disappointed.

One woman cited several 'most helpful' things in various situations: rides to safety, a plane ticket to go home, reassurance from a police officer that her husband's problems were his own.

Most disappointing? When I was staying at his aunt's house and asked her husband for protection, to stay by me so he wouldn't do anything – when he was threatening to kill me – and he just walked away. I felt scared and completely alone even though I was surrounded by all these people [she had identified nearly two dozen network members in her immediate neighbourhood]. Another time was when I called up his father when Ricardo was doing drugs ... he said he'd talk to him, but he never did.

This account is supported in later discussion about Relational Pairs (see p. 94–5) and reveals the cultural context for one's assertion of feeling alone in a crowd, even if the crowd consists of one's natural social network (Benson and Hughes 1983: 138).

When scores from the Social Network Questionnaire are interpreted in reference to information obtained from interviews and participant-observation, however, they take on more significance. First of all, the range of network contacts supports the women's self-evaluation regarding family relationships and agency use, as well as the Values Index by network members (discussed in Chapter 7). That is, most social network support came from *natural* versus formal network members. In the network assessment during battering, out of a total of 72 network members cited by five women, only 10 (14 per cent) represented formal institutions. After battering the proportion was similar: 20 per cent of 65 network members were institutional representatives. This figure drops to 15 per cent if the three college teachers cited by Karen are excluded.

Karen referred many times to the support she received from teachers as she struggled to complete course work, care for her children, and work as a housecleaner trying to keep afloat financially. Such support was very tangible when she was encouraged by her English composition teacher in developing essay titles like 'Marriage and Slavery: What They have in Common', 'The Single Life: Advantages and Disadvantages', 'Why I Gained Fifteen Pounds', 'My Son Is A Lovable Person'. The successful completion of these essays through the support of a teacher and a friend represented for her a successful stage of working through some of her problems as a single parent, regulating eating, stress, and exercise to control weight gain, and weighing the advantages and disadvantages of marriage in her new relationships to men.

The scores of Loreen are the most consistent of the five during (60 per cent) and after (61 per cent) the violence. Loreen was in her late teens at the time; she had regular contact with her parents before going to the shelter and stayed with them for about nine months before obtaining independent housing for herself and her new baby. At the time of this network assessment she was considering a reconciliation with her husband and thus included members of her mate's family among her network. Karen, on the other hand, cited eighteen members of her mate's family as significant to her while she was battered, but noted none of them after leaving her mate. Although several extended family members were screened out during interview as 'non-effective' kin (Barnes 1972: 20), there were still thirty-nine altogether. This is more noteworthy since Karen was living in very close proximity to her mate's tight-knit extended family, yet had to rely on her own family hundreds of miles away and a family friend in the area for the necessary aid to escape from her violent mate. The brother and grandfather of her mate, however, were quite supportive of her. Also, a sister-in-law once intervened in helping her control her fantasy of killing her husband. The *fact* of her initial listing of so many 'ineffective' network members takes on more meaning when considered with this statement of hers in a tape-recorded group discussion of network support:

Karen: Never mind what they feel, what about how they act, about how/

Group Member: When you ask them for help and they shut the door in your face. That's when you know.

Karen: You know. Just like when my mother said, 'You can have a lot of friends but when it comes down to you needing help then you can count some of your real friends on one hand.'

This excerpt illustrates practical reasoning about who does and does not give help. In general, the relationships with a violent mate's family were strained or ambivalent. The response of Yvonne's mother-in-law is illustrated in the following interview excerpt:

One of his aunts and uncles went to California to visit my folks, not knowing that we were even separated. My mother thought they knew and filled them all in. And they went back and called up Robert's [her husband with two PhDs] mother and father. *How did they respond?* They didn't believe it. Well, they didn't believe it initially but then his mother called up and told Robert that they knew. And Robert, of course, denied it. So his mother called my mother and told her that she knew and my mother said: 'How did you know?' And his mother said 'I've seen Yvonne black and blue, but I never thought Robert was doing it to her.' *What did she think was happening?* She thought I was falling. Robert told her I had a clotting deficiency. *So what was her attitude when she finally got the news?* She hasn't called me in three years, so I have no idea. [Yvonne added that her mother-in-law may have felt torn between loyalty to her son and sympathy for her daughter-in-law.]

This example suggests that at higher educational levels, the dynamics of extended family interaction and family dismay about what to do are similar to those observed in working-class families. Well-educated people, however, have more avenues for avoiding responsibility for battering through familiarity with technical language, e.g. 'clotting deficiency'.

Another woman, Gwen, was loved by her in-laws, but deliberately refrained from seeking support from them while battered because she knew her husband's father would never let him in the house again if he knew of his son's behaviour. Here is another instance of the extent of a woman's self-sacrifice to protect and defend her husband, behaviour that suggests the depth of a woman's commitment to others at a very high price for herself. Naomi also said that her mother-in-law called the police several times to intervene in her son's violence.

The women's interaction with members of their mates' families can be understood further by drawing on the notion of 'Relational Pair' (R) as a categorization device used by network members, for example: parent/child; mother-in-law/daughter-in-law; friend/friend (Sacks 1967). Such relational pairs 'constitute domains of rights and duties and ... can be appealed to for help' (Benson and Hughes 1983: 136). This categorization device reveals how people order the set of people they turn to when in need. The rules of R provide two sub-sets of the relational pair: 'Those to whom one may properly turn for help, Rp; those from whom it would be improper to seek help, Ri' (Benson and Hughes 1983: 136). Thus in the R domain of parent/child (blood or 'cognate' relations), it would usually be considered 'proper' to ask for help since such relatives have a natural obligation to their own. In contrast it is less usual or natural to ask for help from one's in-laws (affinal relations, through marriage).

However, members' practical determinations about others – in this case, who has the knowledge, means, and willingness to help if asked – have the property of 'defeasibility'. The practicality of asking for assistance can vary, depending on contextual circumstances (Hart 1951; Coulter 1979b: 24, 54). Consequently, in situations such as a threat to life by one's partner, a woman may claim the *right* to call on 'anyone'. During crisis, a relationship through marriage (affinal) may be considered as 'proper' as one through blood for calling on and ascribing responsibility to help. In Karen's case, besides the 'threat to life' that necessitated her appeal to affinal relatives (Ri), her reasoning was also affected by the 1,500 miles that separated her from her natural relatives (Rp). How strongly these social and physical circumstances influenced her decision to appeal to her mate's relatives for help is more compelling when one considers that she was not married to the violent man she lived with.

The defeasibility and contextual variation of ascribing rights and responsibility to relational pairs is also observed in the case of another woman who stated she was 'loved' by her in-laws. This statement presupposes her right to call on them for help in crisis. Yet she refrained from doing so, knowing that her father-in-law would probably have taken drastic – even violent – action against his son if he knew. Her judgement that her father-in-law would probably 'blame' rather than defend his son represents an exception to the widely observed traditional practice of either ignoring, normalizing, or excusing male violence against wives (Dobash and Dobash 1979). These data suggest that there is a gradual shift occurring in the tendency to 'excuse' male violence in spite of having defined violence as 'illness'.

The scores of Jessica appear very curious with a 21 per cent difference in positive network characteristics during (85 per cent) and after (64 per cent) battering. Contextual analysis clarifies this change. Jessica, self-described as the indulged youngest daughter of the family, said that all four network members cited for the 'during' phase were highly supportive of her. This picture was confirmed during participant-observation with Jessica's mother and other family members. After separation from her mate, four of the new members of her social network included staff and residents of the shelter. Since these relationships were very short-lived, she evaluated them less positively than the secure relationships she kept up with her family. Participant-observation with Jessica several months after completing the Social Network Questionnaire confirmed this impression: shelter residents and staff were there and available if she needed them the first few months after leaving the shelter. Later, however, she was disinclined to continue active contact with other battered women.

Ruth had the lowest scores on positive network characteristics both during (45 per cent) and after (48 per cent) battering, suggesting the least supportive and accessible network among all the women. This is the same woman who expressed general cynicism about even *asking* for help in crisis, let alone receiving it. She also gave the impression in several instances of having the greatest need for privacy and her desire to rise above her difficulties and succeed by her own efforts in spite of the weak response she received when in need. The notion of 'the strength of weak ties' (Granovetter 1973) is useful in understanding this woman's network attachments. During Ruth's crisis of homelessness after leaving the shelter, she was taken in by her mother. Although recognizing her dependency and need for her mother's help, she maintained an air of detachment and distance through it all, assuming that ultimately she is responsible for herself.

Naomi had the greatest increase in network support after leaving her husband, from 56 per cent before to 72 per cent after. Several individual scores are significant here. First, in range of network members the highest number, eight, were family during battering, while after battering *no* family members were cited. This is the woman whose mother had died and whose father told her to leave after she drove 500 miles to his home for refuge against her violent mate. During the post-battering stage Naomi is the most isolated from her family of all the study participants. However, she is also the person who has created for herself a substitute 'family' through a tight-knit network of friends. Significantly, only one of these is an institutional representative, her lawyer, who assists her with child custody issues. Many of the others are members of various self-help groups with established reputations for supporting one another. Naomi's case supports Lindsey's (1981) work on 'friends as family'. Not only does she have the highest score on network characteristics after battering, but she frequently spoke of her new friends as her 'family' and ascribed many more positive qualities to them than she did to her natural family (with the exception of her mother who had died when she was a teenager).

The women's natural network members: strengths and limitations

Individual responses to network questions clarify further the process of interaction between battered women and their network members. First, let us look at natural network members. As already noted, one woman stated that her father and brother said to her in effect: ' "You made your bed, lie in it" ... he [her father] was critical of me as though I'd done something to deserve it.' However, she tempers this description that could be heard as 'blame' with a partial explanation of why her father would not or could not help: 'He told me that he warned me that my husband was an alcoholic. He was concerned but didn't know how to help. He thinks everything is a moral issue.' This can be heard as an excuse and presupposes the woman's belief that certain circumstances provide grounds for the failure of network members to help a battered woman (Coulter 1979a). The complex relationship between personal responsibility, traditional socialization, and the need for social support is illustrated in this woman's statement:

> As I went to people they were less and less supportive, because I was wavering in my decision, afraid I couldn't survive alone, that I needed a man. It comes down to whether you want to live or die ... I even put my children out [this statement is discussed in detail in Chapter 11].

This woman's case illuminates another aspect of network interaction. When everyone seemed to have given up on her and she herself had abandoned most hope of outside help, one friend stood by her. The following interview excerpt with her friend clarifies further the human process of helping and the place that 'caring confrontation' might play in this:

> At the time she was battered I was angry at her, angry at my mother who was battered. Cowardly, stupid, crazy – they should have defended themselves. There's no such thing as couldn't. We can use any means of self-defence. Threats of murder could be a silly threat. For example, she could use her hand to hit back. *What about violence breeding violence?* If you stand up for your rights you'll make your point sooner or later. I kept telling her to do something back, be defiant and test him, but she seemed to have this fear. I worked with her [at the hospital], and I got away with more things with him than she. I'd get so angry because she'd just melt: 'If you don't do something and be less than a coward, so what's the point of survival.' I'd have a fit at her, scream and holler at her: 'If you don't want to do something about it, I don't want to hear it.' *What kept her seeking your support?* We had a special friendship and I'm twice her age and she knew my mother was battered and we had a lot of things in common. I felt so angry at my mother for taking it. That's where I got my strength.

This interview, besides depicting the loyalty of a friend, highlights two other points: the friend's belief in violence as an appropriate response to violence; the importance of reserving judgement about why a woman stays with a violent man and does not retaliate violently. In this case, the woman knew from experience that any physical retaliation would only reap more violence. Her complex reasons for staying, while probably not apparent to the friend, remain *her* reasons, founded in reality as she experienced it.

In response to the question 'If you asked this person for help about general conflict with your mate, how likely would this person respond in a helpful manner?' another woman said this about her entire family: 'Not at all ... They just wouldn't. No one said anything. They heard me screaming.' Yet from participant-observation and interviews with some of the women's family members, they did not appear at all indifferent to her plight once she left the violent relationship. She confirmed this impression as she told of how much more friendly and outgoing her family were once she was separated. Also, when homeless, her family gave her housing and assisted her actively in other ways. Her situation underscores the dilemma family members face around helping battered women while they are still with a violent partner. It also supports Barrett and McIntosh's (1982) argument that families have probably been relied on too exclusively as the source of support for troubled people. One woman's experience reveals yet another dimension of network interaction. When this woman was 13, her family broke up. All the children were placed in foster homes when her mother had a mental breakdown. In response to the question 'What is the probability of your *asking* for help in a family or marital emergency (other than a strictly medical emergency)?' this is what she said about her family:

> What could they do? They were 1,500 miles away. I didn't want to get them involved. I felt my parents had enough problems of their own without having to deal with mine. [Her sense of complete responsibility for herself and all her brothers and sisters was strongly reinforced when she was placed in charge of the household in her mother's absence.] I made my bed and now I have to lie in it. I was always close to my mother so why should I hurt her. And I knew that when I was ready she would be there. My brother Jay came down when Ricardo held the three guns on me. I had asked him to come. He pushed me to come back with him: 'What if something happens to you?' My other brother Jerry said: 'I can help you but I can't carry you.'

When she did return, her father gave her temporary housing. These responses demonstrate compassion, commitment, and respect as well as the strength and resilience of families in spite of enormous problems. But they also underline the complex relationship between family members' good intentions and their dismay and confusion about how to help. They reveal the material and attitudinal barriers to helping, and the battered woman's absorption of the value that somehow *she* is primarily responsible for solving her problem. The interview also recalls earlier discussion of relational pairs (Rp, Ri) and the social circumstances that influence a woman's reasoning about asking for help. When all these complex factors are placed in context, the enormity of the challenge a battered woman faces is brought into sharp focus.

Chapter six

The women's interaction with formal network members

The content of formal network interaction

Responses of formal network members to the women's plight were generally less positive than those of natural network members. But there were some positive responses from individual institutional representatives, which included counsellors, nurses, physicians, police, and priests. Karen said it was 'highly probable' that she would ask her counsellor for help in a marital emergency, because the counsellor conveyed her interest by calling up occasionally to see how she was doing. Naomi enthusiastically praised her social worker:

> My husband had me so scared ... But I developed this network through a separation ... I worked with a social worker for two years and she and her supervisor were excellent. They went to great lengths ... She gave me her home phone number. She supported me emotionally, my children too ... Even after I left him she helped prepare and place the children. Upon an accident – the last beating – she went to court with me that day, helped me get the papers, she set up temporary care for the kids overnight, she was *there*.

But Karen said that another counsellor was 'too busy dozing' to make her feel respected and admired. When asked how much she could confide in this person she said 'quite a bit, though I don't think he ever heard a word I was saying'.

Naomi said her counsellor 'was like a dead fish, a picture ... I got no approval or disapproval from her.' Loreen was so negative about her counsellor that she did not even include the counsellor among her network members. This counsellor saw Loreen and her husband together and focused on trying to discover what Loreen was doing to provoke her husband into beating her: 'She tried to see that I would not stir anything up. I followed everything she said and he still beat me. This proved to me that he had to change himself.' That Loreen arrived at this insight despite the counsellor, underscores what Stark, Flitcraft, and Frazier (1979) see as a typical problem of patriarchal medical practice: that defining the woman as the cause of the problem not only does not help, but actually can make things worse.

Another woman seemed ambivalent about her relationship with a priest. She said that although he made her feel respected and admired, was very concerned and sympathetic, and would quite likely respond in a helpful manner if asked for help, she 'wouldn't ask' and would not confide in him because 'I didn't know him well enough'. The following excerpt from a group discussion concerning clergy support corroborates the woman's views:

Did any of you in your battering situation look for help from clergy and if so, what kind of help did you get?

W1: I was afraid to ask. I didn't get that feeling I could go to him for help ... because he didn't seem to be involved with the people.

W3: He told me 'It is wise if you got out' ... He was supportive.

W1: One told me one time I should pray to God for a husband and I said 'What if it's not God's will?'

W2: I went to the priest when I felt real desperate. He sent me to Catholic counsellors. It was a very cool reception. I was always afraid of priests. I found one alcoholic priest working on his problem. He was very good. He was human. Al-Anon is what brought me to God ... when I got scared and alone and I tried what they suggested.

The women's descriptions of police response varied, though most were negative. Karen said that one police officer who supported her gave her legal information and a ride, and told her

'You're better off without him ... He'll be out in two days.' [When he came] the officer asked: 'Is there any problem here?' and Ricardo [her mate] said 'No, we're just having an argument.' And the officer said 'I'm not talking to you, I'm talking to her.' He noticed that I was nervous and afraid to talk and then asked if I'd stand my ground. If I hadn't stood up then it would have meant to Ricardo 'You can hit me', and there's no sense in anyone helping me 'cuz I wouldn't help myself. I told the officer: 'It's something I got myself into and have to get myself out ... He's got trouble with drugs.' And the officer said: 'That's his own problem that he has to work out' and I have to think of my own life. It was these little things that put a spark of fire in my heart and kept me going ... I would like to get their [the officers'] names and write to them.

Ruth, although generally cynical about health and social service agencies, stated it was 'highly probable' that she would ask for help from police because 'they are supposed to help'. But she also said that it was 'very improbable' that she would receive help. Her belief is supported by her previous experience. After her husband beat her in the stomach (while pregnant) and attempted to push her in front of cars, he said: 'I'm going to take you to the police station and you can tell them everything.' This act of bravado seems to stem from the common knowledge many violent men have that even if they *acknowledge* their violence, the police will support them rather than the battered woman. Men's security that they will 'get by' with violence toward their wives is reinforced by one woman who told the police everything that had happened. They said it was a family problem and couldn't help. She was advised to 'go to court on Monday morning' to obtain a restraining order. When she later contacted the police, she was given the name and number of a shelter to call.

Naomi said that her husband 'slapped me in the face in front of eight cops and they [the officers] laughed. Then he said "Look you're screaming for help ... Look at the last time – it didn't work because you're crazy." ' These women's experiences with police parallel those cited by many other battered women (e.g. Martin 1976). Thus, implementation of State laws requiring that police protect battered women is very unevenly applied – this, in a State such as Massachusetts with one of the most progressive Abuse Prevention Acts.[1]

The women's accounts of their success with formal networks can be interpreted further by drawing on the membership categories they use in ascribing blame and responsibility. Even though police and priests belong to a category of people who 'are supposed to help', the women were sceptical of their ability or willingness to do so. The relational pairs (introduced in Chapter 5) here are Rp (priest/parishioner, police officer/citizen in distress) in which the parishioner/citizen has a proper (Rp) *right* to ask for help and the priest/police officer are *obliged* to help. Whether it was the social circumstances of a woman not knowing the priest well enough, or the belief that she probably would not receive help from the police based on past experiences, for the most part, these avenues of support were not productive.[2]

If people in Rp (proper position in the relational pair) do not respond, then the women's reasoning follows logically from their experiential reality. But one may also conclude that something is awry in the social order when people who make a reasonable request for help are not only denied assistance but instead are blamed for their distress. These findings go to the heart of the process of victim blaming and demonstrate the need for social change in dealing with the problem of violence.

Formal social network members' responses to battered women assume added significance if they are analysed along class lines. In general, battering among working-class and poor women is more visible because these women have greater need to appeal to public services such as the police for help. Although this study does not focus on the incidence of abuse across class, the research reveals a similarity among all battered women when they interact with family and with health and mental health professionals. Both the positive and negative examples of counsellors noted above occurred with *public* mental health agencies used by poor women. The two non-poor women did not appeal to the police, nor did they use shelters for battered women. One woman's experience in seeking the help of a psychiatrist, and her own extensive medical treatment for a gynaecological problem, reveals a continuum of professionals' responses to battered women regardless of class. Two interview excerpts describe the interaction of economically advantaged women with health professionals. One woman, who was beaten so badly that she was in terrible pain, describes her medical treatment in these terms:

The next day – I couldn't sleep all night – I called my doctor and said: 'I need help, I think I broke my back.' And so he said, 'Come over.' And then of course he said 'How did you do it?' And I said I fell off a skateboard. And he looked at me and started laughing. He thought that was funny, a 30-year-old on a skateboard. And he said 'Yes.' I had a big huge black and blue mark on my butt. But it was all covered so they couldn't see it. *Was that by design? Did you really want to hide it?* I did. I was too embarrassed. I didn't think anyone would believe me. *What was the meaning of the doctor laughing? What did you take it to mean?* He probably thought I was an idiot for getting on that skateboard. That was the craze then. *You don't think he might have seen through this as an excuse to cover up the battering?* I don't think so. *But he didn't ask?* No, he didn't ask.

And from that day on, it got more intense and worse. I was always black and blue, from here to here [points to arms and legs]. It wasn't until I got into the graduate programme, at the University when people started asking me why I was black and blue. We were in family therapy after my son was born ... Not once did that therapist say, 'How did you get all black and blue?' Not once. And finally, after I had left Robert, I went to my therapist and said, 'I've been sitting in front of you on and off for the last four years and I have not been without a black and blue mark. And you have not once asked me how I got those.' And he said: 'Well, I didn't think that Robert was ... ' And it was all excuses. And I said 'I don't care what you think.' I was just furious ...

Another woman told of similar experiences:

I remember what my mother said: 'If he ever hit me once that would be it' so I couldn't possibly tell them – they would have thought how stupid I was to have stayed. I was ashamed ... Many times I came to work [in a human services agency] with black eyes and someone asked: 'Does he beat you?' I said: 'Yes, every Friday night' – end of conversation. There was no response or attempt to help. *Why?* I think they don't know what to do with the information. One time I had my arms up and someone saw the marks and asked 'How did you get those?' I think she was also abused and knew. I quickly put my arms down and said 'I don't know.' I had seen all those battered women in our agency so I had lots of stories to use and work into my cover-up.

During one of our bad periods we went to counselling and the psychiatrist was worth less than a nickel. He was absolutely terrible. In 10 visits he *never* asked what we did about anger. *What problem did you present to the therapist?* Alan [her husband] went because he had trouble coping in his studies. The psychiatrist did not know I was being battered. *Why didn't you tell him?* It never was appropriate to the conversation. He asked how Alan was like or unlike my brothers or father. *How did you respond?* There *are* similarities, I can find similarities in any two people, but so what? I didn't tell either because it was deeply entrenched in me that it was our problem and I wasn't to tell anybody. I was afraid he'd retaliate if I brought it up ... He would beat me up because I told some of his friends something *good* about him. He kept me isolated. Because of that one of the reasons I never turned to anybody else was because I had no one I had turned to in any *other* area of my life ...

This woman also had dental problems as a result of beating. When her dentist asked: 'When does the tooth hurt?' and she said 'When I'm hit in the mouth' the dentist responded with total silence.

Like some natural network members, these responses from formal network members reveal a sense of dismay or bewilderment about what to say, what to do. They also suggest strongly that in some instances the women were testing the possibility of receiving a sympathetic response, were probing to see whether a professional would act on his/her obligations to help a battered woman. But in those instances where professionals or colleagues asked directly about bruises, the women deliberately covered up the battering. The reason may be deep shame, fear of retaliation, and absorption of the norm of battering as a 'private' matter. The responses of health and human service professionals to these battered women also reveal the pervasive 'privatization' of violence against women. This cultural value is so deeply absorbed by many health and human service professionals that it overrides their extensive socialization to help others in distress. Their failure to heed signals for help illustrates Dexter's (1958) concept of 'selective inattention' as applied to human service professionals, their lack of training in crisis intervention, and perhaps burnout (Berman 1983; Hoff and Miller 1987).[3] Additionally, it supports Truax and Carkuff's (1967) finding that empathy by mental health professionals *decreases* as the length of time from their original training *increases*. Conversely, these researchers found that non-professional crisis counsellors were highly capable of providing the empathy and support needed by distressed people.

The battered women's shelter movement (Schechter 1982) and this research offer fresh evidence regarding the value of peer support and lay help to battered women (McKinlay 1973). The point is not that mental health professionals are incapable of providing the same degree of empathy as non-professionals do. But a professional degree is not a guarantee in itself of qualifications to help people in crisis. Of related significance is that the two economically advantaged women held graduate degrees in human service fields and therefore had above-average knowledge of how to negotiate the human service system. Their experience with the attitudes of human service professionals, however, parallels that of a woman who worked as a para-professional in a large hospital, and revealed her insights into contemporary analysis of oppressed group behaviour (Hedin 1986) by nurses.

> I used to come in [to my hospital job] with bruises and they [the nurses] would talk about it: 'How can a woman be so stupid and stay with a guy like that?' The nurses were so unsympathetic. I couldn't have been bothered talking to any of them about my situation. But I couldn't help seeing how the doctors would put them down and they stood there and took it. Women are too competitive with each other ... They get that from men. They [the nurses] would complain about how they were treated by doctors and the hospital, but in their relationships you'd have thought they were

perfect the way they acted and talked.[4]

Women from all social classes experienced shame, fear of retaliation if they told, and dismay, bewilderment, or outright indifference from network members. When these factors combine with their own intensive socialization to protect and defend others (especially a male mate) and to feel responsible for making a marriage work, even at the cost of great personal self-sacrifice, it is understandable why battered women feel trapped in a violent relationship. As one of the women said: 'If *I* had a hard time leaving, with no children and a secure professional job, think of the working-class poor women with children, and how much harder it is for them!'

The dynamics of institutional responses to battered women

Because ascriptions of negative responses from formal network members emerged so frequently and intensely from the women, I explored this topic in depth during a group discussion with four of the women. Since the women were so often disappointed, especially by professional institutional representatives, and because I was concerned about gaps between research and clinical practice, the focus was to discover the dynamics of negative institutional responses to them during their crises. I also hoped to obtain constructive suggestions from the women about what they expected from formal network members. Here are excerpts from this tape recorded group exchange. (Code: *LA* = Interviewer; the women are *W1*, W2, and *W3*; empty brackets = unable to transcribe; / = interruption.)

LA : What bad experiences did you have?

W1: I asked him one time, 'Why did he decide to become a psychologist?' And he answered my question with a question ... 'Why did you ask?' ... He told me he was interested in people's behaviour ...

W2: I felt like I was under a microscope ... like I was a bug, a Harvard specimen.

W1: My doctor I see now ... She gives me feedback ... Like my relationship with Jack, she told me 'Maybe he can't *deal* with it. It doesn't necessarily reflect on you.' She would let me know that she was listening.

LA: So you want feedback and some advice ... Going back to the negative, you felt like you were not listened to?

W1: Yeah, sometimes I used to think he was falling asleep on me.

W2: Oh, I had one fall asleep on me last year. He actually sat there like this [gestures with bowed head]. I never went back. I said 'I'm sorry I can't use your services. You don't provide any.'

LA: [to W1] Did he know you were battered? Did you talk to him about the battering?

WI: Yeah.

LA: What was his response to your being battered?

W1: Ah, ah.

W2: Ah, ah.

LA: [to W2] What else about the other one?

W2: I had two sessions with her, one was an information one, an intake and then the first session and she sat there and I was feeding to her the dilemma that I found myself in, seeking counselling about what I should do about it and she just sat there.

She was listening, but I got no feedback, that was the one thing that was most crucial in my life, it sent me into the pits ... she put me on medicine. She's a psychiatric social worker for a State mental facility. I called in desperation about the battering and I thought I was going crazy, why can't I get out of this? What can I do? I need help. I was in a desperate state. She said 'Come up here and make an appointment. You need to learn to cope with the situation.'

LA: You need to learn to cope with the situation?

W2: So, in other words, right there I felt like I was bein' – the situation was being *minimized*, I needed to learn to *STOP* it, not to *COPE* with it. You don't *cope* with someone *beatin'* on you. I'd been coping for *years* with someone beating on me/

Right *away* I was made to feel with that statement that *I* was less than capable as a human being, that *I* was doing something wrong. I went up there and made the appointment with this self-doubt saying 'Well, they're professionals. They know – I'm gonna go to them and they'll tell me what to do.' I went there, I sat there week after week ... They gave me Elavil [an anti-depressant drug] and they, because of my anxiety neurosis, that scared me out. I have more books to identify these words and read up on 'em and find out what's *really* wrong with me and wrong with him – I'm ( ) finding out what's wrong with him, figuring out that he's worse off than *I* am, on my own. Anyway, I'd sit there and talk and this woman would sit there and listen, and I told her all the things I thought a psychologist ought to know about my childhood – she'd ask a few questions about my childhood mostly. Then she had me go in – to see this man ... And this guy asked me one question 'How's your sex life?' and I *burst* into tears, like [said sarcastically] 'My sex life was great, it couldn't have been better!' and I thought he meant 'How often do you get laid?' you know? I, I was so embarrassed that this *strange* man, that this woman brought me in to, here being beaten by the only man in my life for years.

LA: Do you think he knew about it?

W2: Well, I told *her*. I imagine that she communicated to him. I don't know but she wouldn't tell me either. They were very closed about my case, about what they were writing down about me ... I'd ask 'Well, what are you writing about?' I was real shy and timid. I was terrified of them. I thought they could put me away in this institution. I saw people walking around in bathrobes ... I heard stories about some of them. And my *husband* proceeded to tell me how crazy I was, so I couldn't let *him* know I was going there. I was isolated like Karen said. The sessions themselves ... I sat with this woman and told her all this information about me. She gave me nothing about what *her* role was in this supposedly helping relationship, which wasn't helping me at all. All I was doing was filling my gut, being fed pills and told to come back the next week! And when I would ask for feedback, 'Where am I, who am I, what am I, how am I doing?' I got 'Well, we'll talk about it next week.' Finally I went to Al-Anon, I got *IMMEDIATE* therapy – feeling-level therapy ... You're gonna be O.K. – you're not alone, this has happened to other people, you *will* survive, a day at a time ... I called them up and said I don't want to take the pills anymore. They told me I have a resentment ...

LA: When she said you have to learn how to cope, what would you ideally like to have had this person say instead of what she said?

W2: I know how to recognize help, quality professional mental health care ... Some will say 'Sounds like you've had some situations that have given you a lot to deal with. Do you think that counselling – How can *we* help you?'

W1: They've asked you that? [sounding surprised]

W2: I think the professionals should ask that ... a good professional draws the person out and makes the person comfortable,
because they wouldn't be calling if they're comfortable. They're
calling because they're *uncomfortable*. And they would ask 'Why
do you think it's necessary? I can see your reason for calling.
What do you think we can do for you because I'm not sure we're
in a position to do what you expect and we need to know what
you expect of us?' And, I think that that would *right* away make a
person with problems feel very comfortable to open up and say
'These people care, I can spill my guts to them.'

LA: And you [speaking to others] agree with that?

W1: Yeah, 'cuz when you call up and say *'Help* me please!' you
feel so bad, it makes you feel you're not even worthy as a person,
you feel humiliated, it's a feeling of being rejected to have to ask
for help. You call up, you've *made* the initial step. You need
feedback to say, 'Well, I'm here.' You need proof that someone's
gonna help.

W2: You call and you don't even know if they're capable of helping you.

LA: [to W3] B, what was your experience?

W3: I was beaten, and I went to school the next day and I called
my counsellor from school, I'd been bitten, and all kinds of stuff,
hit with the fist, and she said you know, come in ... after school.
And I had my parents meet me at the place. And I went there
and she told me that I did something to provoke this. That I did
something – Wow! I didn't agree with her but all of a sudden,
you know – the way that she said it and how I'm being treated by
this boyfriend who is now my husband – soon to be ex, I hope –
it made me feel guilty that I *had* to have done something, and I
searched myself to find out what the hell and it was nothing ...
She told me that it's my fault, that I did something to provoke it.

W2: I think the professionals have a problem too 'cuz there are
times when people call up in utter fear after a beating ( ) and I
was whispering like an animal, and I don't know what would
have helped ... what I do if somebody calls on the crisis line at
the shelter, I say 'Where are you?' I try to make them feel comfortable right there, 'cuz that's the biggest thing with battered
women, is they feel isolated.

LA: What if you had a battered woman who, let's say either on
the phone or came in, let's say the person responded along lines

you've suggested and your sense is that the woman either isn't ready or is extremely dependent or doesn't want to take the necessary step. What would you do, what would you expect in that kind of case?

W1: You can't really make that person get out until they're ready. You just have to let them know that there's help there.

W2: I know I was in that position. I'd say in a kind way, I'd just share my experience with them, and I usually put the facts out, this has gone on for a while, it hasn't gotten better, there is a place to go, that can help, but only you can do it.

W1: In other words you make them realize/

W2: The reality. I take them out of the isolation ... I say, 'Look, it took me years to become willing to want to pay the price. Everything has a price and getting out of that situation also has a price.'

W1: They don't have enough confidence in themselves and they want to know that there's someone to hold onto ... they're at the end of their rope ... You have to let them know 'When you're ready we're here to help you, but you're the one who has to do it.'

[Interruption to speak with children]

LA: Getting back to the professionals/

W1: Stop trying to tell us what to do and just be there when we need it.

LA: How can they learn?

W2: Get out of the intellect and into a little bit of emotion. Stop sufferin' us with their degrees!

LA: Supposedly professionals are taught all that, but you say they're not doing it for battered women.

W2: You give us equal time with battered women and I'll bet you we'll come up with more success than these educated professionals!

W1: Let them volunteer, or better yet, I'll charge to teach them what it's like to be battered. We could do it, we're the professionals here.

W2: They should know what's going on in a battering situation.

LA: Where can we start with professionals who think they

110

already know?

W2: Volunteering in a shelter would help. Professionals need to know *how* a battered woman *feels*.

[Interruption for children]

LA: What about nurses and doctors?

W2: I had to go to the hospital ... The doctors, there's this secrecy – I'd had some legal experience – I was hit with a chair – I told the doctor 'Please *record* this injury, for a legal proceeding' 'cuz I wanted to be prepared for my lawyer ... And he looked at me like I was *nuts*, and he was non-supportive ... What I wanted to hear was 'Oh, you're a battered woman – We know just what to do. We'll put this down in case you ever need it for court.' He didn't offer. He was like, Oh!!! a creature! A battered – his attitude was like – he gave me a dirty look. I demanded that he make sure it was recorded medical-legal because I may call for it as evidence in court/

W1: And he made you feel like/

W2: He acted like I had balls to ask him something like that and what kind of creature were you/

W1: Sometimes they make you feel inferior/

W2: He made me feel very inferior. I had the strength at that time, but before that – I can imagine a new battered woman/

W1: Didn't they ask you what happened?

W2: He did ask me and I told him ... and he sent the nurse in – I was undressing for the examination – and, and she touched me like I was, this/

W1: Yuk! [gets up and jumps back from her chair to demonstrate the sense of contamination and avoidance she said nurses and doctors seem to feel on learning that a woman is battered]

W2: Like that, like this – a battered woman, ooh!! It was so, so disgusting to me, it was so aggravating to me.

[Interruption with children]

W1: What she was talking about – it's society. You say you're battered and 'Oh, my God, I'm gonna catch that disease! Stay *away* from me.' They *do*! They have you stereotyped.

LA: What gives you that impression?

W1: They don't talk with you. You can sense it. It's a feeling. It's hard to describe but automatically they put these ( ) They get quiet/ ( )

LA: What about when your eardrum was punctured?

W1: I was tired of lying. I had marks on me. Never once did he ask me, and I was too humiliated to even say – it was almost like you have this feeling that you're the only one, and you feel it's because I made the wrong choice – I thought I was being punished.

LA: What do you want them to do?

W1: Stop being ostriches with their heads in the sand. They know what a battered woman is. Say 'What happened? You can talk to me.' Be *caring*. We need help. He only responded to give me medical attention. He never responded to give me any emotional support. He said 'How did this happen?' I said 'My boyfriend slapped me across the face.'

LA: What did he say?

W1: Nothing!

These accounts present such powerful commentary in themselves that detailed analysis seems redundant. On the other hand, entire papers could be written on several themes revealed here. I will limit myself, however, to several general statements directly relevant to social network issues in this research. First, the accounts are remarkably similar to published works on psychotherapy (e.g. Truax and Carkhuff 1967; Orlinsky and Howard 1978; Kaplan 1984).

All these authors point to the quality of the relational bond, listening, and empathy as key components to success in therapeutic relationships. The importance of these elements (plus feminist consciousness) in the process of helping women is based on the fact that women's growth and development is focused on connectedness and relationship to others (Miller 1976; Gilligan 1982; Kaplan 1984; Rieker and Carmen 1984). The similarity between the women's accounts and professional works underscore a key assumption in this study: battered women are not 'cultural dopes'. They *know* how to recognize a 'good' professional. For instance, one woman, with no formal training in crisis intervention, knew that prescribing an anti-depressant drug is not right for a battered woman.[5]

In spite of extensive clinical literature on the importance of network approaches for people in crisis, such approaches are conspicuously absent in these accounts. While authors like Stark,

Flitcraft, and Frazier (1979), Dobash and Dobash (1979), and Kurz
and Stark (1988) cite agency representatives' generally negative responses to battered women, it should be noted that professionals
may also make things worse.[6] Finally, these accounts reveal another
ugly side of the process of victim blaming: the 'taboo' attached to
being a battered woman, similar to the social ostracism resulting
from suicide, cancer, and AIDS (Acquired Immune Deficiency Syndrome) (Goffman 1963; Douglas 1966; Sontag 1979, 1989; Bateson
and Goldsby 1988). This aspect of battering is usually not talked
about precisely because taboo topics and stigmatized persons are, by
their nature, not to be mentioned in polite company. It is noteworthy
that such a taboo may extend to the researcher. Just as those who give
service to devalued groups like the retarded or the elderly are not esteemed, I have sensed several times that my choice of battered
women as a research topic has served to devalue me in the eyes of
some researchers.[7]

The women's accounts underscore the central role that social network support plays in the process a woman goes through in freeing
herself from a violent relationship. Sometimes network members –
especially institutional representatives – are part of a battered
woman's problem. More often, though, natural network members in
particular were part of the solution for women in this study. In some
instances network members the women identified appeared to em-
body all the negative stereotypes and rejecting attitudes that have
been exposed by previous authors (e.g. Martin 1976; Dobash and Dobash 1979). Such negative responses from natural network members,
however, were not found as frequently as had been anticipated. Even
in cases where a woman felt most rejected by and isolated from her
family (e.g. Naomi), the woman herself stated that relatives failed to
help because they were terrified and simply did not know what to do.

The women's accounts present a remarkable picture of their mod-
est expectations from network members, though they did ascribe
blame to some professionals. Their self-recriminations suggest that
these women, like many others, are perhaps too self-effacing, too
ready to accept responsibility beyond what might reasonably be expected. Their reasoning about how to get help and their expectations
of and excuses for social network members conform to the cultural
norms of the society of which they are members. They know, in theory, who is morally responsible for helping, but they also know from
practical, bitter experience when not to ask. Furthermore, in keeping
with the widely accepted practice of victim blaming and the socialization of women toward concern for others rather than themselves,
they often excuse batterers and negligent professionals while blaming themselves. Nevertheless, they were aware of their own role in

eventually freeing themselves from violence even though they wanted and needed help to do so. Their odysseys negate images of battered women as helpless victims or 'cultural dopes', and reveal just how complex is a woman's task of escaping from a violent relationship.

The women needed to know that when the appropriate time came, escape was realistic – usually when there was *no* further hope for change, when there was threat to life, when economic circumstances were right, and when additional outside support would be there when needed. Conversely, if a woman perceived helpers' *potential* negative, non-supportive attitudes, her chances of mobilizing material resources and acting on her desire to leave were reduced. This argument is supported by the fact that most of the women left temporarily several times before their final departure, and that in the process of planning escape, testing the reliability of social network support was one of the important steps.

Implications for human service policy and practice

These findings reveal the highly complex web of relationships between individual, social, and material factors that affect whether battered women remain in or leave violent relationships. They also confirm findings from the crisis literature regarding the role of social support in the positive resolution of crises (Polak 1967, 1971; Hansell 1976; Hoff 1989: Ch. 5). Furthermore, they highlight the crisis in mental health and social service delivery systems concerning poor, disadvantaged, and powerless people; i.e. the need to make these public services more accessible and available to people in crisis. In practice this means that: (1) a concerted effort should be made to correct attitudes among human service professionals that express society's most negative values toward battered women, attitudes that might make an otherwise adequate service inaccessible to such women; (2) bureaucratic service delivery practices should be reformed so that workers are not so burned out themselves that they further victimize battering victims.[8]

Attention to these issues in health and human service delivery systems could affect practice in two additional areas: (1) formal network representatives would enhance their ability to assess natural network members' potential to support a battered woman; (2) when it is clear from such assessment that a battered woman's natural network may be part of the problem rather than part of the solution, formal network members could act as catalysts to link women to substitute social support sources; or they could assist in creating new social networks when necessary. Facilitation might include linking the woman to a shelter for battered women. At the very least, though, it would preclude simply referring a woman to a psychiatric service thus redefining the problem as one of her own psychopathology, and ignoring the social origins and ramifications of the problem. This is not to say that some battered women do not also need psychiatric treatment, but when such treatment is indicated it should be conducted by persons sensitized to a feminist analysis of violence against women.

These findings also suggest that the extended family in the metropolitan area of the study is stronger than public and professional opinion might have thought. Nevertheless, since most of the families in this research were supportive but remained at a loss about how to help, there is powerful evidence that battering is a *public* problem which extends well beyond the family's boundaries and resources. However, the formal network members' generally negative responses to battered women symbolize the failure to define violence as a public problem.

The need to thus redefine violence in socio-political terms is particularly significant in view of the increasing tendency to speak of 'family' or 'spousal violence' as distinct from 'violence against women' and to interpret the violence in an intergenerational family systems framework, in spite of the opposite position taken by feminist activists (Bograd 1984). These developments suggest a backlash against public concern for women's problems. It would be unfortunate if we merely substituted family-blaming for individual victim-blaming in another effort to resist accepting the public, political dimension of this problem. As Barrett and McIntosh (1982) note, it is not so much that the family is dying or evil, but that we have perhaps asked too much of the family and not enough of other societal sources of support for ordinary and troubled individuals.

Chapter seven

Social network members' values

Introduction

Social network members' response to the women reveal how network members' values either facilitate or impede battered women in getting necessary outside assistance. Data analysed from twenty-five tape-recorded interviews with social network members from diverse class, race, and religious backgrounds, focused on their values regarding women, marriage, the family, and violence, and how these values intersected with the values of the women.

Analysis of social network members' values

The interviews were framed around the 54-item Values Index, compiled from theory and research, and from popular knowledge, myths, and attitudes regarding women, marriage, the family, and violence (Hoff 1984b: Appendix A). Seven of the original items were eliminated, either because they had a neutral value, or they depended on very subjective experience, or the participants did not easily understand them. The items were broadly differentiated on a traditional-feminist continuum, and then subdivided into 'values' and 'knowledge' based on the assumption that knowledge may (though not necessarily) influence one's values and beliefs. Statements were assigned scores on a five-point Likert-like scale (from 'strongly agree' to 'strongly disagree') to signify traditional or feminist values.

To reduce bias and the influence of my own values on the research process, the interviews were conducted with network members as early as possible after they had been introduced in person or by telephone. The battered women themselves were interviewed about values during the first structured session. Terms like 'opinion' and 'ideas' were used in order to avoid revealing to interviewees the traditional or feminist value I had assigned to the items. People expressed themselves freely at both ends of the traditional-feminist continuum, which suggests a close correspondence between their responses and what they actually believe about the topics (in contrast to socially acceptable responses). Additionally, the items were introduced as topics for discussion as much as to ascertain traditional or feminist values. Finally, of the sixteen network members interviewed who were also seen in participant-observation, some of their expressed values were also observed interactionally. In general, I avoided a 'forced-choice' approach to this 'objective' tool, and instead, used it to aid interpretive and contextual analysis.

Among network members formally interviewed, only three persons out of the twenty-five, the lawyers for two women, and the pastor for one woman, were members of formal institutions; the rest were 'natural' network members, i.e. family, friends, or peer group.

Network members' scores were analysed according to gender and compared with those of the battered women. The lowest possible score is 47 (signifying most traditional) and the highest is 235 (signifying most feminist). The mean score of the women was 186, somewhat higher in feminist values than either the male (170) or female (175) network groups. The slightly higher feminist scores (7 per cent difference between the women and male network members, and a 5 per cent difference with female network members) could be attributed to the suffering the battered women experienced, and their exposure to feminist values by actually leaving the violent relationship and, in most cases, seeking emergency refuge. The experience of battering – directly or indirectly – may raise everybody's consciousness. The relative equality of scores also supports the concept that family plays a significant role in shaping one's values.

Most of the network members held traditional views on some points, but their values were quite feminist on other points, with the majority tending more toward feminist than traditional values. Such findings suggest caution against stereotyping people as 'women's libbers' or 'hopeless conservatives'. But it is also possible that some network members may have given 'acceptable' responses in disapproving violence and approving economic equality for women, since these issues are currently very much in the public domain. Their sympathy and concern for their sister or daughter who was beaten and was now experiencing economic hardship may also have influenced their responses.

This analysis of aggregate and average scores, however, has two limitations: (1) the small sample size makes it impossible to draw firm conclusions about statistical differences between the groups; (2) there is an inherent limitation in quantitative approaches to analysis of people's beliefs and values regarding such sensitive topics as women, marriage, the family, and violence. Therefore, interview data are analysed further by examining individual scores – including the extremes – in the context of qualifying statements made during interview together with participant-observation data revealing relationships between network members and individual battered women. From this analysis the following conclusions emerge.

Of the nine women, the one with the lowest score (145 out of a possible 235) was only four points higher than her father's (141), although her mother was closer to average scores with 174. These scores assume added significance if related to age and class. This woman was the youngest in the group, in her late teens at the time of the study. She also spent less time in a violent relationship than the other women, and was in regular supportive contact with her parents through the entire two-and-a-half-year battering period. Significantly, her father (a para-professional service worker) obtained the lowest score (signifying most traditional attitudes) of all network members interviewed. However, even this score represents a moderate position between traditional and feminist values.

Throughout her adolescence, this woman observed her father routinely assume daily cooking, food shopping, and child care activities (he was receiving a disability pension from paid work) while her mother worked for pay at a menial job. This man, alone among the eleven men interviewed who routinely performed traditional 'women's work' without apparent resentment (as observed on several occasions by the researcher), nevertheless expressed more traditional values than many others. Of further interest is his similarity to the fathers of two other women: one father, a business worker, had a score of 144; while the professional father of another woman had a score of 181. All three of these men strongly expressed their disapproval of and helplessness to stop the violence toward their daughters. Two of the fathers spoke of their inclination to beat up the violent husbands if they had a chance. The para-professional father was so exasperated trying to answer people's questions about 'What keeps them together?' that he said 'She must love to be beaten ... If she wouldn't like it she wouldn't be with it ... Something must be holding her [the daughter was still working at possible reconciliation at the time of this interview] ... Maybe he's got something on her.' Despite these attitudes, though, he also made frequent statements of concern and support for his daughter. A professionally educated father was equally exasperated and frequently blamed himself as well as his daughter.

Values and exasperation: a case analysis

The parents' consternation, their groping for answers about why their daughters were beaten and what they might have done to prevent it is illustrated in the following excerpts from an interview with the affluent parents of one woman. The woman's father (with a score of 181) held a graduate professional degree, while her mother (with less formal education than her husband) came from upper middle-class New England ancestry, and worked in a managerial position. The couple reside in an exclusive suburb of a large metropolitan area, where the mother is known for her informal 'counselling' of affluent battered women. This middle-aged woman received the highest score (216) on the Values Index and was, of all those interviewed, the most pronounced in her feminist views. This in-depth interview compensates in part for the class bias in research on violence against women. Parents and relatives of the other women expressed many similar ideas and dilemmas but in more spontaneous participant-observation situations spread over several months. Here are excerpts from the tape-recorded interview, with the assumed names of Michael and Carol to preserve privacy. (*F* = Father, *M* = Mother.)

F: To our amazement we didn't know [about the violence] for years. *Why do you think she didn't tell you?* It bothered me very greatly because I wondered what in heck I had done wrong in our upbringing of her in not having given her the self-confidence to say 'Nobody's going to treat me like that ... Get the hell out of here.' Somehow or other I feel I'm amiss on that score. *You mean that you feel it's a failure of your parenting?*

F: Yes, I feel that way very strongly, both of us do ... You know, one of the things I kidded her about was 'You don't need to go to college ... you're pretty enough to find a nice man ... You don't have to go to college.' I was kidding ... I had no intention of not letting her go to college – no way, but apparently it was misunderstood and taken wrong. *Did she tell you that?* I found out about it much later when she told me I had told her that when she said she *was* going to go to college anyway.

M: It was more like 'Thank goodness you're a girl ... We don't have to worry about the expense of putting you through college.'

F: In whatever way it was said it was unfortunate ... You know it's amazing that she would take it that way because my mother was one of the first people that was emancipated in that sense in [a West European country]. We came from a *nouveau riche* family ... She [his mother] had the gumption to say 'I'm going to do it [take up a career].'

M: I would always try to counteract and say 'Your father doesn't mean it ... girls have to go [to college] just as well as boys.'

F: I found out when she was in High School and was upset about it. We'd ask her what she wanted to do ... of course we talked about money ... everybody talks about money. *Do you think she felt less valued as a girl?*

M: Valued in a different way, but less valued for education purposes, but not for me.

F: In spite of the ERA, etc. I still feel that in 90 per cent of cases making a living falls on the men. Women get married and they manage that way somehow, but there hasn't been the pressure on women to earn the money to support the family ... I don't see how we're going to get out of it. It's in the nature of things, if you're gonna have kids who's going to take care of them? It isn't going to be me ... I don't want to be a mother in that sense. *What about being a father?* A father's O.K. *But you don't think fathers should take care of children?* I think this is where we differ. Especially during the Depression ... you have to have not only eight hours at work but substantial amounts of other time.

M: Your brother was willing to partially give up his career to put his wife through medical school.

F: That's his problem. *How did you first learn of the violence?*

M: When she called me up. They didn't separate because of that, but infidelity. *What was your explanation?* ... I said many times to the children I would *never* allow a man to hit me and if he did it was 'Out the door' so perhaps she wasn't ready to take that final step and couldn't tell me because *I* had felt rather strongly about that. *Do you mean that if she had acknowledged the battering to you the next step would have been 'I have to leave'?* That's what I wonder ... I don't really know.

F: ... I didn't know him well enough to have a strong opinion for or against. He was a charming guy. *Why were you against him?*

M: Because during their [courting] relationship one night they had been here and we had gone out for a short time and she was black and blue and she said she bruised easily and denied it. Also, he had other women ... *Why do you feel that your daughter didn't share her problem with you?*

F: Partly it was because we weren't here. *If she had confided what would have been your response?*

M: ... I would have talked *very* seriously with her and said 'Look, you better get him out until he gets help.' I wouldn't have too much hope for a person like that to be able to change ... but it's possible.

F: I would have been fit to be tied ... I would have had a hard time keeping from knocking him out. It would have gotten me extremely angry. I would have thrown him bodily out of the house.

M: We were present at a few of the disagreements they had and Michael [her husband] told me it was none of my business, but I felt that if I was present I went to the extent of knocking on the door and saying 'My, My' or 'Calm it' or 'Is there anything I can do?' – something on that line. And one time talking with them afterwards – he was calling her names, accusing her – I asked him how he could talk that way. *His reaction when you confronted him?* He was just angry, and *later* he confronted me with thinking I was better than him ... It was like a soap opera. It was terrible. He felt inferior, no question. *Would you expand on the dilemma of interfering in a marital fight?*

F: I wasn't aware at times there was a physical problem [of violence]. People argue and some people are not upset at yelling, screaming, etc., but for others this kind of thing is extremely rare. *Do you think you have the right to interfere if there's a verbal or physical fight?*

F: Oh yes, definitely ... I think people need to learn how to disagree and argue ...

What was the response of his parents to the battering?

M: She never told them. [In an earlier interview with this battered woman she said she was deliberately protecting her husband by not telling his parents, as she was very well liked by her father-in-law and felt that he would be extremely harsh with his son if he knew.]

What do you think can be done about the problem?

M: It's terribly difficult. This is something that should be brought up in every home and school as a part of social behaviour, and marital relationships, a no-no, there's too much of it.

F: ... The *key* ingredient that is lacking in these women is that they just can't say 'Hey, that's not the way I want to be treated. This is the end, whatever the consequences are' ... the women still don't have the self-confidence, the self-respect that they should have. *Why not?*

F: ... The most basic thing is self-respect. In my NTL [National Training Lab] course I learned you are responsible for the way other people treat you. At first I thought that was nuts, but it's true. If you're the Queen of England I'll treat you with a great deal of respect, but if you're a washerwoman that's something else. *You* set up how I treat you. *What do you think about the social sources of being a washerwoman?*

M: A washerwoman deserves just as much respect. A woman's *position* in life shouldn't determine respect. *Would you say, then, that your daughter would be responsible for her husband's violence?*

F: She is responsible for continuing to let him do so, because if she would have been properly brought up by us she would have said 'Get out.' *What's his responsibility?*

F: He's responsible for doing it, but she's responsible for letting it continue.

M: The background teaching and customs had so much to do with it, too. I think you have to slowly inculcate it into the women ... The man should go to trial. It should be taken more seriously by the courts ... If a man uses violence it's a criminal of-fence.

F: If you have a woman with a child who can't figure any other way out I can understand that, but in our daughter's case she could have left. So there's something wrong in her self-respect.

M: I don't think we have to take total blame.

F: You get too soon old and too late smart ...

This interview illustrates how values intersect with the occurrence of violence and its endurance by victims. It highlights beliefs (especially the father's) in personal responsibility for violence and its aftermath, while minimizing sociocultural context. This father's painful recall of teasing his daughter about not needing a college education presup-poses his belief that there is a connection between his behaviour and his daughter's later battering (Coulter 1979a). The inculcation dur-ing childhood to strive for traditional roles of wife and mother rather than college and career seems clear in this woman's case. Even though she is now educated at the graduate level like her father and is highly successful in her career, she expressed her 'failure' as a wife and mother more keenly than any of the other study participants. She said:

> My mother had been *very* tied up with her ability to have children (she had 16 pregnancies, with only four living) ... I was thinking about it the other day and if someone told me I have only a year to live, what do I want to do, to have accomplished? And the first thing that popped into my mind is that I would want to be pregnant, to have a child.

Furthermore, her decision to conceal her suffering from her parents as long as she did was influenced by such family factors as her mother's frequent depressions and a two-year physical absence of her parents who were living abroad. Interestingly, she did not include her father's teasing about not having to pay for her to go to college; only the father brought up this item.

Although the daughter does not refer to her father's teasing in her accounts, let us examine some excerpts from the interview in an ethnomethodology perspective, specifically, membership categorization (Sacks 1974) and presupposition analysis (Coulter 1979b). Sacks developed the notion of Membership Categorization Device (MCD) to describe the organized ways humans describe and understand people and their activities (Benson and Hughes 1983: 132). (Code: *F* = Father, *M* = Mother.)

```
 1  F: To our amazement we didn't know [about the violence]
 2  for years. Why do you think she didn't tell you? It bothered me
 3  very greatly because I wondered what in heck I had done
 4  wrong in our upbringing of her in not having given her the
 5  self-confidence to say 'Nobody's going to treat me like that
 6  ... Get the hell out of here.' Somehow or other I feel I'm
 7  amiss on that score. You mean that you feel it's a failure of
 8  your parenting?

 9  F: Yes, I feel that way very strongly, both of us do ... You
10  know, one of the things I kidded her about was 'You don't
11  need to go to college ... you're pretty enough to find a nice
12  man ... You don't have to go to college.' I was kidding ... I
13  had no intention of not letting her go to college – no way,
14  but apparently it was misunderstood and taken wrong. Did
15  she tell you that? I found out about it much later when she
16  told me I had told her that when she said she was going to
17  go to college anyway.
```

123

18   M: It was more like 'Thank goodness you're a girl ... We
19   don't have to worry about the expense of putting you
20   through college.'

An example of MCD displayed in this interview is 'gender' which includes the categories 'male' and 'female'. This man's daughter, in the category 'female', is 'pretty enough to find a nice man', he says, and 'you don't need to go to college' (lines 10 and 11). This statement implies that the male member of the category 'gender' does have to go to college. In lines 2–5 he expresses guilt about his parenting which presupposes the belief that failure as a parent may be connected to his daughter's putting up with beating. He attempts to mitigate his guilt, however, by defining his statement as 'kidding', and disclaiming any intention of 'not letting her go to college – no way'. That his daughter took him seriously shows at least some ambiguity around what, 25 years later, he calls 'kidding'. His present connection of this 'kidding' to his daughter's imputed lack of self-confidence to say 'nobody's going to treat me like that – get the hell out of here' (lines 5 and 6) could be heard as an expression of his desperate attempt to understand his daughter's situation.

On the other hand, this kind of kidding itself, of a girl but not of a boy, even if sincerely intended *only* as kidding, presupposes certain beliefs about the categories 'male' and 'female' and the necessity of a college education for boys, but not for girls. Furthermore, such jesting reveals certain beliefs that girls can depend on being 'pretty enough' and consequently on finding 'a nice man' as a result. These statements also tie the female/male members of the category 'gender' to the traditional association of 'female' with marriage and the categories 'body/nature/private' ('pretty enough'), and the male with paid occupation and the categories 'mind/culture/public' ('college') (Ortner 1974).

The father's disclaimer 'I was kidding' (lines 12–13) is challenged and the presupposition of traditional beliefs about women verified on two counts: (1) the daughter apparently took his kidding seriously – 'She said she was going to go to college anyway' (lines 16–17); (2) the mother redefines his 'kidding' as 'Thank goodness you're a girl ... We don't have to worry about the expense of putting you through college' (lines 18–20).

After this joint interview each parent was interviewed individually with a further focus on the items in the Values Index. At the end of the father's individual interview, after the tape recorder had been shut off, he again made associations to the category 'gender' and certain behaviours around violence. He told about one of his sons who had accepted his wife's nagging until he 'shook her' once as 'the only way to stop her', because he couldn't take it anymore. I asked if this was any different than his daughter staying and 'taking it', i.e. if he can't take her nagging anymore why doesn't he just leave instead of dealing with it by force? From my question during this brief inter-change this father seemed to develop an awakening to the double standard about gender and violence: he had just elaborately inter-preted his daughter's staying and putting up with violence as indicating her lack of 'self-respect'. For his son who didn't leave, self-respect does not enter the picture, but the use of force is seen as a 'necessary' solution. Gender and violence are inversely related here: If women have violence used *against* them and *fail* to leave, they lack self-respect. If men are stressed by *non*-violent behaviour (e.g. nag-ging), their *use* of violence is justified as necessary. This reasoning presupposes the traditional belief that a *man*'s self-respect *depends* on the use of violence in such a case.

The language displays deeply embedded beliefs about the respon-sibility attributed to women for their victimization, the necessity of violence by men as a problem solving tactic in social relations, and the excusing of male violence and/or its redefinition as an 'illness' to be treated rather than as social action to be accounted for. Later ana-lysis in this chapter and in Chapter 10 on homelessness supports this interpretation.

This example also illustrates that the feminist ideal of one's mother does not necessarily influence a daughter to ask for familial support. For this financially independent, highly educated woman, economic factors did not play a part in her staying with a violent hus-band for eight years. But several other factors seemed to operate in a complex interplay to keep this woman essentially isolated during her crises: her father's values regarding education for girls as revealed in his 'kidding'; absorption of this value and its expression in the pri-macy of the wife and mother goal; her corresponding sense of responsibility to make the marriage work; her shame in not living up to her mother's ideal as a woman who would not put up with vi-olence; long-term physical distance from parents. In short, values seemed to intersect with social, psychological, and material factors in this particular instance to inhibit the woman from breaking out of the violent partnership sooner.

This woman's case supports the argument of Chodorow (1978), Dinnerstein (1977), and Keller (1983) about the powerful influence of early childrearing practices and the mother's influential role dur-ing the years a child is developing a self-concept. Her father's professional career did not impress her nearly as much as her mother being 'very tied up with her ability to have children'. This woman's vision of marriage and motherhood as her most important life's work

125

is most probably related to structural features in her family that strongly reinforced the traditional view of women as the dominant influence in child rearing (Poster 1978; Barrett and McIntosh 1982).[1]

Other value statements from interviews with various network members must be examined as well. Items on the Values Index were categorized into these sub-groups: Culture of Violence; Psychological Abuse; Biological Determinism; Medicalization of Violence; Economic Equality and Class Issues; Privacy and Female Solidarity.

Culture of violence

Item 12: Spare the rod and spoil the child.

Of the twenty-five members interviewed, only three were opposed to the idea of physical punishment in rearing children successfully. These three were men: a Catholic pastor, a former child care worker in the shelter used by seven of the battered women, and a lawyer. Only three of the battered women themselves opposed physical punishment. One of these had been to the shelter twice and said she had completely accepted and absorbed the policy of non-violence in disciplining children. Another was childless but was familiar with research literature on the negative effects of physical punishment. The third also was exposed to the shelter's non-violence policy, and was in therapy to control her harshness toward her children. These findings support the national survey (Straus, Gelles, and Steinmetz 1980) results which show how pervasive this cultural value is.

Interviews also focused on how shelter staff deal with the battered women's childrearing practices. The policy of not physically punishing children was devised largely by a consensus of white middle-class women, a population whose values differed significantly from most of the people in this study – working class and middle class, black, white, and mixed ethnic heritage. Yet, we should not assume that the women are therefore cruel to their children, for they are quite clear about the care needed in applying physical punishment, and the distinction between physical punishment and child abuse, a link assumed by most social scientists researching violence (Gelles and Cornell 1985). The complexity of this issue is illustrated in the following statement of a white, male, professionally trained child care worker who is opposed to physical discipline:

> I got hit quite a bit as a kid. The last time my father hit me I was 18 – he slugged me on the side of the head when I swore at him, and I swore I'd never hit a kid. But once I did hit a kid it got harder to control myself from hitting again.

This young man's experience reveals the complex relationship between individual and family influences on violent behaviour and one's struggles to control it. Instead of becoming an abuser himself, this man's experience of abuse as a child had an aversive effect on him: he adopted a non-violent approach to children. Thus even though he deviated from his resolution of non-violence by hitting a child once, his reaffirmed commitment to non-violence raises questions about the popular concept of the 'intergenerational transmission of violence'. It also highlights the fact that non-violent behaviour can be learned just as violent behaviour can. Thus, instead of 'violence begetting violence', just the opposite outcome might occur in response to violence experienced as a child.[2] An excessive focus on the 'intergenerational transmission of violence' can move 'victim blaming' from the individual to the family. One of the problems with 'family blaming' is that it mitigates individual accountability for violent behaviour and the possibility of learning other behaviours, which suggests further interpretation of the young man's statement. Since it 'got harder to control myself' after he had hit a child, it seems clear that once the man acted against his internally imposed taboo against hitting a child, the broken taboo weakened the inhibitions that could prevent future violations. This man's experience suggests that deviation from his norm *against* hitting children intersected with his own childhood experience of violence in a complex effort to remain non-violent in his interaction with children.

Statements by network members reveal the widespread cultural approval of violence that other writers (e.g. Straus, Gelles, and Steinmetz 1980) report. For example: 'A man's place is not to hit a woman ... Some girls need it but I'd never do it ... I'd hit her if she went out with someone else ... Sometimes the wife goes crazy and it's necessary ... It depends on the circumstances.' But network members also disapproved of the kind of brutal beatings their women relatives (or associates) received, and felt that men should be accountable for their violence, e.g. 'I don't know why they get off – Is it because the women back down? ... It's a crime and should be in the same class as for a stranger.' Some feel that a certain amount of violence might be 'deserved' and so do not perceive any continuum of violence from a slap to a brutal beating, while others acknowledge a double standard, 'depending on who you are'. Several men during interviews spoke of their urge to beat up the men who had been violent with their daughter/sister. Generally, the cultural approval of violence appears deeply embedded in these network members.

The battered women themselves – except for one – disapproved of violence for men *and* women, except in self-defence. Several of the women, however, did engage in retaliatory violence with their mates, though those who did also cited how futile and dangerous it was to respond to violence with violence.[3] The woman with the lowest score (most traditional) strongly agreed that women should slap men if insulted (Item 16) and also said regarding Item 15 that 'if she deserves it, she should get it'. Other statements by this woman about 'the woman upstairs' who was frequently beaten suggested that she believed the woman 'deserved it' because her behaviour was unacceptable. This woman was more conservative than her father who, though more traditional than all others interviewed, believed 'a man's place is not to hit a woman'. These statements by a battered woman reveal the extent to which a woman can absorb the centuries-old value of women as appropriate objects of violence (Dobash and Dobash 1979). Several men during interviews spoke of their urge to beat up the men who had been violent with their daughter/sister.

Psychological abuse

While the study emphasizes physical abuse of wives, psychological abuse was included among the women's general descriptions of the violence they suffered, e.g. calling them insulting names, putting them down, criticizing and complaining. In the Values Index the women and network members were asked to discuss the proposition: 'psychological abuse of women may be even worse than physical abuse' (Item 54). While this item was not assigned a feminist or traditional value and therefore not included in scoring, the responses should be reported. All of the battered women either agreed or strongly agreed with this statement. Of the twenty-five network members interviewed, all but three either agreed or strongly agreed with this statement. Two women relatives of one woman disagreed and the male lawyer said he was not sure. Only the pastor commented that psychological abuse is 'more deeply harmful'.

Biological determinism

Item 36 focused on the participants' attitudes toward the role of biology in determining 'appropriate gender' behaviour: it's in the nature of men to be aggressive and sometimes violent.

Society is more accepting of men being aggressive. (Woman lawyer)

It's the way they're brought up. When things don't go their way they get violent. (Grandmother)

128

There might be some biological element as well. This is the way
God made us. (Pastor)

In response to Item 37 regarding the 'natural' gentleness of women,
this pastor said: 'I think they were created that way. *How then do you
explain women's violence?* By the kind of society we have today.'
The topic of whether men are aggressive and women gentle by nature led to a new question related to the issue of 'salutogenesis'
versus 'pathogenesis' discussed in Chapter 4. Instead of asking why
men are violent, it seemed important to ask 'Why are many men
gentle?' or, 'What keeps them from being violent?' This question assumed more importance in relation to the difficulty most researchers
have in obtaining male participation in research about violence.
Three men discussed at length their views regarding this topic. All
three men conveyed an attitude of gentleness – in voice tone, man-
nerisms, and concern about the problem of male violence. The first
was already quoted in respect to his resolve (though broken once)
not to hit children as a response to being knocked around a lot as a
child himself. Responding to the question: 'What do you think keeps
men from being violent?' three men stated:

When I was a kid I hit my sisters and they hit me. When I was in
third grade I hauled off and hit a girl who called me names ... I gave
her a black eye. The school called my parents, but they didn't say
anything to me because I didn't say anything. I felt terrible socially
to have hurt her ... What would people think? I know a lot of really
gentle men who had violent fathers and were roughed up as kids.
My life is a history of getting beaten up and not defending myself.
*What do you make of the fact that your parents didn't reprimand you
for hitting the little girl?* The meaning is 'That's O.K.'

My foster father, learning patience with him. I was moody and self-
centred, a wise guy. He straightened me out ... his ways. He cared
but he'd do things to aggravate me until I learned to trade. He was
owner of the sub-shop, like a second father, he got me into art and
sports. Everything was set back in our family [the eight children
were placed in foster homes when the mother was admitted to a
mental institution] ... You find yourself with that – we grew up faster. Strength is from my mother. There's always violence in me at
times. *What keeps you from acting on it?* Mind over matter. If I'm
angry at someone I take it out in a different way. I think the situation over.

They've [non-violent men] always had additional information,
availability of more choices. If you'd have known me before, you'd

probably call me a violent man. If you threatened me I'd have broken your arm. It all comes from fear – my reaction to threat and fear was violence. For example, there was a bat in my house ... I caught the bat and pulverized it, out of fear. The next day I read an article about a woman down the street who called the fire department [for a bat] and I said 'Gee, why didn't I think of that.' When I was a kid I knocked a nun down when she confronted me about my temper, and I kicked a priest in the shins. I fought my way through school. I used to be labelled angry and obnoxious. I was programmed. I had to be tough and that made me fearful. I was also a role, and angelic, an altar boy and president of my class but I could do no wrong. I was two roles. There was a kind and gentle me even then ... I helped old people. I loved my mother ... She was an example of warmth. If the nun had told my mother [about his violence] I'd have been heartbroken. *Do you think she should have told?* Definitely. I don't have to be tough anymore, because of the emergence of that part of me that is kind and gentle. That kindness and gentleness feeds me, not the toughness. It's the spiritual dimension that is the primary influence of my life so it's no longer my instincts controlling me. We've got to make men thirsty, tell them there's another way. I believe in the goodness of my fellow-human beings and that at any moment you can reach someone by saying 'Hey, there's another way.'

Another man, upper middle class and living with one of the women in the study, discussed his violence with his first wife and ascribed it to his immaturity and a lack of communication because of cultural barriers (she was Asian, he white American). At the time of this interview he expressed total commitment to non-violence in his relationships with women. He also spoke extensively about his growth as a person, especially in respect to his relationships with women. His view regarding the immaturity of violent men is shared by the affluent father of one of the women who expressed the need for self-control and responsibility: 'I think it's an irresponsible form of behaviour.' These views contravene theories of innate male aggression (e.g. Goldberg 1973/74).

The men's responses also led to discussion of Item 47: there's nothing that can really be done to stop men from being violent, so individual women that it happens to just have to do the best that they can to help themselves. Women and men network members were almost unanimous in their disagreement with this statement. Only three women said they were 'not sure'; all other members either disagreed or strongly disagreed.

It's crazy to think like that! Plenty can be done ... Women *could* get together in self-help groups. They have to organize. They [the men] definitely should seek psychiatric help and the woman can talk to him ... Society's got to change, for example, education showing people how to get rid of aggressiveness without violence ... Courts should push it: 'You get out of there' has more substance than 'I'm sorry' if he doesn't know any other way ...

Network respondents were quite optimistic about the prospect of stopping violence against women. They had no sense that male violence is inevitable. They emphasize social change and public control of violence (e.g. arrest and incarceration), support groups for the women, and re-education and treatment for the men. Nothing in their remarks suggests placing the responsibility on the victim rather than the assailant, although many held the prevailing view that the women can leave. For many, though, the theme of social disapproval blends with a view of violence as something to be 'treated'. The use of the term is appropriate, considering the widespread belief that violence is a medical phenomenon.

Medicalization of violence

Network members frequently and the women occasionally shared their belief that men who beat their wives are sick. To explore this popular belief, Items 20, 23, and 48 of the Values Index were particularly relevant. Item 20, 'If a man hits a woman it's usually because he just can't control himself, so he should be forgiven', elicited the following responses:

Women who keep forgiving are being irresponsible to themselves – They're losing their identity. (Male peer group member, AA)

It's true he's out of control, but he should take steps to come to terms with it. (Health professional and member of AA)

Maybe women feel guilty and responsible, like with the alcoholic. (Mother of battered woman with alcoholic brother-in-law)

Forgiveness is the key to good living. (Male lawyer)

Some can't control themselves, but they shouldn't be forgiven. (Sister)

Item 23, 'Men who beat their wives are crazy' ('crazy' was specified to mean a person's state of not knowing what he/she is doing, rather than the colloquial sense of the term, e.g. 'I think I'm going crazy'), provided these observations:

> Even if he is he's still got to be punished. (Brother)

> Some men are brutes, bullies. (Pastor)

> They know what they're doing and just don't want to learn how to control it properly. (Sister)

> They lose self-control in a fit of anger. (Father)

> If they're drunk they might not know. Plenty of people do things in a blackout. (Al-Anon peer group woman)

> That's really sick. It's easier to deal with things in terms of health. Some men are really mean, but that's a form of insanity. (Student in a health profession)

> Some men do have psychological problems, but others? It's kind of a way of life. Everything's too medicalized. (Woman lawyer)

> They should be put away somewhere. Some beat their wives every-day and they [the wives] don't deserve it. (Male friend)

> Not crazy, but they do have some psychological problems ... 'I didn't know what I was doing' – it's a cop-out. (Mother)

> Not necessarily. Some women like to be beaten before sex. (Father)

> There's something wrong somewhere. They need help. They have no respect – no discipline or respect. (Grandmother)

> You can take 'crazy' in so many ways. Men do know what they're doing. I think it's because of the role they think they're supposed to play. (Sister)

> There's something wrong with them. (Cousin)

Although most network members saw some association between alcohol and violence, they were quite careful not to reduce the problem of violence to alcohol. The majority either disagreed or strongly disagreed with the statements linking violence to alcohol abuse, e.g. 'It doesn't help, but it's not the source of the problem. It releases inhibitions.' This finding is noteworthy since most of the women's mates had problems with alcohol or other drugs. A few of those interviewed were active in AA, but did not locate the cause of violence in alcohol abuse. These findings support previous research (e.g. Gelles 1974) suggesting that alcohol should be interpreted more as an 'excuse' to avoid responsibility for violence rather than as a cause of it.

The network members' general unwillingness to attribute violence to too much drinking is somewhat surprising in view of the popular tendency to interpret alcoholism as a disease, and therefore to excuse acts of violence committed while under its influence. Several women in the study accepted this view. Most dramatic was the willingness of one woman to excuse her *husband*'s violence, but not her own while under the influence of drugs.

Another woman stated repeatedly and emphatically that she believed that 'drinking, alcoholism, and being battered as a child have direct effects on a man who batters'. She included in this judgement her husband, whose battering was frequently associated with drinking. She held the same belief in defining her own addiction of over-eating as an illness. Her symptoms were induced by, or became more pronounced, she said, because of her husband's violence. But since she had been afflicted with her 'illness' since childhood, she also felt that it was in some way responsible for why she allowed herself to be beaten.

At first glance her reasoning suggests that her 'illness' of overeating was both cause and effect of violence.[4] The relationship between food addiction and this woman's vulnerability to violence could be interpreted as interactional rather than causal, drawing on the concept of 'resistance resources' (Antonovsky 1980) and the relationship between stress, crisis, and illness discussed in Chapter 4. In this woman's case, overeating represented a personal response to stress originating from an interplay of physical, psychological, and socio-cultural factors (e.g. metabolic rate, low self-esteem, loss of mother, cultural norms regarding female thinness, etc.). The resulting obesity aggravated the social-psychological problems already there, while eating itself acted as a tranquillizer to deal with anxiety generated by new stressors such as violence. Thus, while this woman often cited her 'illness' of compulsive overeating and her husband's alcoholism as the chief reasons she was trapped in a battering relationship, the situation appears much more complex than that for the following reasons.

Twice in five years this woman left her husband and went into a shelter, while her compulsive overeating continued. Moreover, she left a third time and drove 500 miles to stay at her father's house only to receive a cool welcome. She had also left for numerous other shorter periods, staying with friends or by herself, but always returned. Her need to return was not because she was a compulsive overeater, but rather the combined results of the economic and social circumstances she faced each time she left. For example, she had documented in detail the inadequate response of police and social service workers she appealed to for help over the years. It could be speculated that if this woman were not so personally vulnerable as a result of her food addiction she could have overcome the social and economic obstacles she faced. Yet, one is led again to question the appropriateness of applying exclusively *individual* solutions to external problems such as violence by another and lack of social support.

The complex dimensions of violence were supported by evidence other women in this study offer, none of whom had significant personal dysfunctions according to ordinary mental health criteria. Although individual action has a place in resolving a problem of social origin, the multi-dimensional aspects of such problems require a tandem approach. If a woman decides to leave a violent relationship, for instance, and there are no social constraints on the husband to prevent her from having to live like a fugitive, and if she lacks means to achieve economic independence, she will probably endure violent attacks for many years. Alternatively, even if many options are available but a woman decides not to use them, she also will endure violence for many years. Yet it is simplistic to conclude that a woman is not 'motivated' to leave (e.g. Rounsaville 1978). Instead we need first to consider the complex interplay between personal and sociocultural factors which contribute to a woman's decision to remain with a violent partner.

The woman who claimed that 'illness' was a major contributing factor in her situation can be interpreted as follows: her contention represents one instance of the widespread public and professional medical interpretation of the problem. Most network members thought there was 'something wrong' with a man who batters, and that he needs treatment. The pervasive medicalization of violence is an instance of our failure to understand 'illness as metaphor' (Sontag 1979). As Sontag says: 'it is diseases thought to be multi-determined (that is, mysterious) that have the widest possibilities as metaphors for what is felt to be socially or morally wrong' (1979: 60).[5]

Economic equality and class issues

When the responses of men and women were compared on values around economic equality, some interesting outcomes were noted. Some women and men held traditional values, though most responses pointed to feminist values. However, Item 4 revealed that both men and women thought that 'a woman should have the same chance as a man to develop her talents in a job' (on Item 4 the mean scores were 4.5 for women and 4.9 for men). In other words, while all men and women agreed with this statement, more men than women strongly agreed on job equality for women. Here are their statements about it:

A woman has just as much brains as a man. (Sister)

Have the kids first, but now it's turned around. That's why there's so much crime in the street – there's no one to take care of the kids. (Grandmother)

That's why a lot are putting off having kids. (Female cousin)

As long as they're not too competitive. (Pastor)

If not *better* chances, to balance things out. (Male peer group member, professional)

The grandmother's statement as well as that of a middle-aged pastor demonstrate the prevalent attitude that women work at paid jobs only out of economic necessity, that they ought to maintain norms of not competing with men, and that it is women's responsibility to care for children and prevent crime. The last statement by the young professional man expresses the intent of 'affirmative action' in public law for women's equality in the paid work sector.

In Item 6, 'Most men don't carry their share of responsibility for child rearing, chores at home, etc.', the mean scores reflected a wider difference between the sexes: the women's mean score was 4.2, while the men's was 3. Here are some of their remarks about this item.

It depends on the man and the relationship. Some women let that happen, but not me. (Sister)

If they did, the kids wouldn't be as bad. (Grandmother)

It's changing and it's for the better, including for us. (Mother, whose husband did routine cooking)

There's a trend towards reversing roles. (Pastor)

A lot more *are* doing it. (Male peer group member)

The pastor's remark suggests a fear often seen in the press that if men assume a share in traditional 'women's work' they will somehow become 'feminized'. The grandmother's statement, if viewed with her statement above, presupposes her belief that both parents are responsible for the conduct of children even though she ascribes the cause of crime to women working outside the home. Interview data around economic values and gender roles of these network members support other research on this issue (e.g. Hartmann 1981; Burden and Googins 1984).

In spite of their supportive attitudes about women's 'double jobs' in the paid and unpaid work sectors, one man's response bears

135

particular examination. He strongly disagreed with the statement for the following reasons (and therefore brought the mean down to 3 with his score of 1): he was divorced and trying to gain the co-operation of his former wife for full care of one of their two children. He also participated equally in doing household chores with the woman he lived with. Like a number of contemporary men, he regretted his deprivation of child-rearing opportunities.

These outcomes are influenced by a number of factors. First, economic equality between women and men has been publicly discussed and contested in the courts. Child rearing is still considered a woman's responsibility, evidenced by the fact that after a divorce, child custody is still overwhelmingly awarded to mothers, a practice which reflects the widely held belief that child rearing is 'women's work' because they are more 'naturally' suited to it (Chodorow 1978; Elshtain 1981). Thus the man who strongly disagreed with the statement about child care, might have been influenced by his own divorce and not being granted child care. This is one case of men personally suffering from deeply embedded cultural norms about women's purported 'natural' superiority as parents.

This man's concern draws attention to the growing critique of traditional research methods which measure or assign scores – in this case to traditional and feminist values – without examining these scores in context (Cicourel 1964; Coulter 1979b; Schwartz and Jacobs 1979). Thus, this man had a very 'traditional' score on this item, though his actual behaviour was very close to feminist ideals. The example underscores how misleading it is to categorize people as either traditional or feminist regarding controversial topics like women, marriage, and the family.

Other class issues also influenced the responses to the interviews. Most people disagreed with the statement that 'Most violence occurs among racial minorities and poor or unemployed people' (Item 49). The stories of two men who were violent with their wives elucidate this issue. One, a college-educated businessman, was the friend of a study participant. He had slapped and knocked around his first wife on several occasions and spoke of his violence primarily as a symptom of a failed relationship, the inability to communicate once their relationship began to deteriorate:

> Relationships fail because individuals fail, and it's just as easy for individuals to fail who have come from privileged backgrounds as opposed to underprivileged backgrounds ... And then towards the last two years of our relationship she had a relationship with another man which I contended less and less well with. It spiralled down very quickly. I slapped her. She had much more of a violent

temper than I. She would fight with her fists although she was only 95 to 100 pounds ... I would try to conciliate her by hugging her or holding her close. She hated that. And so she would fight loose of it. In other words, instead of leaving the scene entirely, sometimes in order to prevent her from hitting me, I would, you know and that made it worse. I disliked myself intensely because of reacting in a manner which wasn't befitting of my image of myself.

This story resembles that of Bob, a working-class man, who slapped around his wife, although he rejected the term 'battering' to describe his behaviour:

I hit her, she hit me ... I just don't feel as though I'm a brutal person. I hit her five or six times. After the first it was easier, but there was always like a thought before it ... Sometimes I might fly off, but these hittings weren't – I'm not going to say batterings because I'm not a batterer – they were *provoked* by her. For instance the last fight we had was a particular situation where I was going through a lot of changes at my job as a short order cook. I worked with waitresses, women, and one particular woman I don't like and she gave me a hard time that day, and the argument that Darlyn and I had was 'You know, it's really cold out, why don't you wear a hat' because a lot of times she doesn't wear a hat – how she can stand it I don't know. I hate to see her go out without a hat on, just caring ... maybe she thought it was just trying to show I was in charge, but I just felt as though it was my way of caring, to wear a hat. So she said something really sarcastic and I said 'Why do I have to go through this at home too?' because I was really going through the mill, and she just kept on going on and on and I lost my head and slapped her. I hit her ... It was a couple of slaps, but as I think about it now a slap is an insulting thing because I know when I was a kid my mother slapped me and I've hated it ever since. I've never wanted anyone to slap me. The first two times I was pretty controlled about the way I slapped her ... It was never like, you know, to really hurt her. *You mean it was deliberate?* It was a deliberate slap, but a controlled slap. *What were you intending to achieve?* Nothing. *Why did you do it then?* It was just a reflexive act ... I can still say controlled but I can't say deliberate because I knew I didn't want to hurt her – A reflexive slap that was controlled that could have done more damage than it did physically. Most times I was thinking about her, but as the beatings got on I just lost my temper and just got hateful toward her, but after it happened was another thing   I felt hurt that I had done it and hurt that I could hurt her. [This man said he had been intensely in love with his wife who was only 20, eight years younger than he. They had a child of only a few months; he was eager to settle down into family life while she wanted to have more fun. In a separate interview she acknowledged that marriage turned out to be much more confining than she had anticipated.]

These findings question Wolfgang and Ferracuti's (1967) concept of the 'subculture of violence' which they associate with a 'working class', mostly non-white, ethic. Instead, violence seems to cut across class lines (Straus, Gelles, and Steinmetz 1980). This study also supports Dobash and Dobash (1979) who found that a violent man's desire to control his wife was frequently coupled with the availability of a culturally approved object of violence – his wife. These factors, the release of inhibitions after the first act of violence, the male's generally greater strength, and a woman's socialization to feel that she deserves the violence for behaviour which doesn't conform to traditional female roles, illuminate the *process* by which violence occurs in the first place and continues, once begun.

Class issues were also discussed by one woman's mother. She noted that women in her upper middle-class neighbourhood confided in her about violence in their marriages:

I care ... if they come around me they don't stay. The husband of one woman, believe it or not, told his wife that *all* husbands beat their wives [a powerful technique for 'normalizing' violence and keeping a woman isolated]. When she came in [to work] black and blue one too many times I said 'O.K. now, what is it?' People talk to me ... they run from ages 20 to 50. *What do these middle class women say about why they stay?* They say 'I love him, I have children. I have no money, I do not have the education. I can't leave my husband with the children because he's sometimes violent with them' and they want to protect the children – but not always, and that's *very* difficult for me to understand, except where the husband has charge of the funds, for example, a nurse in Oregon just packed up the station wagon one day and came here with her children ... she'd been married 20 some years. The ones that stayed with their husbands were not ready to take off, admit it to the world ... I think the shame would be *very* great. *Do you think middle class women stay because of creature comforts?* That has never come up. They don't see how they could leave the children with the husband.

That violence occurs among all classes and groups is apparent from Straus, Gelles, and Steinmetz's (1980) survey findings. Perhaps only the statistical visibility is greater among the poor and people of colour because they have fewer economic, legal, and medical avenues to keep it hidden.[6]

Marital privacy and female solidarity

If breaking away from a violent partner is usually so difficult by purely individual effort, what then are the conditions to be met if help is to come from social sources? We have already noted the dilemma some network members faced about how and when to intervene in marital fights, a dilemma compounded by the issue of marital and family privacy and the need to balance privacy and intimacy needs with the need for community support and involvement (Hoff 1989: Ch. 5). Many factors may prevent a person from fulfilling one's privacy, intimacy, and community needs. For example, if a person feels too insecure to establish satisfying intimate or communal attachments, or if a couple establishes an intimate attachment that is essentially closed and turned in on itself, they limit need fulfilment from a larger social network (O'Neill and O'Neill 1972). So too if a battered woman is kept isolated from a support network or is threatened with death if she tries to sever attachment to a violent mate, her needs for both intimacy and community are unmet. The privacy/intimacy/community issue touches on a central question in this research: What links exist between the personal trouble of battered women and public matters of women's status and culturally embedded values about marriage and the family? Therefore, three items on the Values Index (11, 51, and 52) were designed to ascertain network members' ideas regarding the presumed relationship between privacy, intimacy, and community.

The statement, 'If there is trouble between a woman and her partner, it's nobody else's business', elicited these comments:

It depends on the nature of the trouble and how close you are. (Mother)

About money, etc., yes, but it's different if there's violence. She kept going back. I said to her 'If you go back again, how can we help you again?' (Brother)

Not unless it's getting completely out of hand. (Mother)

That's the way they want it. My husband wanted it that way. (Divorced grandmother)

They can't turn the responsibility over to others. (Father)

I am my brother's keeper, though one needs to be careful and not be a busybody. (Mother)

That's why we stay out of their problems. (Father)

Only if it doesn't affect anyone else. It is definitely someone else's business if there's violence. (Father)

A lot of situations can't be resolved by the parties alone and they should seek advice or a third party referee. (Pastor)

One of the women said that her mother-in-law tried to help but 'didn't know what to do'. In a similar vein when describing her efforts to get help from her family, she said 'they were terrified' of her husband's violence. A male friend (student health professional) of this woman shared the following experience (not with this study participant) when discussing this topic:

It's up to the woman to ask for help. It's really difficult to know how to set up letting women know you're there to help. It's difficult to know how to intervene. When he was in town she'd let us know and we'd get in touch and call *her*, as she often couldn't call us. For example, she couldn't talk, you know, and I'd say 'Do you mean such and such?' and she'd say 'Yes' and we'd say 'We'll be right over.' *He'd* say 'It's nobody else's business' and we'd say 'Who are you to say it's not.' Sometimes she'd want privacy too. Women need really strong community support networks. One time I was there and I was terrified. As soon as a *man* walked into the house he turned into a pussy cat.

This example shows the impact that social disapproval of violence against women can have, and the need for men as well as women to express such disapproval publicly. But the illustrations also suggest that the problem of stopping violence and offering assistance to battered women extends beyond natural social network members such as family and friends, since they may be as terrified as the women themselves and not know exactly how to intervene. The people in these two examples (the mother of one battered woman, and the male friend of another) had the highest scores on the feminist attitude scale (216, 210 – most feminist) of all network members interviewed. Their dilemmas about how to help underscore the limits of family intervention in a problem that is deeper than the family and consequently requires involvement by formal institutions. Let us return now to additional examples of the network members' values regarding privacy, intimacy, and community.

When asked to respond to the statement that 'Almost anything, even violence, would be better than living alone' (Item 52), all network members interviewed either strongly disagreed or disagreed with this statement. Here are some of the things they said:

She's never known such happiness (since she's been without him).

Maybe they would leave *sooner* and support each other (if they weren't afraid to live alone).

Is it desperation for a man or hope for change? (Mother)

These responses are interesting, particularly in light of our culture's attitudes that people are incomplete without a mate. Significantly, eight of the nine women in the study either strongly disagreed or disagreed with this statement about living alone. One woman said she was neutral about it now but acknowledged that 'two years ago I thought that was so'. Although it is possible that fear of living alone operated as a motive in the other women's lives, this did not emerge during in-depth interviews. The reasons the women did cite, their obvious happiness after leaving and their deliberate care not to rush into other relationships, suggest that they do not have an unbalanced need for intimacy.

To the statement, 'If women got it together more among themselves, there would probably be fewer women beaten' (Item 51), respondents had this to say:

If women would only unite, get together and discuss what men are doing to them, so if it happens they know what to do.

Women need to stand their ground, but some don't want to hear it.

It also helps to see that men without warped minds sympathize with the situation.

They could gang up on them. (Father)

Men and women are the same regarding competition for each other. (Mother)

That's only one step.

Sometimes if you congregate, the other party might get even angrier. It might help the woman but not the relationship. Men don't like to have things said outside the marriage. I think she loved him too much. (Woman friend who stood by for years)

It is interesting and paradoxical that this woman expresses concern for preserving even a violent relationship, although she continuously urged her friend to leave it; her behaviour suggests that she is at least ambivalent in her agreement with the common male value of abhorring outside interference since she helped her friend over the husband's objections. It also points to the prevalence of the traditional value of maintaining family stability no matter what the personal price for battered women and children.

These responses highlight the dilemma members of a woman's natural social network face, a dilemma more noteworthy when viewed along the spectrum of greater/lesser orientation toward feminist values. For example, the father of the woman with the lowest score, 141, who said in response to Item 11: 'That's why we stay out of their problems', tended toward the traditional end of the continuum. Yet, the individuals with strong feminist tendencies (the mother of one woman and a male peer group member of another) and conviction about the need to help, each expressed clearly the difficulties of intervening appropriately and effectively even if they believed in their obligation to do so. The more traditionally oriented father, however, while believing he should not actively intervene, nevertheless was there for his daughter with emotional and material support after she left her husband.

The public dimension of violence

Maintaining a hands-off attitude *during* violence but supporting the woman after separation was observed in other families as well. Thus, a network member's values seem to influence whether one would or would not intervene actively in violence between marital partners. The majority said that violence is not a sufficient reason to maintain the norm of privacy between couples. In other words, violence is not merely a personal act relevant only to the marital pair. According to these people it violates publicly accepted norms of behaviour. Furthermore, one's fear and difficulty in intervening, even when strongly committed to do so, is compelling evidence of the need for assistance beyond the family.

Public laws define violence as a public issue by protecting family members from violent attack by other family members. However, such laws are of fairly recent origin. As a result of the latest phase of the women's movement in the US (1960s, 1970s, and 1980s) States have updated their Abuse Prevention Acts to afford wider protection to battered women, including mandatory arrest in some instances. Public laws, however, are only a partial step toward protecting women so long as traditional values about women prevail in male–

female relationships (Yllo and Straus 1981).

Recent research conducted with the Minneapolis Police Department underscores this argument. The study's authors, Sherman and Berk (1983:2), express the dilemma succinctly:

> Does punishment deter criminals? Or does it just make their behavior worse? Nowhere is the debate over these questions more evident than in police responses to domestic violence. Some police, like labeling theorists in sociology, argue that arresting people for minor acts of domestic violence will only increase the seriousness and frequency of the violence. Some feminist groups, like some deterrence theorists, argue that arresting suspects of domestic violence will reduce the suspects' use of violence.

These hypotheses were tested in a field experiment. 'Three police responses to simple assault were systematically assigned: arrest, "advice" or informal mediation, and an order to the suspect to leave for eight hours' (Sherman and Berk 1983: 2). In six months, the recidivism rate was 10 per cent among those men who were arrested, 24 per cent for those who were sent away for eight hours, and 17 per cent for those given advice and mediation assistance (Sherman and Berk 1983: 7).

These findings support the feminist argument that assaults against wives should be treated as criminal offences rather than as a 'private' squabble to be defused or mediated. But two objections surround this research. Most vocal have been Emerge, a men's collective (with a feminist philosophy) for counselling men who batter, and the Pennsylvania Coalition Against Domestic Violence (Hart 1983; Wald 1983). Their arguments revitalize the issue, noted earlier, about the problem of inferring rates from 'official' records in which the poor and people of colour are usually disproportionately represented. The Minneapolis research can thus contribute to the popular stereotype that violence is primarily a problem of the poor and ethnic minorities. Mandatory arrest also raises questions about the victim's civil rights, it deprives her of choice in pressing charges against her husband, and implies that victims are not 'knowledgeable, capable' agents.

These complexities underscore the importance of social change around values and *prevention* of violence in the first place. A group discussion with four of the women illustrates their awareness of the limits of current legal approaches to woman-battering.

Woman: They have a law for professionals to report abuse of children. *Why* don't they have those kind of morality laws for pro-

143

fessionals like doctors in emergency rooms where someone confides in them that they are being physically abused by someone. Why shouldn't they be required to file a complaint about that? Wouldn't that help? I mean if that were the case, I think my ex – the only people my husband was afraid of was authority figures – doctors, lawyers, cops. The cops he could even manipulate. *Why do you think we don't have laws like that?* Because men, doctors, big money, doctors, lawyers, some of which may be battering, who knows, you know I'm sure, I think they don't want to legislate that. Not only that, it requires them to be responsible and they're gettin' away with avoiding the issue and it's at very high cost to human beings.

This comment focuses the problem squarely as not merely a medical or legal issue, but a moral one, since it entails blame, rights, and responsibilities. Just what the role of social support and advocacy for battered women is in the public arena is explored in Chapter 8, where the women discuss their experiences in shelters and beyond.

Part III

Social life without violence: struggles and visions

Chapter eight

The shelter experience

Introduction

The third phase of the women's experience involved their lives after leaving violent partners. Seven of the nine study participants were contacted in a shelter (referred to as 'Woman House') in order to determine the nature of their experience there.

The research was not intended to focus on the shelter itself. In fact, had such an interest been explicit or implicit, I would never have gained the shelter staff's co-operation nor resolved my 'problem of access'. However, the women's stories would be incomplete without reference to the shelter Collective, and the research would have suffered without the help of staff members who examined the proposed research, judged it to be non-exploitative, supported the researcher, and collaborated in the research process.

Several ways in which shelter services affect battered women and their children are considered: (1) the particular shelter's philosophy of service to battered women and their children, and how shelter staff approach social change regarding the status of women; (2) how the shelter meets the immediate and long-term needs of the shelter residents; (3) what role feminist models play in achieving the shelter's objectives.

These issues emerged during my volunteer work in two shelters and again during the several months I spent with the study participants after leaving shelters. My volunteer work was important politically because had I discontinued it after finding a sufficient number of research participants, I would have been viewed as 'just another exploitative researcher'. My continued involvement with the shelter also facilitated the Collective's participation in the research process.

The women's accounts and my own experience and observations are examined from three perspectives: (a) that of a feminist activist;

147

(b) that of a mental health professional, specially trained and experienced in crisis intervention; (c) that of a social analyst.

Philosophy of shelter and social change strategies

The 'problem of access' alluded to in Chapter 1 relates directly to the philosophy of battered women's refuges. Are shelters just another type of human service agency, or are they an aspect of the political struggle to end violence against women? If they serve both ends, how are both objectives reconciled? (Schechter 1982). Fundamental to the radical feminist philosophy of Woman House is the issue of power. It should be noted that the 'problem of access' concerned the women who *operated* the shelter, not its residents.

Radical feminists view violence as the result of women's powerlessness in the social structure, the political economy, and their personal relationships with men. Accordingly, the staff of Woman House believe that battered women need to experience a sense of power and control over their lives. They view the shelter, therefore, as the women's temporary residence, *not* as an institution in the traditional understanding of that term. Thus every effort is made to help the women feel that this is their home for the time being, their space to do what they need for themselves and their children in order to build a new life free of violence. The staff take great pains to eliminate all vestiges of traditional institutional settings. For example, there is no strict schedule and no particular person in charge, etc. People who commit themselves to work there are trusted to act on their commitments without threat or coercion from authority figures. Power is shared among all members of the Collective, volunteer and paid. Decisions are made by consensus of the Collective's members. Each woman's opinion, whether resident or staffer, paid or volunteer, is heard and respected. Every meeting is open to anyone in the House wishing to attend.

The physical setting for this re-created 'home' is a two-family, three-level, frame house, indistinguishable from similar dwellings on the block largely for security reasons, since some violent men go to great lengths to seek out their wives, even holding an entire house of residents hostage until a wife is 'turned over'. At the beginning of my volunteer work, the shelter's physical amenities left a lot to be desired. As one staff member complained: 'This place is gross ... You or I would never choose to live here if we weren't forced to through violence.' She was referring to a never-ending battle against roaches, leaking plumbing, inadequate heating, shabby furniture and finishing. The only places for clothes in some of the rooms were wall hooks or clean garbage sacks, despite the constant work of a volunteer and one part-time staffer devoted to maintenance problems and capital improvement with the meagre funds available. Over the years visible improvements have been made.

The shelter's sub-standard physical features served as a symbolic reminder of society's devaluation of women: not only are the victims of violence, rather than their assailants, required to leave their homes, but for many their substitute 'home' represents a drastic reduction in their standard of living.

The women's experience in the shelter was affected by several unavoidable factors intrinsic to the situation. Each had to cope with: (1) the presence of up to seven other women, each with varying numbers of children who had similar needs and expectations regarding their temporary residence; (2) the fact that often the women who come here for physical refuge are in emotional crisis as well, and/or may have had a history of excessive dependency; (3) the necessity for a structure and process that assures that the shelter will exist after an individual's six to ten-week stay; (4) the suspicion of funding bodies about agencies that do not operate according to traditional organizational patterns with clear lines of authority, client service hours delivered and accounted for, qualifications of staff, etc. The latter is related to problems of physical maintenance because the Collective's members recognize that some of the shelter's material needs could be readily alleviated by additional grants, public appeals, etc. The Collective has turned down outside funding to avoid being pressured to compromise certain aspects of the operation through routine site visits by funding bodies.

These factors raise several questions. First, given the size of this 'family', what are the probabilities of each member exercising expected responsibilities, such as food preparation and cleaning chores? Even in an 'average' household, most people are familiar with the normal family struggle of getting each to do his or her part of necessary household chores. In a 'family' of twenty to twenty-five members where previous acquaintance cannot provide a context for resolving conflict, it is understandable why individual members might rebel, give up, or withdraw.

Moreover, women who come to these shelters are often in a state of emotional crisis. One possible manifestation of such a crisis state is a woman's inability to function at her usual level of responsibility. And if her children are tense and upset, then the picture is even more complicated. Furthermore, many battered women have developed dependencies that may have already complicated the process of leaving violent mates. Or, a woman may simply be exhausted, burned out, or frustrated from her repeated efforts to get help, so that her predominant need at this time is simply to be taken care of. The challenge, then, is to balance a woman's need for support and material aid during crisis with her need for emotional, social, and physical space so that she may once again experience herself as in charge of her life.

If the requirement of assuring that the shelter continues beyond the stay of individual residents is added to all the conflicts and tensions inevitable among a group of twenty-five virtual strangers, then the complex challenge of providing material necessities and social survival without compromising the political objectives of creating an atmosphere in which the women feel both at home and in charge of their lives becomes clear. But how does one document the accomplishments of such non-traditional objectives to traditional funding bodies that evaluate service adequacy primarily in terms of numbers and hours served?

These questions took formal shape after several months of volunteer work. I worked on them in two ways: (1) as a volunteer working within the Collective structure, I proposed whenever possible various avenues for more active input from the residents into the running of the house; (2) I gradually evolved a way of asking staff and the study participants their views about my observations and some of the issues that were emerging as themes. These were incorporated into interviews with some staff members for this research. These efforts resulted in a 'Goodbye Information Sheet' which actively solicited the women's opinions of their experience in the House and their desires for future contacts (see Brosnan 1976).

This shelter's philosophy of empowering the women invited their participation in decision-making. But avoiding traditional institutional controlling tactics is apparently not enough, since the women's participation was often less than ideal. Many of these women are very traditional, and therefore are not immediately comfortable with this radical feminist value. Thus exposing battered women to feminist values must be done carefully. Such exposure cannot *im*pose these values despite the staff's political commitment to changing traditional values they believe are related to women's vulnerability to violence. These complex dynamics and values regarding violence and women's empowerment complicate the problem of including battered women in the everyday concerns of their life in the shelter. Strategies of inclusion are needed, but they must be used sensitively since women in active emotional crisis or with dependency problems have varying capacities for active participation and the acceptance of responsibility.

Some problems concerning participatory shelter work and larger political considerations remained unresolved. A significant finding here concerns the similarity between observations of the staff and those of the residents:

> We waste so much time in those meetings. I feel alienated in those meetings. Third-world women feel alienated in those meetings, working-class women feel alienated. So many people feel alienated in those meetings ... I don't think anyone has sat down and thought about how we do meetings. Our meetings are such an effective way of weeding out all the people who don't fit into this sort of idea that being a feminist means having long discussions into the middle of the night.

> The thing that bothers me [about the meetings] is knowing some of the other women may be excluded operating that way, because it's my education and middle-class experience that I can even tolerate that.

This staff member also said that she wished that there was more opportunity for the women to work through grieving for the relationships they are leaving (discussed in Chapter 9). Another white, middle-class staff woman said that racism, not sexism, is the most significant issue in her life. The experience of many at this shelter represents a microcosm of a vital issue in the women's movement as a whole: the concern that feminism primarily serves white, middle-class women, and that enormous energy and commitment are needed to transform the movement so that it recognizes the needs and gifts of all women, and uses these gifts for the good of all.

The staff's sensitivity to issues of racism and empowerment of battered women is evident in all the shelter's meetings. Ironically, even though many complain about meetings, they nevertheless deal with issues of vital concern about the general problem of violence against women of all colours. Hours of painful discussion dealt with what we could do about racism amongst ourselves. Thus, while one resident may observe that the staff is 'talking among themselves all the time', the resident may not have known the content of the discussion, even though all meetings are open to residents.

Several reasons prevent most residents from participating actively in these meetings. One is the urgency of their immediate problems. A second reason is that few residents have had prior experience of such group processes, and have rarely confronted sensitive issues such as one's personal racism or homophobia. Third, the philosophy of 'open' meetings must become a reality through concrete mechanisms that make individual women feel welcome.

Such bridging activity is required because of the alienation people often feel in traditionally organized service settings such as mental hospitals (see, for example, Farberow 1981). For example, the weekly meeting agenda of the governing Committee concerning overall house affairs may be posted on the refrigerator door for all to see; but if a specific verbal invitation does not accompany it, the women may not perceive that they are generally welcome.

Concrete efforts to include the women have consequences for both the shelter's direct service and its larger political objectives. First, a woman may interpret the staff meeting time as evidence that she is not getting all the personal support and help she needs. Second, because a woman in crisis may focus predominantly on her own problems (see Hansell 1976; Hoff 1989), she may fail to understand that she is, in fact, welcome to attend this meeting. Ironically, she thereby also may deprive herself of an opportunity to gain more experience and success in other areas of problem-solving (Caplan 1981). For battered women attending a Collective meeting, success could be something as small as contributing an opinion regarding some issue, or doing the artwork and receiving positive feedback for a project such as the Goodbye Information Sheet. Finally, limited participation deprives the Collective of the diversity of ideas and contributions from all shelter residents. Over time, the deterioration of participants' involvement can contribute to the very thing the Collective hopes to avoid: a process of gradually assuming the characteristics of traditional institutions in which the division between staff and client is clear and unequivocal. Frequent meetings of the Collective members discuss ways to detect and avoid such deterioration.

A similar dynamic was observed regarding the conduct of other meetings in which the focus is on the day-to-day concerns of residents and in-house staff: division of chores, discussion of parenting problems, etc. Here there is more explicit attention paid to including the residents in the meetings, but this objective is often complicated by two other factors that demand attention: (1) the need to balance the residents' active involvement in decisions concerning their daily lives with the need to ensure the existence of the House beyond the stay of its current temporary residents; (2) commitment to the principle of fostering women's self-determination, while dealing with the fact that some residents' immediate desires (e.g. consumption of alcohol, entertaining men on the premises) conflict with the long-term goal of preventing total chaos, damage to other residents, breakdowns in necessary security from violent men, and threats to funding support and future existence of the House.

152

Residents' reactions to the shelter experience

The Goodbye Information Sheet illustrates the participatory process that Woman House uses. Residents were actively involved in the several phases of the form's development, while frequent staff discussions about the service/political goals of the House provided background for the project. The form was developed on two premises: first, that providing adequate service to women in crisis is one of the most effective ways of involving battered women in helping other battered women; second, that an organized means of contacting the women is necessary to get them involved and maintain their interest. But the women are not expected to volunteer their services at the House beyond the immediate needs of the group living there. In fact, women are not permitted to work at the shelter until several months after leaving in order to discourage using the House as a convenient means to avoid developing more stable support networks. Typically, women return every week or so to do laundry at the House (washing machines are rare for these women) for a while if they live in the area, or they return just to visit or for holiday celebrations. Some, including two of the women in this study, occasionally do volunteer work.

Both residents and staff responded to efforts to include women in the good-bye interview and the post-shelter contact. The staff was very enthusiastic even though the women's participation was irregular. Of the women in this study, all wanted to be contacted after leaving the House in one or several of the ways listed. Most evaluated their experience at the House as very good, and provided specific comments about the positive aspects of their experience there:

There was always someone to talk to – staff or another woman ...

It's excellent that places like this exist. The staff are very liberal and let women lead their own life and give information when needed. I feel kind of let down on some things, but I got stronger ... No man will run my life anymore.

The last group of women were great – I think I'll continue talking with some of them ...

Support from other women. The staff are really good, especially at listening and letting you be yourself. I could *be* myself. I didn't have that with my husband.

Meeting [the researcher] and finding out more information about dealing with stressful situations and with children. The house was a safe place for me to stay at before I returned on my own.

153

The opportunity and freedom to change my life again.

A roof over my head, security. It was a fighting experience, fighting for myself and my children to think positive.

They helped me a lot, to forget everything inside my mind, my husband, and me. They listened when I told my story. I liked the staff and other women. I felt safe. It was nice and quiet, nobody pushed me.

The one persistent criticism concerned the bickering and petty conflicts among the residents themselves, and the residents' perception that the staff were not able to intervene effectively in these conflicts. They also complained about 'too many meetings', overcrowding, dirt, a 'rat in my room', not enough linens, and 'kids running around the house'. One woman said she thought that men should also be staffing, 'so there's another viewpoint ... for example, they could come in once a week so that the idea doesn't stick that all men are animals'. A resident also suggested that there should be a group on developing constructive relationships with men and on 'how to let them go'.

Conflict among the residents can be traced to the difficulty of suddenly creating a 'family' of six to eight adults and fifteen to twenty children with irregular staff and in a marginal or sub-standard physical setting. Moreover, the women's tolerance for conflict and ability to deal constructively with others depends to a great degree on the attitudes and state of mind of individuals, which varies of course among the women in each group. Nor is there ever a discrete group as such, since women constantly enter and leave the shelter. Thus, four or five women may arrive within a few days of each other, and develop a certain cohesiveness which is nurtured through the several weeks of their stay. Additional women who arrive intermittently over the next couple of weeks may or may not be integrated into the existing group, because of a variety of social factors such as prior group living experience and material circumstances.

Some women are forced without preparation to reduce significantly their standard of living. Such women have a harder time dealing with the added stress of inadequate housing when already in emotional crisis. It is too facile to offer platitudes about the need to overlook such deficiencies when one's life is at stake. A woman's response to inadequate housing needs to be considered in cultural context. Historically, women have been strongly socialized in American society to domesticity and to associating status, well-being, and self-respect with a nice home (Hayden 1981). To suddenly discount this value in one's life in a materialistic society is like asking one to shed one's culture. As one woman put it: 'The pictures of how bad a

shelter is were true.' Remarks like this are more significant considering that they come from women who have never known much
material luxury in the first place.

Shelter staffing issues

The residents' assessments of shelter life can be compared with the
accounts of the staff and set within the context of larger political considerations. First, the woman's recommendation that some staff
members be male will be examined. The decision whether or not to
have male staff members flows directly from the philosophy influencing shelter operation. Schechter (1982: 258–60) has reviewed the
debate within the battered women's movement about the role of men
working in shelters. Those against it argue that abused women 'need
environments in which dependence on men is challenged, not recre-
ated', and that because many women are socialized to see other
women as competitors, 'a shelter environment should demonstrate
that women can support one another and take care of themselves',
thus learning through role models and experience how to take control of their lives. Also, an all-female environment is thought to
permit more open expression by the women free of male judgement
and intimidation.[1] Finally, experience with battered women suggests
that many would be initially upset to find men on the premises of a
shelter. Even though the man is non-violent, a woman's recent experience with being terrorized may make it difficult to quell her fears
while in crisis around male violence.

The argument favouring non-violent men staffing shelters coincides with the view that battered women need a 'corrective'
emotional experience with gentle men. The idea of a 'corrective' experience needs to be seriously challenged, since it implies that
women are inadequate in the way they relate to men (Schechter
1982). It is also too much to assume that six weeks of counselling
work with a 'gentle' male can undo the effect of years of violence.
Counselling by male therapists, moreover, may reinforce the
women's traditional expectation of male rescue. Psychotherapy research supports these political considerations since studies show
definite trends toward greater client satisfaction and benefit from female therapists (Mogul 1982; Kaplan 1984: 3).[2]

Whether male staff members will be included is still an unresolved
question in the women's movement as a whole. The shelter Collective in this study resolved the issue by including men as child care
workers to present non-violent role models to children (see Chapter
11 for further discussion of this). Significantly, however, Woman
House opposes not only the idea of male counsellors, but female

counsellors as well, on the premise that counselling can reinforce the popular notion that battered women are emotionally or mentally disturbed.[3] It is not uncommon for women coming to this shelter to ask about counselling assistance soon after their arrival.

Such requests are handled as follows: the woman is told that the shelter is not staffed with professional counsellors; at the same time the philosophy of peer support and self-help is explained. The woman is also encouraged to talk with any women there – residents and staff – before seeking formal therapy or counselling. If after a few days the woman still feels the need for a professional counsellor, she is given the names of referral sources known for their feminist perspective regarding battering and its after-effects. In most cases the women find that they no longer feel the need for professional counselling. This finding supports the principle of empowerment which seems to be instrumental in changing a woman's belief that she was battered because of something wrong with her.

These issues reflect the tremendous challenge of avoiding the flaws of traditional 'total institutions' in which residents are essentially prisoners (see, for example, Goffman's *Asylums*, 1961). Yet the staff recognizes that the House faces many of the problems and requirements of all institutions: that policies, regulations, and programmes are necessary to prevent chaos and damaging interpersonal conflict among relative strangers; that a support system is required so that the staff do not suffer the burnout so common in front line human service work.

Meeting this challenge is particularly difficult. The large scale development of battered women's refuges originates from a political vision that includes deep suspicion of traditional institutions. Self-help groups, a collective decision-making structure, and an emphasis on peer support and self-determination, offer legitimate alternatives to traditional service delivery systems. Such alternative service groups sprang up in great numbers, particularly during the protest decade of the 1960s, especially to serve people with suicidal and drug abuse problems (McGee 1974; Hoff 1989). As Schechter (1982) points out, some traditional institutions have historically sheltered battered women (e.g. the Salvation Army). However, this study and other research (especially Dobash and Dobash 1979; Stark, Flitcraft, and Frazier 1979) have documented how traditional social services and medical institutions have often *contributed* to rather than alleviated the problems and crises of battered women. But because of pressures from governmental and funding bodies to operate shelters according to more established patterns, often accompanied by threats of funding cut-offs for non-compliance, many shelters have been co-opted into becoming just another professional agency (Ahrens 1980).

Battered women's shelters and other social movements

With a vision and agenda aiming to correct some of the deficiencies of traditional service institutions, the founders of alternative human service programmes have moved in the direction of less rather than more structure in their organizations. The early abundance of good will and boundless enthusiasm about a new-found mission tended to obscure some of the problems inherent in group living and the sustained effort required for fund-raising and other means of keeping a venture afloat. Individual motivation and a sense of personal accountability make it possible to get along with less hierarchical authority structures. After a while, however, the reality of staff stress sets in and personal survival starts to take precedence over whatever the mission was. Burnout is one of the unfortunate results.

In comparing the battered women's movement with other alternative services, such as suicide prevention, several differences and similarities emerge.[4]

The similarities. Both groups emphasize the use of non-professional helpers at the front lines. Both have contributed remarkably to community service needs for distressed people who had been ignored by traditional agencies. Those served, suicidal people and battered women, have much in common. They are considered taboo by many professionals and have often been ignored or denied service, either because they elicited conflicted feelings or because traditional service providers did not understand the dynamics behind their despair or plight. Both rely in part on formerly suicidal people and former battered women as staff. In each case the prospective staff member is expected to be out of personal crisis before assuming staff responsibility. Once recruited, though, they work without stigmatization from a suicidal or battering history.

Both groups have also struggled to compete with long-standing traditional agencies for scarce funds. Some individual agencies from both groups have been co-opted by traditional agencies, often forced into this position by lack of funding (Ahrens 1980; Hoff and Miller 1987). Both have often been demeaned by more 'professional' agency staff as 'naive do-gooders' who lack professional insights and expertise, interlopers who will probably disappear from the scene if they are ignored long enough or are squeezed out by politically more powerful rivals for funds.

The differences. One of the major differences between these two providers of service for people in crisis is in their organizational structure. Most suicide prevention centres have an identifiable hierarchical structure formalized through organizational descriptions, though in practice a consensus model is highly visible in most. Some shelters for battered women are indistinguishable from professional social service agencies in hierarchical lines of authority, staffing patterns, and approaches to 'clients'.[5] Others operate on a consensus model as feminist collectives. This difference is a matter of whether the objectives of the organization include explicit political action to end violence against women. Such a philosophy – illustrated in Woman House – assumes that violence against women is primarily an issue of power relationships between the sexes as expressed through all of society's political-economic and social arrangements. Shelters that operate more traditionally may include radical feminists on their staffs, but political action is usually not explicit. Such shelters acknowledge a woman's individual psychological problems, generally by making therapists available to them.

A closely related difference between shelters and suicide prevention centres involves their different organizational and staffing structures and the use of professionals. All suicide prevention centres explicitly rely on professional consultants to assist with certain aspects of service.[6] Shelters for battered women vary here according to whether they are more professionally or politically oriented. Unlike suicidal people generally, battered women are not assumed to be in need of therapy, although as we saw in Chapter 3, all the women in this study (and many others, see for example Hilberman 1980) considered suicide during the battering phase of their lives. Some shelters are staffed to meet the special needs of women with emotional or substance abuse problems. For the most part, though, shelters screen potential residents for psychosis, suicidal tendencies, alcohol, and other drug abuse.

But because many battered women are in desperate situations and/or because staff lack experience in such screening, some women with very serious problems are sometimes admitted. When this happens, staff lacking professional mental health expertise face a serious dilemma. In spite of well-founded apprehensions about how a battered woman might fare in a traditional psychiatric agency, they now feel compelled to turn to psychiatric specialists in the event of a psychotic episode or acute suicidal tendencies of a woman. What usually happens is that once a woman is referred, there is little communication between the psychiatric agency and the shelter; a woman may receive adequate or inadequate service, but no one in the shelter movement really knows.

There is yet another difference between suicide prevention and crisis centres and shelters for battered women. Both serve people in crisis, emphasize listening skills, values clarification, and sensitivity to controversial issues, and 'politically correct' attitudes in their training. However, shelters, unlike crisis centres, do not usually include the basics of formal crisis intervention in their training protocol. Both groups emphasize the human element of helping people in crisis, but crisis centres have combined this aspect of the process with well-founded principles and techniques of intervention culled from specialists in the field. When shelter staff do not take advantage of this knowledge and skill on behalf of battered women, it could be interpreted as an over-reaction against establishment protocols. In other words, while there is much in traditional health and human service practice concerning women as a whole (e.g. Ehrenreich and English 1979) and battered women in particular (e.g. Stark, Flitcraft, and Frazier 1979) that deserves vigorous protest, there are some elements that can be used to the advantage of distressed women.

One of these, I believe, is crisis intervention with a feminist perspective as an adjunct to the general support, and perhaps psychotherapy, needed by some women. There is no question that crisis intervention is practised intuitively and informally in the shelter of this study, much as the women themselves practise it around battering episodes – i.e. 'natural crisis management'. Considering, however, how highly effective the staff are already, and how positively the battered women regard them in contrast to formal institutional network members, it is important not to overlook effective humanistic assistance simply because it comes out of formal training. As Truax and Carkhuff (1967) emphasize, the *quality of the relationship* we establish affects the outcome of our work with people in crisis more than theoretical and technical knowledge does.

The challenge, then, may be to examine closely what formal crisis theory has to offer to the battered women's movement, especially since the crisis movement has already demonstrated effective alternatives to the most offensive aspects of traditional human service systems. My experience suggests that there is a certain duplication of effort going on and that the battered women's movement can benefit by learning the strengths of other alternative services. By anticipating and tackling these problems shelters may avoid co-option and can maintain their innovative philosophies and service modalities. Formal crisis intervention skills would complement natural helping ability thereby enriching the already highly successful peer support approach to assisting battered women during crisis. To be effectively applied on behalf of battered women, however, such training should be conducted with a feminist framework which assumes the origin of battering in social inequality and cultural attitudes about women.[7]

Specifically, crisis intervention skills would aid in determining if a woman's state is so acute that self-direction is temporarily impossible, or if a woman's demands for more service arise from chronic dependency problems, and thus acceding to her requests for more service increases her excessive dependency needs. Crisis intervention training could dispel some of the common myths surrounding suicidal people (Hoff and Miller 1987). The following example illustrates the havoc and stress that can result from lack of current knowledge about suicidal people and their needs:

Jane was one of a group of eight women at the House. Despite screening of residents for acute suicidal tendencies, addictions, and mental disturbance, Jane became suicidal one night and locked herself in the living room to protect herself from acting on her suicidal tendencies with kitchen knives. When she slept she did so on the office sofa so she would not have to ever be alone. Jane had not told her fellow house members why she did these things, though the other women did know that she was suicidal. Tension among the residents grew because they did not understand Jane's behaviour. They were afraid that if they asked she would become more suicidal. One of the residents said she would leave the House if the staff 'didn't get rid of Jane'. Regular staff were highly concerned about the crisis in the House and Jane's safety.

Assessing the situation at the beginning of my staffing shift, I called a meeting of the residents to discuss the problem. I explained to Jane that other residents were worried about her and asked 'Are you willing to meet with them and explain what's happening with you?' To which Jane replied: 'Sure', and eagerly jumped off the sofa. I added that I had experience with suicidal people and was not afraid to discuss suicide. This brought a sigh of relief and 'Thank God!' from Jane.

When asked, Jane explained her behaviour as self-protection, not hostility, as her fellow residents had perceived, and shared with the group that she felt the most protected and least suicidal when another resident had gone for a walk with her. Jane also reassured everyone that in the event she hurt herself or died it was her responsibility, not theirs. All residents expressed relief at having the problem out in the open and agreed to keep open future communication with Jane instead of trying to second-guess her.

This example attests to the fact that battered women are capable agents, even when in acute emotional crisis, and illustrates the advantages of formal crisis training in dealing with anxiety-provoking and potentially life-threatening situations in a shelter.

Human service models for women in crisis

More widespread action to include formal crisis training seems timely since the battered women's movement stands in some respects at a crossroads with more than a decade of experience for the earliest ones. The growing security of the whole women's movement means that women in shelters can more easily share their vulnerabilities (e.g. funding and staffing problems, mistakes, etc.), and acknowledge that their agencies are no more imperfect than many others, without fear that they will be dismantled or co-opted by funding and licensing agencies.

Traditional agencies, on the other hand, can learn from shelters, rather than assuming that professionals always possess greater knowledge and skill in offering human services. The feminist co-operative approach to decision-making and peer support of battered women rests on solid theoretical and practical foundations (Hansell 1976; Withorn 1980; Hoff 1989). Management and personnel research long ago demonstrated that workers who are actively involved in the decision-making structure of agencies are more satisfied and ultimately more productive than those who must function by rote obedience in a chain of command. Therefore, collaboration might well replace an atmosphere of antagonism in relationships between some shelters and traditional agencies.

Similar principles are evident in the success of those psychiatric and human service programmes which actively engage clients/ patients in developing and implementing a service plan. Failure to take these principles into consideration results in creating still greater dependency in distressed people who may also have chronic underlying dependency problems. The shelter staff's solid commitment to the principles of women's empowerment made it possible to consider residents' minor complaints that people did not do enough for them. An empowerment philosophy helps a woman regain control of her life by actually taking control of her life, even when in acute emotional crisis. In psychology this is called 'experiential validation', the beneficial effects of which one may not recognize immediately while in emotional pain.

These clinical observations, however, do not negate the fact that the weakest link in the co-operative approach is its lack of efficiency. This is supported by my own experience working in this collective, the experience of members of other collectives, as well as from interviews of several staff members and the negative comments of residents. For example:

> There should be more emotional support for the battered woman the first week or two of her stay there. When she comes to the House, she's frightened, nervous, and usually drained. She doesn't know where she is going in the first week, but given some sense of physical and emotional security, she can regain her self-confidence – or at least some sense of it – and with some help she can set some goals of what to do, and how to go about it. She needs to know the 'ropes' about obtaining an apartment and a job and she needs information and encouragement about what obstacles are ahead of her and how to overcome them. Being an aggressive person I was able to swing on some of these ropes, but had I been a passive person, I don't believe I would have come as far as I have.

Balancing the needs of battered women in crisis without fostering unnecessary dependency or compromising opportunities for individual empowerment is a great challenge. An extremely 'efficient' environment can result in a battered woman feeling like she is in a strait-jacket, but extreme inefficiency, on the other hand, especially in the contrived substitute 'family' of strangers that constitutes the shelter population, can add to a battered woman's sense of confusion about how to organize the next steps of her life. Excessive inefficiency, if uncorrected, also leads eventually to staff burnout, fatigue, and subtle loss of motivation.

What should not be concluded, though, is that inefficiency is necessarily inherent in collective organizational structures. Nor should the greater amount of time spent in the consensus decision-making process he equated with inefficiency, since a consensus-derived decision is likely to yield more fruit in the long run than one imposed hierarchically. Nevertheless, conscious attention to improving the efficiency of feminist co-operatives would serve to lessen the dangers of reverting to hierarchical structures, since even people committed to co-operative structures become impatient over the time expenditure, and may simply give up, which can pave the way for returning to traditional structures.

Classism and racism also affect the structure and operation of a shelter. One staff member noted that her tolerance of long discussions seemed directly related to her white, middle-class background. This observation was confirmed by many statements of black staff members who more frequently than white members expressed the need to move on with the agenda, since they had duties and children waiting for them at home. Implied here is that only white, middle-class women have the luxury of sufficient time for such a lengthy process of getting work done.[8] These practices suggest that certain structures of talk and the problem-solving process can mask racist and classist social structures and the division of labour between races and classes.

Since consciousness-raising has been so successful for achieving certain political objectives in the women's movement, it should be used in feminist co-operative structures to preserve and improve the many positive aspects of such structures. The willingness and ability to examine these issues is made easier by explicitly acknowledging the enormous accomplishments of feminist co-operative structures. Thus, for example, although residents suggested improvements in the shelter operation, the overall picture they presented was highly favourable compared with that of the formal network members described by the women in Chapter 6. There we heard stories of indifference, victim blaming, and failure to respond to direct appeals for help.

Training in group dynamics is another way to improve the efficiency of meetings and provide greater attention to the needs of residents without compromising the collective's philosophy of consensus decision-making. Staff with more group work skills could balance an individual's needs with those of the community by fostering the principles of self-determination and empowerment for the residents without sacrificing the need for long-term stability of the House. Such stability is assured, in part, through policies that cannot be uprooted and voted out on a whim by members of the resident group. Since battered women have years of survival skills and common sense, they can understand these survival necessities if they are presented honestly. Thus, for example, an individual in a transition state with attendant high anxiety, may resort to immature behaviour (e.g. over-indulgence in alcohol) that might have been tolerated in one's old role. In such an instance, peer support, role modelling, and skilful group work can be instrumental in disapproving the *behaviour* without withdrawing necessary support from the individual engaging in it. Skilful assistance of women with difficult tasks during life passages enhances the process of empowerment that has been such an asset to battered women rebuilding their lives free of violence.

If the shelter movement is co-opted by the establishment, it would mean the loss of valuable progressive policies, such as effective implementation of affirmative action hiring procedures. Of a total of ten staff members in this shelter, five are women of colour and four are former battered women. In its employment policies and its progressive practices regarding child care for staff, this shelter can serve as a model for more humane and just work practices everywhere. The exchange of philosophies of service and individual skills by people in alternative and traditional agencies could be potentially enriching to each and could help to bridge the gaps that currently exist in these two approaches to helping distressed people.[9]

Staff members were asked what they found most rewarding about their work. Here are some of their comments:

> It's great to realize how much people accomplish without a hierarchy, and that in itself is worth working for ... It's more productive. I like the fact that you can voice your opinion in a way that's going to make changes. [This woman had worked previously as a counsellor in traditional human service settings.]

> The most rewarding for me is the fact that the shelter's there and makes a difference and that I'm part of that. There are so many frustrations, but after a good night there, it feels great to watch women go out and get an apartment ... being exposed to these women who've left their situations. These women are really strong. Working here is not like this depressing thing, you see the women pick themselves up. Plus, I like the connections with other women.

> The opportunity to have known so many different kinds of women ... Seeing the women get out of those bad situations. I've looked at people like plants, e.g. I'd walk in and see a little garden like little posies popping out. I like being associated with the other people doing the work, with people like me, not feeling so alienated.

> It's personal, I'm able to give back some of what it takes to make it – Anything to help women overcome the domination of men, anything I can do to help a woman realize her power, that she doesn't have to take that abuse, that she's a real woman.

> Seeing a woman leave here, getting her own apartment and make it. Sometimes when a woman falls apart it's a real hard thing, but it's also a growing opportunity. Former battered women have a great deal of understanding of what a woman goes through. Some battered women only want to talk with someone who's been battered. [This staffer was a former battered woman.]

Staff accounts are supported by other collective members who say that few, if any, other work settings afford them the sense of freedom to do what they can and lack of pressure to do what they can't. Through the work of shelter staff and the atmosphere they create for battered women to help themselves, women experience that they are not alone. Free of violence and in charge of their lives, battered women observe other women in charge of their lives. In this refuge, women feel the security of a temporary home free of fear and the threat of violence. They take the first step toward rebuilding their lives, creating a new domestic environment for themselves and their children. As Chapter 9 illustrates, however, this first step, though critical, is not enough.

Chapter nine

Rites of passage to a life without violence

Introduction

Shelters for battered women may provide salvation for women and their children who have been battered or are threatened by violence. But women who are in such a crisis are in a 'liminal' (in-between) state, which often extends well beyond their few weeks in a shelter. This chapter discusses what happens to women who embark on the difficult passage to a violence-free life. It also examines how the process of conducting this research provided the women with social support and insight which they were unable to obtain elsewhere, illustrating how collaborative research can contribute to the healing function. The chapter concludes by showing how important support is for women who must grieve for the various losses suffered through violence.

The research process, the participants, and the researcher

The women's accounts document the effects of collaborative research on them and put the 'problem' of access in a broader perspective. In early phases of the study, I had envisioned contacting former battered women through shelter follow-up programmes, only to discover that such programmes did not exist – at least not in a formal sense. As it turned out, though, the research process itself served as an avenue for certain follow-up services to the women. While I took extraordinary care to avoid any exploitative interaction with the women, I also had to avoid doing too much for them and thus creating possible unhealthy dependencies. This demanded distinguishing between research, advocacy, therapeutic, and friendship relationships with the women.

This dilemma is not new to field workers. Participants contribute essential information and the researcher typically offers to return favours in the form of goods and services. Relationships inevitably develop from such extended involvement. Although some researchers pay participants, reimbursement was not involved in this study. What I did do was assist the women in baby sitting, transportation, cooking meals or bringing food or treats to their home, loaning my car, writing advocacy letters, being available on the phone, calling lawyers, going on outings, etc. At the end of the information-gathering phase, I told the women that they would share any book royalties if the study was published.[1] Juggling various kinds of interaction with the women was sometimes helped and sometimes complicated by my commitment to a collaborative research relationship where the traditional boundaries between researcher and participants are at least partially blurred.

An unintended but welcome outcome of the research process was its impact on the women participants. Throughout the project the women found it very painful to recount their experiences associated with the battering. Whenever such difficulty became manifest, they were asked to reassess their decision to participate in the research. None of the women withdrew once they became involved in the project. A trusting relationship developed, one which created a context in which they could explore sensitive, painful experiences. Several times the women stated that they found it valuable to participate in the project despite the emotional strain and time commitment it demanded. At the end of the formal process of data-gathering, the women were asked explicitly to comment on how the research affected them and why they decided to take part. Here are some of their responses:

I realize that a lot of women have gone through this ... the understanding helped. You have truly listened to me and were objective. I don't talk to my family. I finally wanted to speak out about my situation. My mother says my depression is getting disgusting to her. [This woman was still forced to live with her parents several months after leaving the shelter.]

It's gotten me in touch with how far I've come. It's been kind of an honour to participate ... just the whole thing of being a woman, how men's role affects women ... It's been therapeutic but emotionally painful. It got things out that may never have been gotten out ... I've told you things I've never told anyone ... I wanted to make a contribution more than I wanted to bury it ...

It helped me to see on which track to go. It took me further than the House did ... I saw things even clearer. From the questions I kinda took a step back and looked at it, and then I took ten steps

167

back and then really acted. It was good that you didn't say anything [when she was considering reconciliation with her husband] or react and that was good and it kind of told me it was up to me. There was no sense of intrusion. I enjoyed the whole thing.

That [a lengthy research interview] was the most incredible experience I've been through. I took about five steps forward. It helped me so much. You were the first person I could really marathon with. I answered a lot of my own questions, but I didn't realize how little I thought of myself before we talked. I even started making meals for myself. [This woman had been seeing a psychiatrist but had terminated on his advice.]

Now at the end it's boring because it's all behind. At the beginning it was interesting. Sometimes it would cause me to think. Sometimes you were rushing. I needed more time to think. The questioning made me draw some conclusions about how I wouldn't let that happen again. Getting it out helped put it behind me. *Why did you take part?* Because I knew you, I thought it would be interesting. It might do good for other battered women if they just read it. Sometimes my own situation seems so unimportant.

A few things tied together. It has brought up topics I've never discussed with anyone ... There's a therapeutic benefit in examining things. It could be a real burden if the interviewer made one feel more guilty. Interviewers have to be thoroughly screened in their expertise and values. [This woman has some training in research methods.] *Why did you take part?* It's hard to say no. It's a worthwhile cause. I'd like to be able to contribute to helping other women to get out of their situations, to get out sooner or not get into them at all.

It's very interesting, especially doing the one about the people, classifying my network. Like my mother always said, you can have many acquaintances, but the ones that will always be there when you need help you can count on one hand. It was encouragement for me to keep my commitment to not going back ... I've had really trying times and felt like giving up. I think just the fact of having contact with you and meeting other women and just finding out more about other things has given me more determination to make it. By asking me questions it made me realize many things. I didn't feel I was being picked apart, but it was so emotional at the time. The research has been a stepping stone to better express myself, like my English course has ... I could be open and honest with you because you understood. *Why did you take part?* I thought if I could be honest and open maybe it could help someone. I've always wanted to share, so someone can draw strength from it. I didn't even know there was literature about this. I felt very isolated, like people with leprosy. Some people want to stay away from battered women, like they're going to catch that disease. I want people to know that I'm a human being, that I'm not a bad person, and that I don't feel that I was *responsible* for the battering ...

Such positive accounts of the research process may be attributed to the extent and stability of time spent with the women, factors related to the collaborative methodology used. The time spent with the researcher extended over several months for all the research participants and over a year for some. Even though the research process was separate from therapeutic intervention,[2] the very fact that the women received sustained attention and interest from the researcher resulted in secondary therapeutic effects. Anthropologists have described such relationships and positive side effects for decades, which in extreme cases accounts for a phenomenon called 'going native', i.e. an anthropologist becomes totally absorbed into the culture being researched.

Even if the researcher does not 'go native', the participants' dependency on the researcher must be considered. There was only one instance of such a problem in this study, which my preparation as a mental health professional helped to resolve successfully. Generally, I have maintained a collegial relationship with the participants, which includes mutual interests in follow-up research and other activities concerning battered women. I also sense the potential of life-long friendships with most of the women. As a result of the research process, my own life will never be the same. The women's accounts have left me with moral outrage at their unnecessary suffering, inspiration from their strength and courage, and a reaffirmation of my feminist vision for social change.

In the case of the shelter Collective, however, I was only partially successful in bridging the gaps between feminist activists and academic researchers.[3] The differences reveal a polarized 'us and them' mentality in the feminist community, one reminiscent of the adversarial method and dualism in male thought and action that feminists have criticized (Riddle 1974/75; Flax 1983; Moulton 1983; Segal 1987). The conflicts also suggest the need to become more aware of the role of knowledge both in the oppression and the emancipation of women. For their part, the women who participated in this research have made a valuable contribution to the development of a knowledge system through their accounts of violence and its tragic effects.

169

Rites of passage

The women's experiences may be viewed along a continuum of 'rites of passage'. Kimball's (1960: xviii) introduction to van Gennep's (1909) classic work on rites of passage emphasizes the place of rituals in modern life. He states that mental illness may arise because an increasing number of individuals are forced to accomplish their life transitions by themselves.[4] Van Gennep (1960: 11) distinguishes three phases in the ceremonies associated with an individual's 'life crises': rites of separation (prominent in funeral ceremonies); transition rites (important in initiation and pregnancy); and rites of incorporation (prominent in marriage). A complete scheme of rites of passage includes all three phases. For example, a widow is *separated* from her husband by death; occupies a *liminal* (transitional) status for a time; and finally is *re-incorporated* into a new marriage relationship (Goody 1962).

In this framework, battered women leaving a violent relationship are in the 'liminal' or transition phase. The women's accounts of what the research meant to them suggests that their role as research participants resembled that of the 'initiand' in traditional rites of passage. That is, the women re-lived the pain they felt during the months and sometimes years it took to leave their violent partners.

Thus, the women's participation in the shelter and the research were integral parts of their successful 'working through' of experiences and behaviours associated with a previous life phase, and fulfilled a pre-requisite need if they were to move on to the next phase – in this case, a life free of violence. The ritual aspect of the research process and its resemblance to psychotherapy rituals was very visible with one of the women. Almost routinely she was late for our interview appointments, even those in her apartment. When we talked about the meaning of this she explicitly associated the lateness with the pain of the interview. More than once I asked if she wanted to continue with the study, and she insisted that she did and reaffirmed how helpful it was to talk in spite of the emotional pain.

In traditional societies, 'ritual experts', with the help of the community, assist individuals through such transitions (e.g. Spiro 1967; Turner 1968). Such assistance assumes that the entire community is concerned with the needs of individuals. It is precisely here, however, that the parallel between traditional societies and the plight of battered women ends, since violence against women has traditionally been defined as a 'private' rather than a community matter. To define violence as a public issue implies that it is of communal concern, and that various members of a woman's formal network can function as 'ritual experts' to assist women in crisis. That mainstream agency representatives often do not function in this manner is abundantly evident in this study.

Thus, apart from the shelter experience, the few examples of formal network assistance cited in Chapters 5 and 6, and the incidental effects of research collaboration, battered women are left to resolve crises originating from violence with only their personal, individual resources for the most part. One woman's poem poignantly expresses this idea:

> The walls are closing in
> I can't breathe
> There's no space to move around in
> There's nowhere to go
> No one cares
> No one wants to help
> No one seems to understand
> What it is like to be battered
> To be so emotionally abused
> that you don't know your own mind any more.
>
> To be beaten so much that you
> deprive yourself of the right to be free
> With what strength you do have, you
> try to escape and start anew.
>
> But again, you stand alone
> A war only you can fight
> No one can help you – no one
> Deep inside you've got to find that
> strength – You've got to find that will
> – whatever is left and strengthen it.
> Sometimes you look around to find that
> strength and you find that you're alone.
>
> No one seems to know what to do
> What to say.

The assistance shelters provide expresses their definition of violence as a public, and therefore, political issue. Not surprisingly, shelter programmes resemble those in traditional communities that provide explicit support to individuals experiencing important changes in status and role.[5]

Beyond the shelter, however, formal assistance to battered women is minimal, as the following excerpt from a group discussion illustrates.

W1: There are support groups and there were support groups. What I don't understand is why they're not used so much. You know what I think it is. Just the conditions that a battered woman has to come out with, she's got to survive first. I found that I didn't have time to go to the support groups ...

W2: Because they have it at a certain place and at a certain time, but if you can, if we can form our own group, then have it like one day at my house, another day at another person's house. It's more convenient – you don't have to feel like you have to dress up and go to a business meeting. And you can just come and relax and if you want to come naked, I mean, so what! You can just be yourself.

W1: I'd be more than happy. And I found my support groups. I got out of a situation I was in because I sought support groups up there that were developing. Once I came into that, I got information that changed me.

Clearly, the women had to find alone whatever help they needed. Only one found a regular group, though it was geared to people with various addictions. Later in the same group discussion, one woman told of her quest for public seeking of recognition in a setting specializing in ritual, the church.

I went to a healing Mass one time to help me strengthen my faith ... and when he [the priest] started to stand at the microphone and asked me what my problem was, she [the lady – in a screening role – she had told that she was an unwed mother and battered] went and cut in and put her hand over the microphone, and I thought 'I want the world to know I'm an unwed mother, so I'm not the only unwed Catholic woman out there, and I want them to know,' but I feel discriminated against. I still feel discriminated against and I feel left out because there's not any support groups that are convenient for me to go to, like the Bible study/

Thus even in one of the few remaining publicly recognized settings for ritual cleansing, forgiveness, acceptance, and re-incorporation into the community, a battered woman who is unwed feels left out.

Another woman described God as 'love and acceptance' and also expressed traditional religious notions such as her expectation of rescue and protection from the battering situation, and looking to the silent, submissive, and humble Jesus as a model of suffering. Because God can be relied on to be 'there' when no one else helps, some of these women may substitute divine support for the support they did not get from humans.

If a woman cannot successfully resolve the difficult changes that violence forces on her, she may remain in a 'liminal' state indefinitely, neither completely separated from her past, nor ready to be incorporated into the community with a new status and sense of self. What is crucial for such assimilation to occur is group support, understanding the demands of the new role, and role models to chart appropriate behaviours in the next life phase. And, for battered women, considerable material aid such as money, transportation, housing – the 'supplies' necessary to avoid emotional crisis (Caplan 1964) – are also required. Battered women often obtain such supplies at the shelter as well as various other resources available there such as peer support, information about housing, legal aid, etc. When women are thus amply supported and supplied with the necessities for transition to a new life free of violence, their need for 'therapy' and the inclination to return to a violent partner seems to be greatly reduced.

Grieving losses suffered from violence

The effects of 'privatizing' violence and leaving battered women to disentangle its tragic web on their own are clarified through the concept of 'grief work', a process of mourning significant losses. Grief work serves a bridging function in a person's passage to building a new life free of violence.

Research examining the effects of life events on individuals' physical, social, and emotional health over the life span sometimes categorizes them as 'stressful' or 'catastrophic' to distinguish the degree of life disruption an event causes. Thus the loss of a loved one by unexpected death is commonly experienced as highly stressful, but not catastrophic (Holmes and Rahe 1967), while loss of one's home and children by fire or disaster are regarded as catastrophic (Gibbs 1982). The trauma of being battered by one's mate, however, generally embraces both categories. The woman's life (and often that of her children) is threatened and she commonly loses her residence and any financial security she had if she was not independently employed. It is not uncommon for a woman to feel forced to flee for her life, abandoning house, furniture, all but a bagful of clothes, and objects of emotional attachment such as photographs – not unlike flood victims fleeing the raging waters.

Because these tangible losses are so immediate, the loss of an important interpersonal relationship tends to become obscured temporarily, especially since the first emotions regarding the lost mate stem from relief from his violence. The delayed realization of the lost relationship is heightened by the woman's almost total absorption during the crisis phase in a shelter with finding alternative housing, initiating legal proceedings for divorce or separation, and meeting the hourly demands of a new living arrangement with a houseful of strangers. During this crisis phase, feelings of anger against the violent mate, caution regarding other men, and the comfort of temporary security against violence tend to subsume whatever feelings a woman may have about losing an important relationship.

But battered women resemble all bereaved persons who must come to terms with loss through grief work, especially if it is a relationship in which one has invested enormous time and energy. The acuteness of the women's losses and their need to mourn them is directly related to their shattered ideals regarding love, marriage, intimacy, and the family. 'Intimacy' as used in this study may include but is not limited to sexual intimacy. The following question addresses this broader definition: Was there anyone you felt really close to and could rely on? In a life history perspective, even before the women were battered, only five of the nine stated that they had someone to rely on. Their responses revealed the general sense of isolation the women felt when they were battered. Even those women who still found their mates sexually attractive during earlier phases of the battering said they did not feel 'intimate' toward them. The five who said there was someone to rely on during this phase named their mother, sister, or woman cousins. These responses underscore the psychological, social, and material factors contributing to the women's isolation, e.g. shame, threat from the man if they sought help, physical distance from relatives, sense of responsibility for making the marriage work. Their accounts also suggest that their ideals regarding marriage clashed with the reality of violent relationships. What we have is the women's ideal of love and friendship as 'sharing, caring, peace, pleasure, support', juxtaposed to the actual behaviour of their mates that resulted only in terror, insult, physical injury, threat to life, and homelessness.

When battered women finally leave a violent partner and find themselves in a shelter or alone, at some point they usually feel acutely the pain of loss of a relationship they hoped would eventually conform to their ideals of friendship, love, and marriage. This loss can assume crisis proportions, though not usually catastrophic proportions, as do housing loss and threats to one's life and safety. But even though such survival issues dominate a woman's attention while in a shelter, the need for grief work, though less obvious, is nevertheless just as essential as it is in other crisis settings. Since battered women are highly vulnerable at this time, inadequate support and the failure to grieve may be pivotal influences in the decision of some to return to their violent mates. We have only informal data about the number of women who return to the men after freedom from violence in a shelter, though impressions from police and emergency facilities suggest that many women do return repeatedly.

Studies of loss, grief, and mourning (e.g. Lindemann 1944; Parkes 1975) now widely recognize that a person who has suffered a serious loss needs the opportunity for grief work, or serious negative consequences can result. The emotional pain attending loss originates from our attachment to others as social beings. But many people resist coming to terms with loss. Grieving is the process of suffering that a bereaved person goes through on the way to a new life without the lost person (Lindemann 1944; Parkes 1975; Hoff 1989). The main features of bereavement include: realization of the loss that eventually replaces denial and avoidance; an alarm reaction including restlessness and anxiety; an urge to look for and find the lost person; anger toward the lost one and oneself, e.g. 'What else could I have done to make the marriage work?', often followed by guilt; bodily distress such as numbness, plus emotions such as depression; feelings of internal loss, e.g. 'He was a part of me'; identification phenomena, e.g. trying to build a new relationship of the same kind.

Normal grief work with battered women consists of helping them to: (1) accept the pain of loss, including dealing with the memory one has of the lost spouse; (2) express openly their pain, sorrow, hostility, and guilt; (3) understand the intense feelings associated with the loss (e.g. fear of going crazy) as a normal part of the grieving process. The ritual expression of grief, as in support groups, greatly aids in this process; (4) eventually resume normal activities and social relationships without the lost person.

A battered woman's failure to communicate explicitly her feelings of anger and rejection about her broken marriage can result in her harbouring wishes for reconciliation based more on fantasy than on reality. The failure to do grief work can also block the process of finding replacements for the person lost. If such grief work is left undone, a woman remains in a liminal phase and is less able to accomplish the tasks of reincorporation into the community in a new role. Just as some divorced people have developed 'divorce ceremonies' to conclude a liminal phase, battered women also require an opportunity to ritually put behind them a life of violence and thus release emotional and social strength for developing a life free of violence. The following poem by one of the women, written a year after leaving the shelter, expresses this sentiment:

Insecure
So unsure
Afraid because she's
still feeling the punches
The scars still haven't healed
But the salt from the world still rubs into her wounds
It's so hard to heal when people act so unreal
with their con-artist games
playing with emotions
They think they know it all,
but they've not the slightest notion
of the unseen buildings destroyed in the war
of the shell still trying to heal
with weak supports
so badly shaken.

The pain and personal price both of violence and of grieving alone are vividly portrayed in the following excerpts from letters and diary material. One of the women shared letters she received from her ex-husband over the course of a year following her divorce. Some are reproduced here to illustrate the need for grief work by violent men as well as by their victims in order to move beyond bitterness after losing a spouse through violence.[6]

Well, My Dear:
This is where I'm staying for the week – one of the best, most expensive hotels in the world.

I'm hard at my new job as a sales manager for _____ . My old bosses are now our customers. I'm meeting people all over the *world* (Japan, Germany) as well as the country relating in all manners to our product – 1200 store chains to 100 store chains. This my dear is a 5–8 year climb – done in 10 months, a multi-million dollar, hi-powered sales force of young, well connected, driven, hungry, highly paid smoothies – selling, selling and it's all legal. I did it myself with no modesty – but aggressiveness – without booze, without drugs – without you. I'm tempted to tell you to take your lilly white, holier than thou attitude and shove it ... But I won't – not just yet ...

I don't worry about your opinion of me anymore. I worry about me – only me and my opinion of me. You'll never know angel, you'll never know what we could have had. All I needed was a woman who could string a sentence together. You couldn't – it didn't concern you to communicate. Communicate to your empty womb now 33 year old ... and I'll send you a quitter's award on your

40th birthday. You're the loser. I played and strayed for fun – you for keeps – keep it.

Pay your wages for equity in a house. I'll put mine in the stock market. May the better person win! You won a lot from me lady – an awful lot. Now eat those gas bills, tax bills and well earned gay divorcee's stigma. It's all yours babe – you wanted it – you got it. Right now I could pay the whole smear and still buy you.

Take another art course and another and another and count your time in meaningless menses.

Significantly, when she received the letters, this woman's response was a completely private one – in her diary. She said she had no intention of ever sending her letters as she knew it would serve no purpose other than to maintain

some connection that I did not want. So not feeling that my thoughts should be burdened on a friend I wrote them to get them out of my head and chest – to be able to organize them somewhat – to give them form and hopefully be able to examine and discard them.

Following is the woman's journal response to this letter:

Received your latest love-hate letter today. I guess you're still not too happy with yourself. You need to tell me how wonderful you and your life is and how awful and empty mine is ... I did everything thinking of you first and then our marriage – What did I win?

A distrust of men and a hatred of you. A fear of men – and memories of bruises and swollen hands, black eyes and loose teeth. Jerry I hate you and I hate you for my hate. I hate you for the fear I have of getting involved with another man. I hate you for the 10 years I so naively wasted on you.

I hate you for the hate I feel towards myself for my incredible stupidity – how could I have married such a creature – you left no area of marriage unspoiled – you committed every crime possible within a marriage.

I am only thankful that I was finally able to realize my catastrophic mistake and divorce you before your cruelty drove me to insanity or suicide. May you die of emphysema.

Following is a diary entry about a month later:

I've been alone now about one year. It's depressing – I guess I thought by now I would at least be dating some men and enjoying life a bit more. But the truth of the matter is there is no one on the horizon. No one who shows any interest in me that I'm interested in.

I'm having some trouble accepting my rejections in life. It makes me feel totally unworthy of anyone. No one has wanted me for long before – why should anything change? Maybe that's not totally true but I still feel that way. I feel ugly, unattractive, dull, clumsy and stupid – total Blah.

I don't think about suicide quite as much as I did about a month or so ago. At least not to the same depth. If this is the healing process I don't think I could ever go through it again ...

Why were we raised on such awful fairy tales – where is Prince Charming anyway? How could adults living in the real world ever allow their children to grow up thinking that life as an adult was great, that marriage is the be all/end all to life and that one Prince/husband would always take care of us ... never to teach us to be self-sufficient. That Love is wonderful – when it stinks. Where are the beautiful children that I was supposed to devote my life to? Not from my womb. If ever.

I wish I didn't need anyone else. I wish I could be self-sufficient. Why is love so God damned important? I have everything else – health, a good job, nice home, good friends – nice living arrangements. Why isn't it enuff. I'm so bound with my own depression. When will it end – Can it? Is it really all my own fault or is it beyond my control? Life is rotten even for us 'lucky' people – I don't understand how people without their health or other advantages choose to live. Sometimes I hang on for the smallest thread. I think I need to get involved in a group for divorcees. Maybe that would help.

Following is a diary entry one month later:

Looking through some old pictures – and remembered a poem I wrote to Jerry about us long before we decided to get married. After reading it and remembering there was no *real* change in our relationship after that I realize that a large percent of the reason I got married was because I was in love with 'marriage'. Even tho intellectually I knew that it was the solution to nothing I did it because emotionally it was the whole future for me. The poem read:

> I feel as a caged animal
> I want to scream my frustration out of me
> Out of my cage

Someone has gone with the key
And won't listen to my plea

Please, please open the door and set me free
Free to love and cage you in me.
But if I cage you, then you will cry
So we must both be free
To grow in love, you and me

The key is my capacity to love
Open the Door!
Open the door and I'll love you
Until Eternity.

The bars are closing in on me
This pressure frustrates and angers me
Spread them wide and let me loose
And I'll show you my kindness, understanding and love.
Then you shall never see
Any anger or hurt in me.

Even then I felt totally trapped and helpless in our relationship. I felt I had no choice. I felt doomed. I don't know why I felt I had to go on with the relationship. I guess part of it was the being so sought after – so desired. Would anyone else ever chase me so hard, so long, so determined – that must be real love – maybe, but probably not.

Two months later she received this letter from Jerry:

I wish I could say all the depressions and pain were gone when I stopped drinking but they aren't. They're still very much there – sometimes sharper and keener than ever. Something painful will enter my mind like a dart and cause me to lose my stride when I walk, water my eyes, cause silence and distraction but I find myself still walking, getting through it, traveling somewhere and discovering that I can live with pain and profound loss. There are many times when I enjoy my life and keep trying to accomplish things. Rejection and inadequacy are still there but I am coping. I'm very much alone now and sometimes prefer it that way. I've pushed many people away without realizing it over the years. Some very good friends of mine are over there with you on the indifference side. And I've lost them as well as you. I guess it takes a lot for me to learn. But, take heart, I'm learning.

179

At this point in this letter I really don't know why I'm writing to you. You're just always with me. Always, always on my mind. Whenever I see cats and kittens, clean kitchens, patched jeans, back yard gardens, homemade bread, houseplants, summer camps, maps of Vermont on and on, I think of you. It's there, I love you. You have affected my perception of the world, the way I see many many things I learned from you and they will be a part of me until I die. They are the few good things in my life, the gentleness that has been lacking and I miss having it around. With the pain of dealing with contemporary society getting into shape I believe I can handle the pain of living without you only with much difficulty.

I cannot seem to generate strong feelings for anyone however. Not as yet. Your influence is too profound. I see a woman with a child, especially a young child and I vacillate between tears and smiles. I remember the trips to the hospitals, the hopes, the thermometers the charts and the nights that were perfect. I regret more than you'll ever know not giving you a child. People, upon finding out I'm divorced, ask if there were any children and I reply NO. They always say I'm lucky or that's good. And I smile and say nothing. My ignorance would *empty* volumes.

So, I can survive without you now but that's all it really is, is survival. Possibly, I can learn to live without you. I know completeness isn't attainable – healthy or unhealthy as you put it, it's fact. My regrets are *almost* insurmountable. But I'm a different person now – still somewhat weak, still angry and still in love with you.

About one month later the woman wrote this poem:

> Life begins again!
> I still have clouds of depression
> But they are shorter and less intense
> Replaced by elated moments,
> Sheer joy to be young, healthy,
> Free!
> Free to see the beauty and subtle colour in a
>   bleak cold winter's day.
> Free to dance, to laugh, to sing, to ski, to paint, to sleep!
> Free to form new friendships
> Free to love again.
> Free to explore, to learn who I am.

I am becoming who I want to be.
Life is opening new doors
and now *I* hold the key!
Sometimes I make mistakes,
take the wrong path.
But I'm just exploring, soon
I find my way again and
I'm humbled by my errors.
There is *no cage*
I set myself free!

It's a little frightening just yet.
In a cage I was safe from the outside,
But not from my insides.
There are no fences to protect me
or limit me now.
Which way should I go?
Which path to follow?
I will try to be brave,
Remain open
Explore as many paths as possible
that I can seek out.

I like the emerging *ME*!

In a letter accompanying these materials, the woman cited the letters from her former husband as

> good examples of how men like Jerry keep their women unsure, unhinged, and immobilized by subtly (or obviously) making them feel guilty, responsible, loved, and that the man is trying and desirous of being a good mate. Somehow even now when I read them part of me can't help but feel – maybe if I was more patient, more communicative, less judgmental, more understanding, more supportive, tried just a bit harder, a bit longer ... It still makes me sad; sad for me and all the unnecessary unhappy memories and changes in me that I still haven't totally recovered from; sad for Jerry that with or without my help (and that of family and friends) that he had to fall so low before beginning to put himself together and that he may never be truly 'together' (although I hope I'm wrong); sad for our families and friends who felt helpless to help us.

This letter, written five years after the woman's divorce, expresses poignantly the human tragedy and waste of violence. It also suggests that contemporary rites of passage for women leaving a violent relationship might help them to rebuild their lives free of violence. This woman's long struggle to heal the emotional wounds from her traumatic experience was essentially hers alone, with no formal sources of assistance, only the individual support of friends and family. Her experience – and Jerry's – suggest that more could be done to shorten the grief work and lighten these burdens.

Together these accounts also support previous analysis about the traditional socialization of men and women, and the internalization of conflict. Some of the most poignant statements about the poverty of traditional male/female roles are the woman's lament about the 'fairy tales' she was taught about marriage as the 'end all and be all' of life,[7] while the man complained 'You see I was never married before. I never went to school for it.' Of course, neither did the woman, because for her all of life was like a school for marriage. More powerful evidence is hardly needed to support feminist arguments for radical changes in childrearing practices and relationships between women and men.

In the shelter where seven of the nine study participants stayed, grief work or small group 'ritual' was evident in informal sharing among the women about woman/man relationships. Conversations among the women also revealed their desire to find non-violent relationships with men as soon as possible. Statements by some suggested that the long-term prospect of living without a man was quite unacceptable, an impression supported by the women's generally traditional values. In fact, shelter residents' (not particularly the study participants) single-minded focus on re-instituting a relationship with a man, combined with their less than enthusiastic response to the political issues concerning violence against women, often prompted the staff's keen disappointment. The staff, however, avoid explicit political tactics. They assume that excellent service and the role models they present of women in charge of their lives and performing capably in a job, are political statements in themselves.

The issue of beginning new woman/man relationships raises some questions about interactions between shelter staff and other professionals working with battered women. First, should staff members explicitly facilitate support group discussion around the issue of developing non-violent, mature relationships with men, or should they merely listen and respond when the women themselves bring them up? A philosophy which supports empowering battered women would suggest that staff not actively direct such discussions. Yet, given the traditional socialization of many battered women, shelter staff may miss an opportunity for consciousness-raising by not addressing this issue overtly.[8] Similar dynamics seem to operate among some health professionals who find it difficult to initiate communication with traumatized women on the topic of violence. Yet when human service professionals do not make explicit their concerns about violence and victimization, women may interpret the silence to support the old notion of battering as a private issue. Besides the value of open communication in the 'ritual' of a helping relationship with battered women, it is no longer acceptable for human service workers to assume a 'neutral' position on the issue of violence.[9] To do so may contribute to the process of internalization, where victimized women continue to blame themselves for another's violent behaviour.

Important as sheltering and rites of passage are for battered women, these social/psychological measures are not enough to meet the multiple problems they face. The next two chapters focus on housing and public policy issues affecting battered women and their children for months – sometimes years – after leaving a violent relationship.

Chapter ten

After shelter: poor and homeless women and children

Introduction

Delores Hayden's (1981) landmark study of the reciprocal relationship between housing, architectural style, and the political economy shows how society maintains women in primarily a domestic role. Physical shelter of some kind is basic to survival. Homes, on the other hand, go beyond survival needs to fulfil social and emotional ones as well. While a man's home may be 'his castle', it is still largely women who turn physical space into an environment called 'home'. Even though labour statistics still do not include unpaid domestic work, this is nevertheless where most women perform many hours of labour for the family and society. Some women consider this their primary job; others view it as secondary to a job they may perform in the paid labour market.

Most women, regardless of class, assume primary responsibility for the domestic side of life either by choice, necessity, or default. Many women do not readily relinquish their traditional control of domestic matters, for example, in the kitchen. Some say they never will until power in the public sector is shared more equally between women and men. Add to these factors the traditional socialization of women to think of their 'proper' place as the home, and it is not difficult to understand why many women feel highly attached to their homes.

Consequently, the very necessity of emergency shelters for battered women is a powerful symbol of society's devaluation of women and children. Considering how societal representatives reinforce the idea of women's primary, biologically determined place in the domestic sphere, that women and children are forced out of the domestic dwelling when *they* are the victims of attack seems a cruel paradox. To reflect on this reversal of justice for victims of crime illuminates the frequently heard question: 'If she doesn't like to be beaten, why does she stay?' For, since the woman is the victim, not the assailant, and since she is imbued with the idea that the domestic scene is her most appropriate place, the appropriate question should be: 'Why should she leave?' That battered women are almost always the ones forced to leave to save their life and those of their children, is a measure of our failure to treat violence against women as a public problem. Since societies define rules regarding interpersonal behaviour, often including prohibitions on attacking others, the following scenario seems ludicrous:

> Several women and more than a dozen children hide themselves away in a secret house with no address, only a Post Office box number. There are stringent security policies around this house: if the location is revealed or the woman allows a friend to accompany her home from an outing, she can be expelled from the house without a hearing. The reason for this tight security policy is the history of certain violent men seeking out their wives at the house, and holding all the residents hostage if they fail to turn over the desired woman.

Nevertheless, the shelter described in this scene provides battered women and their children with a substitute home for the one they have had to flee. Once their time limit in such shelters is exhausted, however, housing crises and chronic problems may continue. This chapter addresses the poignant results of policies and practices that provide battered women and their children, already victimized by violence, with physical shelter that mocks any vision they had of 'home'. It also argues for re-thinking the future use of shelters.

General housing status of the study participants

The women's housing problems were compounded by the inconsistent interactions between individuals, political action groups, and public institutions concerned with housing. One major problem was poverty; another was the generally inadequate housing for low-income residents in the study setting; and a third was housing authorities' attitudes regarding the needs of homeless battered women and their children. In short, class and cultural values regarding women and violence created an interacting cycle of crisis and chronic housing problems for some of the women, a situation that lasted months beyond their stay in a shelter.

Housing and financial status varied among the nine women. Before being battered, only two women had even been moderately dissatisfied with housing. Seven said that their residential status was good or excellent. Even during the battering phase, only two of the nine women had serious problems around housing. Their self-evaluations about housing support a common judgement about why some battered women do not leave violent relationships: putting up with violence is the price that many women may pay for the security of housing. This thinking is borne out by the fact that, after battering, all of the women had to find inferior housing.

The women's evaluations, however, need to be analysed in context. Three of the women went immediately from the shelter to their parents' home. A fourth woman went to her parents' home after temporary stays in shelters and in the home of a shelter staff member. Four of the women moved from home ownership to rental housing. One moved to a single room in the YWCA, then to a room in a family home and finally to an apartment, and then only because she had temporarily relinquished custody of her children. Only two women had satisfactory housing after leaving violent relationships. These were the two women with graduate degrees and adequate independent income. Even one of these, however, moved from a $100,000[1] owned home to a much smaller apartment in a housing complex. The other purchased a home for herself and also owns a vacation home in the mountains. The other two women in owned housing prior to and during battering had no readily marketable skills to maintain this housing standard.

Lacking job skills or adequate financial means, most women paid a heavy toll during their struggle to obtain even minimal housing once they had left a shelter. The housing problem is exacerbated because culturally-embedded values interact with the political economy and a woman's personal circumstances to keep her chronically deprived of adequate housing.

Housing and the political process

In the community of this study social and political policies regarding the poor and disadvantaged are generally highly progressive. Public services, special legislation, and social activism on behalf of the needy are exemplary. Situated in the 'cradle of the American revolution', the community prides itself on upholding historical ideals and acting on the liberal tradition of social largesse. Yet the community is also known for its racial tension and for maintaining Victorian ideals and traditions. The housing situation has been complicated by a highly-touted urban renewal programme and a revitalization of the downtown area, which some claim has been carried out at the expense of the poor and neighbourhood cohesiveness. 'Gentrification', political corruption, and mismanagement of publicly owned housing has created a chronic shortage of affordable housing, especially in low and moderate income categories. Thus the city's vacancy rate for rental housing has been critically less than 5 per cent for several years, even though 70 per cent of the city's households rent, and three-quarters have incomes low enough to qualify for public assistance with housing. While an emergency housing programme exists, hundreds of people who qualify for emergency placement are often placed on a 'waiting list', causing delays that can last for months. Each new cold season brings a repeated outcry about the plight of the city's hundreds of homeless people and pledges from public authorities to respond to the problem.[2]

The acute housing problem was evident during the several months study participants attempted to find housing. While shelter staff offer concrete assistance in finding housing, many women quickly become discouraged by the obstacles they face.[3] Theoretically, of course, women can seek housing in a large number of municipal jurisdictions in addition to the urban centre. However, those communities closest to the central city have similar waiting lists and rental rates. While the vacancy and rental rates are less forbidding in outlying areas, transportation to such housing presents a serious problem. And for those women who came from the central city and who try to maintain or regain social contact with their families and friends, distance only complicates the problem. Only the two financially independent women had cars. While these obstacles are formidable enough, if a woman also has children and is non-white, she faces further trouble in obtaining housing in this metropolitan area. These general housing problems assume concrete meaning through a description of what transpired for these women over several months around housing needs.

Immediately after leaving the shelter, Eileen moved to her parents' house with her small children. The atmosphere was chronically tense for several reasons. (1) Her father was one of the few family members who was unsympathetic to his daughter's plight. He was also chronically ill, which elicited Eileen's sympathy even though he expressed none toward her. (2) A brother had a problem with alcohol and other drugs, and was sometimes physically abusive toward Eileen. (3) Conflicting views among family members around child rearing caused additional stress to Eileen and her children who were already scarred from years of observing the abuse of their mother. Eileen qualified for housing assistance, but could not find an apartment in the specified price range. Nor could she find a job to supplement her welfare payments and expand her housing options. Eileen was chronically depressed about her inability to break out of

the cyclic problem of housing, unemployment, and forced dependence on her parents. She said:

> My social worker says I'm lucky to have my own place [i.e. a room
> in her parents' home] – 'There are a million other people in ident-
> ical situations.' She's a kind lady, but she said I should be happy my
> mother took me in. She said I should smarten up or she'll take
> away my kids. She's on my back about getting a job *first* and then
> get an apartment ... I disagree that my situation is identical to
> others ... But I kept my mouth shut. One thing I've learned is that
> raising your voice to them they judge you. She's already asked me
> to go to a psychiatric clinic. *Housing* is my problem. One landlord
> put the rent up by $75 when he found out I had kids. People do dis-
> criminate against married women who are single parents.

As the months wore on, Eileen's conflict with her brother became
more intense and her mother asked her to leave. She stayed with an
aunt temporarily, returned to her mother's house, and after her
brother physically attacked her again, entered another shelter for
battered women. Complicating Eileen's problem was her chronic depression which she attributed to inadequate housing. The severe
shortage of housing, particularly if children are involved, and if personal depression inhibits full attention to the large task of finding
scarce housing, completes the formula for extended homelessness.
Thus, a year after her first shelter experience, Eileen and her three
children were still homeless.

Jessica found an apartment on a summer sub-let basis only, but
even after several months she could not find an affordable permanent residence for herself and her child. Ultimately she had to move
into her mother's home for six months. Her full-time employment
both as a computer programmer and hostess finally allowed her to
rent an apartment. These successes were possible in part because her
mother took an active part in caring for her 3-year-old.

Loreen's post-shelter housing situation was similar to Eileen's
and Jessica's since she too had to move back to her parental home.
Here she stayed for eight months while awaiting available housing
even though she had been approved for housing assistance months
earlier. The fact that Loreen, Eileen, and Jessica were *able* to move
back to their parents' home reveals the general supportiveness of the
women's family members. Eileen's experience with this housing arrangement, however, suggests the limitations of a woman's reliance
on such family support, especially if there are other family problems
and if even one member lacks sympathy for the battered woman.
Even without such problems adult women who are mothers and have

already experienced independent housing, suffer a loss of self-esteem and independence when forced back into dependence on their parents. Public officials who ask 'Why don't you stay with your parents?' are totally unaware of this issue. This problem was less acute for Loreen since she was in her late teens when she returned to her parents' home and had not yet given birth to her first child. She therefore interpreted this necessity as less of a deviation from the norm of expected behaviour for married women.

Naomi similarly experienced a loss in housing status but under different external circumstances. She spent several months living in the YWCA, a particularly trying experience for her since many of the residents were women discharged from mental institutions or with other highly visible personal problems. This environment served to remind Naomi of her struggle to reject her former husband's constant accusations that she was 'crazy'. Living among discharged mental patients made it difficult to convince herself that she was not mentally ill just because she had been battered for years. Naomi's next move was to a single room in a family home. Here she had to struggle against the family matron's tendency to treat Naomi as she treated her teenage children. After years of experience successfully managing her own household, this new dependency position in her mid-30s provided a source of continuous stress. After several months of employment and freelance consulting work as an office manager, Naomi was able to obtain an apartment that suited her needs for privacy and independence.

Welfare practices and beliefs about the poor

Karen faced different problems. She was able to find an apartment immediately after leaving the shelter. It was a one-bedroom flat with a large kitchen, dining area, and living room (which doubled as the children's bedroom), but no central heating or refrigerator. There was also a problem of rats and mice and an insecure door. Marginal as this place was at $300 per month, she would not have been able to obtain it if a shelter staff member had not posed as her 'former landlady' and stated that she earned $250 per week. To maintain herself and her two children in this sub-standard dwelling, Karen worked two or three days each week as a housekeeper to supplement her monthly welfare budget of $379.20 for three. One of these cleaning jobs was provided by the Welfare Department as part of its work incentive programme requiring welfare mothers to work outside the home at least part time in return for public support. One month a computer error was made and Karen's benefit was cut, requiring her to ask her father for $100 in order to meet regular bills. Karen became very discouraged with her situation. She was living in sub-standard housing, going to college full-time to improve her job skills, caring for two young children alone, and working outside the home as well to subsist on her meagre public assistance budget. Any pro-gress she made in becoming financially stable meant that her benefits were cut, thereby defeating the purpose of working to enhance her budget beyond $379.20 per month, or $4,550.40 per year. Addition-ally, she received $120 per month ($1,440 annually) in food stamps, financial aid at college, and a $150 per year children's clothing allow-ance. Her total annual income was $6,140.40, $2,070 below the official poverty level in the US at the time of this study for a family of three (US Department of Labor 1983). She therefore decided to pro-test the cut in public benefits by requesting a hearing. Prior to the hearing a caseworker made a routine review of her case. Following is a transcript of Karen's meeting with the caseworker and the hearing on the budget cut that followed (both were tape-recorded and ob-served):

Karen: It was scheduled for yesterday [on such short notice]. What's this about child support? I don't need to fill this out, I don't have a husband and I've already filled out the 'good cause' form. [The 'good cause' form refers to grounds for not revealing the husband's name or presumed whereabouts, in this case, the fear that he would thereby be able to trace his wife's location and commit further violence against her.]

Worker: If you don't want to fill it out, don't do it.

Karen: Why do I have to fill it out?

Worker: It's mandatory.

Karen: Each time? The children's father has not changed, the situation has not changed.

Worker: You know, but I don't. Just fill out whatever you think is necessary. [Speaking to Karen without looking at her] You have checking account? [*sic*] Savings account? Life insurance? Medical insurance? [English was a second language for this worker.]

Karen: Just medical.

Worker: You receiving food stamps?

Karen: Yes.

Worker: Bank account?

Karen: $19.27 ... It's such a big amount [said sarcastically as she shows her check book and account number].

Worker: You know why you're on WIN [Work Incentive Program]?

Karen: I was told they'd pay for my schooling but they won't – only if I work 20 hours a week which is ridiculous. If I work 20 hours a week I have to go to school at night and they won't pay for a babysitter. [There are long pauses here, staccato mumbling that was not clear, no eye contact between worker and Karen as he finished with the following:]

Worker: Just fill it out or suffer the consequences.

Karen: ... I've just learned how to fight back. [Karen walks out of the office with no formal closing of interview observed. A few minutes later she is called for the formal hearing regarding her protest in cut of benefits.]

[The Hearing Officer reads the terms of a Fair Hearing as provided by State law, including the right to be heard before a Judge if dissatisfied with the decision.]

Karen: $379.20 totally is a budget for three. If you make more than $597.30 you go off all aid. I didn't even have beds for my children or sheets. How am I supposed to acquire that if I go out and work? That was my whole reason for working so I could go out and save money so I could get beds for my kids to sleep on and sheets ... I can't do it ... It's not fair for me to go to work and go to school at night. What's the sense of having that when my children will be out on the streets ... there's a lot of drug addicts out there. I got away from their father. He was one and I want to better myself but I'm not going to do it if it's going to be a disadvantage to my children. How am I supposed to get ahead and eventually get off welfare if I try and then I'm *penalized*? [Karen is sounding increasingly emotional with a pleading tone in her voice.] You know what I'm saying? I'm not trying to live high and mighty off of welfare. It's something that I have to depend on because I don't have the skills to go out and get a good paying job that will give me some kind of medical insurance because with children you know how susceptible they are to whatever is going on.

Case Worker:: [in calm voice] She [looking at Hearing Officer] can't change policy. I can't change policy.

Karen: It used to be that you could get beds and things ... They wouldn't even give me a refrigerator. What am I supposed to do?

Case Worker: [calmly, with controlled 'professional' concern] It puts you in a difficult position.

Karen: The cost of living is ridiculously high. I can't even save up to buy a sewing machine so I could make [the children's] clothes ...

The Hearing Officer and Case Worker examined the records and confirmed that a computer error had been made and agreed to adjust Karen's monthly payments so that she would receive the original set payment of $379.20 monthly.

Karen's experience is significant in several respects. First, the purported reason for the State-sponsored Work Incentive Program is to reduce welfare mothers' dependency on public assistance, by providing a woman with incentives to become self-supporting through contributing at least partially to her monthly income from public sources. The programme represents a microcosm of the free enterprise system; that is, rewarding a person in accordance with initiative taken. In fact, the programme does not reward but rather penalizes a woman for any personal effort she makes to reduce her dependency on public subsistence. When, through personal sacrifice, she moves herself a few dollars closer to the official poverty level, her public benefits are cut, telling her, in effect, that she is really better off financially if she remains *completely* (rather than partially) dependent on welfare, while at the same time effectively eliminating the financial leverage needed to make long-term strides toward eventual self-sufficiency.[4]

Ethnomethodological analysis of Karen's interaction with these three representatives of the Welfare Department reveals clearly her ascription of blame. She categorizes the agency as one from which she can properly expect more service than she has received (Sacks 1967). The fact that she is given the public hearing at all presupposes the belief – as provided in official policy – that actions taken against certain welfare recipients may in fact be in error, may be unfair, and therefore are subject to adjustment. The public policy decisions can be examined further in this brief statement of the case worker: 'She [the Hearing Officer] can't change policy. I can't change policy' which presupposes the worker's belief that policy *should* be changed, since her statement followed Karen's lengthy complaint about welfare policy and there was no challenge or rebuttal to Karen's complaint (Coulter 1979a). Thus, even the representatives of the Welfare Department suggest that Karen has grounds for her complaints about the prospects of eventually reducing welfare dependence.

In spite of such built-in disincentives to reduce welfare mothers' dependency on public subsistence, Karen remained determined to pursue her goal of eventual financial independence through a professional career as a certified public accountant. Suppose, however, that Karen had a history of welfare dependency, had already abandoned hope of ever being self-sufficient, and had deeply set patterns of general dependency on others. In such a case, welfare officials intent on reducing such dependency patterns would need to examine the system of casework approaches to these mothers. In this study it became apparent that a welfare mother rarely could identify a case worker she routinely contacted for case review, questions, etc. Thus, a fundamental premiss (a stable relationship between the case worker and a particular welfare mother) for resolving excessive dependency problems is missing in this bureaucratic approach to casework. Each time a welfare mother appears in person or telephones the welfare office about her case she more than likely will talk with a different worker. Thus, while publicly promoting programmes with the alleged purpose of reducing welfare dependence, the disjointed, impersonal approach to service is likely to result in the exact opposite effect: greater dependence fostered by uncoordinated service and the lack of stable client–worker relationships.

Karen's hearing revealed that the individual women examining her complaint had some concerns about her plight, but were virtually powerless to improve Karen's circumstances even though they were themselves in authority positions (albeit lower level). The case worker's statement 'It puts you in a difficult position' is a stereotypical example of the 'professional' empathic response. If considered, however, in relation to the worker's earlier disavowal of personal responsibility ('I can't change policy'), it represents in effect a band-aid approach to Karen's problem in spite of her diatribe against the Welfare Department. Altogether, this interaction reveals the rigidity and intransigence of depersonalized, bureaucratic agencies even when their own representatives apparently believe in the necessity of change.

If an outcome like this occurs for someone like Karen, who is very assertive and leaves no stone unturned to improve her circumstances, it is not difficult to understand why some welfare mothers give up and focus simply on daily survival. Karen's experience underscores the enormous need for evaluation and reformation of public welfare services in the US, a need repeatedly expressed by State and Federal authorities, but yet to be acted upon nationally. In spite of more generous benefits to the poor and disadvantaged during the 1960s and 1970s as part of the 'war on poverty and hunger', Karen's case and thousands like hers suggest a return in the 1980s to punitive attitudes and practices toward the poor, implying that people are poor through their own fault and that greater *personal* effort is the main thing needed to correct their poverty. Karen's case reveals the fallacy of this assumption and also illustrates the processes involved in the 'feminization of poverty', which should probably be redefined as the 'pauperization of women and children'.

The struggles of these battered women with housing and economic survival provide additional answers to the question: 'Why don't battered women leave?' As noted earlier, only two of the women described their housing after battering as better or the same as before, and even for them there were problems of forced dependency on family or others. Many women who call shelter hotlines suggest that insecurity about housing and daily subsistence enters into their decision to leave or stay. Evidence from this study suggests that battered women's fears about economic insecurity (especially if they are poor and have no marketable job skills) are well founded.

The women's struggles despite institutional obstacles show their determination to live free of violence and gain economic independence. These obstacles reveal why some women give up and eventually return to violent husbands. It was precisely these kinds of hurdles, combined with their beliefs about their personal responsibility to make a marriage work, that constituted major reasons why Eileen, Naomi, Karen, and Sophia returned to violent mates several times before making their final break. As Eileen said:

> I'd go to my friends' and mother's house, but I just couldn't make ends meet. I didn't have a baby sitter, money, or the physical and mental strength ... I was depressed about everything. My mother stuck it out for 40 years. I didn't believe in divorce, I believed in marriage, but this was not my idea of marriage. Basically it [the reason she didn't leave earlier] was my religion and for financial support.

Attitudes within the legal system constitute an additional hurdle. When Sophia left the final time it was directly from the hospital after her near-fatal suicide attempt. Upon leaving the shelter she moved directly into an apartment and began divorce proceedings. Meanwhile, she struggled to get by with minimal furnishings while caring for her three children. Several months into these lengthy, complicated negotiations, her husband's lawyer said that given enough time, he was sure Sophia would go back to her husband; he didn't understand why she didn't go back this time. He also seemed very sure that 'they like it' (i.e. women from Sophia's ethnic group). 'It's part of their culture. You'd never see anything like that from "my kind".'

The lawyer's judgement, considering the lengthy entanglements of trying to get a divorce when a partner objects, suggests a self-fulfilling prophecy. It is a dilemma similar to those a woman often encounters in trying to obtain a restraining order on her husband so that she can remain unharmed in the marital dwelling. Yet, if a woman finally returns to a violent partner out of hopelessness in overcoming all the obstacles in her path, some then naively assume that she would have gone back anyway. Significantly, during all the months of waiting for a divorce and house sale, Sophia's husband enjoyed the comforts of the co-owned marital dwelling, while she and the children lived in an apartment with lead paint hazards and a landlady who would walk in unannounced and pry into Sophia's cupboards and activities.

The response of housing authorities to homeless battered women

A related obstacle battered women face is revealed in Ruth's problems with housing after leaving the shelter. During the maximum stay of ten weeks, Ruth was unable to find an apartment. First she lived with a staff member of the shelter, while she continued to seek independent housing on her limited public assistance budget. After several months she finally moved to another shelter for battered women. Again, the several weeks' limited stay was exhausted before she found permanent housing. Ruth was lucky since the lawyer who was handling her divorce (he donated his service to Ruth) also argued for her acceptance on the city's 'emergency priority' housing list after her request for emergency assistance was denied. The grounds for refusal were that homelessness because of battering and threat to life by a violent husband did not constitute adequate criteria for emergency assistance. To qualify, a person's homelessness must be 'through no fault of one's own'. The letter from the Housing Authority's Director of Occupancy stated:

It is the recommendation of the Committee and I concur, that your request be denied for the following reason(s): Inadequate evidence as to basis for homelessness. Homelessness as a result of domestic conflict does not constitute an emergency under the provisions of the Tenant Selection and Assignment Plan.

Ruth's attorney appealed the Housing Authority decision and was given a hearing by the State Superior Court judge. The judge ordered the Housing Authority to review the case. Ruth's lawyer also tried to bring public pressure to bear on the case by sending a story of her plight of homelessness to one of the two leading newspapers. It was not published. By this time Ruth's time was up in the second shelter and she and her young child were forced to travel daily from the City Hospital to an outlying public mental hospital that had been set up as an additional emergency shelter for the homeless. Ruth by now was in her ninth month of pregnancy and her child was out of school because of Ruth's itinerant status. Following is a summary of Ruth's hearing with the Director of Occupancy of the Housing Authority. (This summary is drawn from recall by Ruth, her lawyer, her mother, and the researcher, since the tape-recorded interaction could not be transcribed due to a defective tape.)

> Ruth described in detail how she had been brutally beaten and choked by her husband while pregnant, ordered out of their apartment, and threatened with her life if she didn't go. Her mother testified to her knowledge of her daughter's beating over several years, stating she was unable to support Ruth and her child in her own home in spite of her sympathy and emotional support of Ruth. The Director explained that the issue of battering as an eligibility requirement for placement on 'Emergency Priority' basis was discussed at length by Housing Authority representatives. He also explained that to be placed on this list, a person must be homeless 'through no fault of one's own'. In a hesitant, cautious explanation, he seemed to have caught himself with the conclusion that since battering was deliberately excluded as a criterion after thoughtful and long discussion, a woman homeless for this reason must be so through 'her own fault'. He seemed embarrassed at this point with Ruth directly before him, attempted an apology and said he hoped Ruth would not get the impression that the Housing Authority thinks that battered women are to blame for their battering. After two hours of testimony by Ruth, her mother, and her attorney, the hearing was concluded with the Director's statement that her eligibility for 'emergency priority' would be reconsidered after they received written 'evidence' of her homelessness resulting from domestic conflict. The specific 'evidence' requested was police and medical records.

Public policy and homeless battered women

Meanwhile, the statewide problem of homelessness had become so acute that public hearings were scheduled before the Committee on Human Services and Elderly Affairs of the State Legislature. Shelter staff who knew of Ruth's housing problems urged her to testify at the

196

public hearing. She agreed to prepare a two-minute statement with the help of a shelter volunteer and arranged to have the volunteer present her testimony if she were unable to attend. The volunteer read the following testimony after introducing herself as Ruth's advocate and noting Ruth's inability to appear due to the imminent delivery of her child.

I left my husband several times after he beat me but went back because he was in the service and always promised to change, and we had a little girl. Then one night last June I thought he'd kill me. We were out walking and arguing about me being pregnant. He pushed me toward the cars so I'd get run over. I resisted, so he threw me in the bushes. Then he pushed me up against an electric power outlet. He choked me and kept hitting me in the stomach and insisting that I have an abortion. I didn't want an abortion. We went to the police station and they told me to come back in the morning and file a complaint. I started to bleed and was afraid I'd lose my baby. The next day my husband told me to get out of the apartment and threatened to kill me if I didn't go. So I left and went to a shelter for battered women in Middletown and started looking for an apartment. When my ten weeks were up there I moved in with a staff member for a couple of months and kept on looking for an apartment. I applied at [names central city Housing Authority and six neighbouring jurisdictions] and a couple of others. I didn't even try Middletown because they had a 10-year waiting list.

After two months I had to leave the staff member's house so I went to another battered women's shelter and had to take a leave of absence from school. This shelter told me I had to leave after six weeks. I'm getting more and more discouraged because it seems like no matter what I do nothing works out. I'm due to have my baby on January 25 and I'm worried about how I'll manage. The [central city] Housing Authority told me that domestic violence was not a good enough reason for getting on the Emergency Housing list. I don't understand that. My lawyer is appealing that decision, but I'm afraid I still won't have a place by the time my baby comes, no matter what my lawyer does.

I crashed at my sister's house for a couple nights, then had to leave. I went to the City Shelter and stayed two nights. I couldn't stand it ... alcoholic men screaming all night long and a matron standing and watching me undress and take a shower like I'm a criminal or something. I had to take my little girl out of school because I never know where I'll be from one night to the next. I hope I find a place to stay before my baby is born.

197

Unlike others who testified, Ruth's advocate was unable to complete the two-minute presentation because of interruptions by the presiding Committee Chairman. Following are excerpts of the volunteer's protest letter recounting the interaction around this testimony:

> *Twice* you interrupted her testimony ... pounded your gavel, and made it appear that I was usurping the time of other more worthy people. After publicly denigrating Mrs R's testimony, you implied that I had inappropriately used the public hearing time ... Ironically, this is just what happens to battered women: they are brutally beaten and then told that it is their fault ...
>
> What makes your response even more ironic during a hearing on homelessness is that the only reason Mrs R is homeless is because domestic violence – even when it is life-threatening – is not a legitimate reason for a woman and her children to receive emergency housing in this State ... Mrs R's story is only a single example of indifference faced by battered women who try to free themselves from violent marriages – indifference and scorn from police, courts, housing authorities, and others. There are thousands like her. At today's hearing several people referred to the problem of homelessness as 'obscene', a 'crime' in the richest country on the face of the earth. It is also obscene to continue to blame homeless battered women for their plight and not grant them the same attention accorded people who are homeless for other reasons ...

Ruth's experience reveals how violence against women is defined as a 'private' rather than public issue. There was no time or appropriate place in this 'public hearing' for the problem of homeless battered women. But even if there were adequate permanent housing available after leaving a shelter, policies are written to exclude battered women and their children from eligibility criteria. Once officially excluded, however, battered women and their advocates tried another avenue of appeal, the 'public hearing'.

It could be argued that the Committee Chairman's hostile response to Ruth's testimony resulted from the 'accidental' circumstance that he was not listening when the advocate introduced the testimony. Yet even after the advocate re-explained the testimony's relevance, the response was the same, with the additional exhortation about not misusing the Committee's valuable time when many 'homeless people' were waiting to testify. It could be argued further that had Ruth been present with her advanced pregnancy highly obvious, the Committee Chairman would have responded more sympathetically. This argument fails as well, since he judged the testimony as irrelevant to the issue of homelessness after a repeated explanation. Without a full-term pregnant woman present, the public policy regarding homeless battered women can be interpreted independent of the emotional response most persons might have to a visibly pregnant woman.

Drawing on the notion of Membership Categorization Device introduced earlier (Sacks 1974; Benson and Hughes 1983), the relational pair in this interaction is Deserving Homeless/Undeserving Homeless, or Homeless through no fault of own/Homeless through own fault. The chairman's twice repeated 'cutting out' procedure and lecturing about misuse of a public hearing on homelessness presupposes his belief that a battered woman belongs to the homeless category of 'undeserving' and 'through their own fault' (Lemert 1962; Smith 1978; Helm 1981). This interpretation suggests that the Committee Chairman was not merely displaying bad manners or impatience; rather, his words display his reasoning, while the pounded gavel symbolized his authority to reinforce the public policy regarding the needs (or, according to this logic, the 'non-needs') of homeless battered women. Or, if battered women do have needs, this interaction underscores the belief that they are not a concern of public officials, not even those with the term 'human services' in their title.

This display resembles that of the Housing Director's 'objective' reasoning about the long and thoughtful discussion held on the issue. That decision, coupled with the eligibility clause, 'homeless through no fault of their own', dramatically reinforced in a public hearing, leads to this conclusion: public officials apparently believe that battered women and their children are homeless because of their own fault and therefore do not qualify for emergency housing assistance, even if such housing were physically available. These policies support an archaic belief that if women are beaten it is because they deserve it; and if they escape with their lives or are thrown out, they also deserve their homelessness. They also support feminist analysis about the centuries of exclusion of women speaking in the public arena even when they are in desperate physical need and when the context is specifically designated as a 'public hearing' with the assumption of a citizen's right to be heard there (Okin 1979; Elshtain 1981; Smith 1987).

Even if a woman is not considered responsible for her battering, though, another argument exists to exclude battering as a criterion for emergency housing eligibility. Legislation already exists in this State to protect battered women from abusive mates. Thus, the Housing Authority officer repeatedly asked Ruth why she did not return to the marital dwelling and obtain a restraining order on her husband. Several intersecting factors are overlooked in this argument. First, the husband pays the rent and therefore claims primary rights to the residence, an economically based claim that is strongly reinforced in the traditional patriarchal system. Second, a man relying on that authority as well as his superior physical strength, has ordered Ruth out of the home and threatened to kill her if she returns. Thus, since he has previously threatened to kill her, and has already beaten her severely, Ruth takes his threats seriously and fears for her life even though the technicalities of the Abuse Prevention Act are in her favour. Unless police stand 24-hour guard over a residence, the restraining order a woman obtains may have *moral* force but cannot assure physical restraint unless it is violated. This means, in effect, that a woman could lose her life if she trusted the law over her practical judgement of whether or not her husband will act on his threat and attack her again – with or without a restraining order. Homicide statistics are graphic evidence that many wives have not been saved by either personal or public efforts (FBI 1982; Wolfgang 1986).[5]

Ruth's experience makes dramatically visible the *process* whereby the needs of battered women and their children for public support are side-tracked by other issues considered more important, or by the internal workings of the legislative process. Copies of the advocate's protest letter to the State Committee Chairman were sent to the State Senators, the Governor, and various other public officials and advocacy groups. Polite responses were received from the Governor's Commission on Homelessness and the two Congressional Senators. A note from Ruth's lawyer to one Senator in Washington DC connected Ruth to her previous letter to this Senator. The Senator's telephone call to the local Housing Authority may have influenced Ruth's eventual placement in emergency housing, though there is no firm evidence of this. Meanwhile, Ruth and her two children were taken in by her mother in a household already overcrowded. At this point her monthly welfare payments were reduced although her mother was in no financial position to support three additional people.

In this State, noted for its sensitivity to social issues, one year after Ruth's testimony a similar process was observed and protested by battered women and their advocates. The following quote comes from a newspaper report about another day 'designated for testimony on any aspect of the proposed state budget', attended by more than 200 people, all but a few of them women.

Upstairs, men in dark suits debated the big issue of the day before a full House and Senate. Downstairs, women with dark tales addressed themselves to empty chairs. In the deliberative chambers

... the oratory of the lawmakers was framed in democracy's most formal parlance. In the airless room one marble staircase below, the whispered voices of the women had a more awkward cadence. 'It's very important for you to hear this ... You need to know what really goes on out there', [one woman testified]. 'It absolutely stinks, their lack of attention,' said Ruth DiTommaso, lighting a cigarette in the corridor after tears cut short her testimony about state funding of shelters for battered women. Two legislators were there ... Like most of the women who testified – about the need for shelters for the abused, programs for children, help for displaced homemakers – DiTommaso had never addressed a public forum before. 'I don't know if we could get them to come again,' said Cindy Chin of the Coalition of Battered Women's Service Groups, who convinced many of the victims of domestic violence to appear before the committee. The explanation offered by embarrassed legislators for the sparse attendance – the competing demands of crucial legislation being debated overhead – 'doesn't wash,' said Chin. 'What was the big issue last year and the year before that? Every year, it's the same. Empty chairs. If these people ever do want to find out what's going on outside in the real world,' she said of the State's elected representatives, 'they are going to have to stop talking to themselves and start listening to us.'

These examples illustrate the constant struggle to gain public support for the most basic survival necessities of battered women and their children. While publicly visible activity has focused on emergency shelters, Ruth's case and the experience of other women in this study reveal how pervasive housing problems are extending well beyond the crisis phase of a battered woman's struggle for a life free of violence.

Ironically, these cases illustrate that 'home' is beyond the reach of some women who decide to take a stand and not put up with violence from their mates under their own roof. After being violently driven from the home they have been led to believe is their 'proper' place, battered women may then also face callous archaic policies regarding public assistance that are designed and consciously reinforced in a male-dominated political-legal system.

Their experience also suggests a need to re-think the place of emergency shelters. Perhaps violent men should be required to remain in detention centres until there is reasonable assurance that they can safely be allowed to return to homes where women and children also dwell. Abuse Prevention Acts might be re-written to actually prevent abuse of women while they dwell in the homes that have for so long been designated their 'proper' place – not because only women belong there, but because everyone has the right to a residence free of violence. Finally, the right of violent persons to their usual place of residence bears reconsideration. Thus, whether one accepts the premiss of a woman's primary position being in the home or not, as a matter of simple justice, the emphasis should be on maintaining the woman in her original home rather than on finding her a new one when her *mate* – not she – has engaged in violent behaviour. This does not imply disregard of the controversy noted in Chapter 5 regarding arrest of violent men without their wives' consent (Hart 1983; Wald 1983). Nor does it deny the life-saving necessity of shelters so long as women are abused with impunity and their assailants get by. It is intended to jar our usual reasoning process about the use of shelters, and to make dramatically visible the ironies of our present response to the problem. While continuing to offer emergency assistance to individual women, we must carve out more time to look 'upstream' (McKinlay 1979) and focus at least as much energy on changing the structure and public policies that allow so many women to fall into the stream of male violence and the homelessness that often follows.

Chapter eleven

The children and work of battered women

Introduction

Children play important roles both directly and indirectly at various points in battered women's life cycle. For the women in this study, motherhood was an important goal. Arguments about pregnancy and/or disciplining children frequently occasioned violent eruptions; and concern for children was sometimes pivotal in moving a woman toward separation from a violent mate. Children of homeless battered women were forced to remain out of school, and had to adjust to living with strangers in a shelter, or were caught in intergenerational conflicts concerning child rearing when living with grandparents. This chapter focuses on the specific effects violence had on the children of these women and related issues concerning 'women's work' and child rearing as a single parent.

Analysis of the participants' values and those of their network members regarding women, marriage, the family, and violence, revealed that most believed in the necessity of occasional physical disciplining of children. In the shelter some of the study participants used, as in most others, there is a policy to urge women to refrain from physically disciplining their children, a policy meant to reinforce the general philosophy of non-violence in the solution of any problems. Such a policy, however, may create two complications. First, since most parents believe in the necessity of physical punishment, it can evoke values conflict and give rise to new stress at a time when women are already struggling with other problems. Consequently, the policy is not rigidly enforced but rather, is presented as an alternative form of adult–child interaction which the staff emphasize primarily in the form of modelling. Second, rigid adherence to this policy implies that violence is transmitted intergenerationally, a position which weakens feminists' *political* interpretation of violence against women.

Although this research deals only marginally with the question of the intergenerational cycle of violence,[1] it does provide insights into the more immediate effects of violence on children. Despite their predominantly traditional values regarding physical discipline, these women were intensely devoted to their children, who were often the focus of their most acute pain and struggle. The effects of the battering on children were evident during the battering phase, the shelter phase, and for months after the women left their violent mates, and included conflicts around discipline, custody issues, and scapegoating of children through the divorce process.

Effects on children during the battering phase

The children were affected both through direct abuse and through observing the abuse of their mother. During the battering phase the women took great pains to protect their children from observing their father's brutality. Direct abuse of a child was often the occasion of violence toward the mother, particularly if she intervened on a child's behalf or protested against the father's harsh discipline of a child. One woman said that the most typical beating occurred when she defended her children. One time, for example, the man's glasses fell off while playing with their little girl. He blamed the child and kicked her across the room with his booted foot. This incident escalated into the final episode and near-fatal suicide attempt of the mother. She said: 'After I took the overdose Maria [the little girl] looked at my face and said "Oh, ma, what happened?" I said "Guess." She asked: "My father?" '

Another woman said she didn't know how the abuse affected her child: 'He won't talk about it except to say "He won't hit on my mommy".' To protect the little boy, this woman had him stay with relatives for a couple of years. Another woman told of her 3-year-old son coming to defend her, saying:

'No, daddy, no!' And he came behind his father and started hitting him. And I was afraid his reaction would be to just knock him down or something and Jane [the 2-year-old] she couldn't even watch it. She would stand there and get hit and just hold on and scream, you know. My daughter is the way she is now from seeing it, when things get too much for her to be around she has her own world to which she can escape. She doesn't do it so much now, but she still does it ... I saw her do it the other day.

The 10-year-old son of one woman called the police more than once. Often, the women were torn between wanting to protect their children from observing or having any part in the violence and needing to rely on them as the only human source of support available.

The damage these occasions had on the children was quite visible when the women came to the shelter. Of the six women in the shelter with children, two did not bring their children with them. One woman's child was in the care of a maternal relative because of a custody issue around alleged child abuse. Before this mother finally left her violent husband he had also abused her child. However, when child protective authorities investigated, family members revealed that this woman had accepted the responsibility for the child's injury and she subsequently lost custody of her child. This is one of the most dramatic examples of the extent to which some battered women will go to excuse a violent mate.

Another woman put her children in the care of foster parents or relatives. The legal custody status took years to work out. The woman's ex-husband had made some moves to obtain custody. However, he was found in contempt of court for failing to pay child support for several years. Periodically during the research participation, this woman poured out her feelings about the painful decision to put her children in someone else's care for a year until she could get herself together and provide for them again:

I need money and an education. I don't have the energy to face them ... no social worker. God is my advocate. I hate to have the kids get rooted in with the other families. They're [the foster parents] judgemental do-gooders. They condemn me by their attitudes. It's just so *painful*. On Easter, the first alone, I just couldn't talk to them. Nobody called for my birthday. Robby [her son] said 'Daddy won't let me call.' I called him and told him 'I still love you.' I can't do anything about it. I can't go through continuous upset for my children. It's real tense to talk to the kids ... It's so painful. It makes me so mad and hurt. I say OK I'll make my own life and see what happens. I've got the motherhood complex. It's been in me for 30 years and I'm trying to get rid of it. It's gonna take a long time getting rid of trying to be perfect. I'm a sick human being trying to take care of four other human beings. I did it all. I went to families and agencies. They helped but not enough ... 'Fill out this paper, come in two weeks.' The reason I didn't call the kids is that it tears down everything I've built up. The new attitude is 'Screw you, I'm living.' But it's real hard ... Motherhood is the hardest thing I've ever had to deal with. They'll understand when they get older, I hope ... I don't know if they'll have psychological damage that will last for years. I'm just counting on the fact that my actions in the past will tell them that I love them, I'm just counting on that.

Considering the general social condemnation of mothers leaving their children, this mother's pain and conflict will probably extend through her life. For example, a foster parent called one day threatening to put the children on the street, leaving her again flooded with guilt for placing them in foster care. Her ex-husband tried to pressure her to give his sister custody of the children 'so she won't be so lonely'. Periodically, foster parents called to threaten stopping the children calling unless she provided money for them, even though they received public support for the children's care. Each time this happened the woman felt overwhelmed with guilt about not having her children with her, even though she felt this decision was necessary for personal survival. Periodically she fantasized abandoning them so she would not have to face the constant conflict and guilt associated with their foster placement.

Her ambivalence about her children is understandable since 'two of my kids were conceived from rape sessions after I was badly beaten'. Whenever an occasion arose such as a child's birthday or a holiday with traditional family memories, there was a new surge of grief, conflict, and guilt. After missing an appointment for an interview, she said that she was feeling depressed thinking about her son David's birthday, not knowing what to do and not wanting to do anything, but feeling very guilty and crying:

> I just don't want to be me ... I don't know who I am. I do so little for them [the children]. I can barely do for me ... I don't even want to talk to them. I just can't do what I'm supposed to. I stuff the feelings down my throat because of my low opinion of myself.

After talking with her support group she said: 'I realized I did all I could for my kids with what I had. I asked for help and didn't get it.' Clearly, this woman faced a continuous dilemma between what she needed to do for her own survival and what she felt obligated to do for her children.

Children in a shelter and beyond

Among the four women who brought their children to the shelter, several sources of stress were apparent. Children of school age were taken out of classes for security reasons, since violent men intent on tracking down a woman find the child's school a good avenue to locate mother and children. While youngsters may welcome staying home from school, the shelter presents several new sources of stress for them. They are suddenly thrown in with a group of strange women and children in close living quarters. Their mothers, though at least temporarily out of physical danger, are still under a great deal of stress looking for housing and handling legal issues.

Consequently, a child who was already frightened and confused may continue to be so. A child's expression of anxiety takes many forms: aggressiveness, withdrawal, regression in toilet and eating habits, crying, demanding behaviour. Sensitivity to these issues demands that shelters provide special child care services for the duration of a mother's and her children's stay. Staff are selected and trained for their particular skills in addressing the effects of battering on children.

One such staff member, a young man, was interviewed as a network member of one of the study participants. He had formerly worked as a volunteer in the shelter's child care service. Asked to discuss this experience he said:

They're incredibly emotionally deprived. They're confused kids. *Do you think they are really damaged from the experience?* Yes, one of the most damaging things is having to take sides, and that's just devastating. We men working with the young boys were really threatening. They didn't know who we were. They wanted to be with their fathers, though they want the violence to end. For example, one 13-year-old girl was watching her father choke and beat her mother. She jumped on her father and choked him. He threw her on the floor, and dragged her by the hair across the street and told her not to come back. Boys asked us: 'Are you queer, are you faggots?' It was a real shock to them to have soft affectionate men around. The girls were more used to it. The boys, though, eventually accepted the affection, and clung to us. They really pushed us to get angry ... It was hard to deal with my guilt for the actions of other men.

Children's confusion in the wake of domestic violence is poignantly revealed in this account of a woman's interaction with her 3-year-old boy:

Child: 'Mommy, Daddy hit you, huh?'

Mother: 'Not any more, he can't find me.'

Child: 'Mommy, only big men can hit Mommies, huh? When I get big can I hit Mommies?'

Mother: 'No, big men that hit Mommies are bad.'

Another woman, after leaving the shelter, said that her daughter has

> a fantasy of having a perfect father ... my son is more rough and outgoing. They've been damaged by the experience and are over-protective of me. One time he [her husband] had me pinned up against the wall with a broom and said 'I'm either going to perma-nently paralyse you or kill you!' The kids all started screaming. Their school work is affected. I'm getting counselling. The social worker told me if I don't smarten up they'll have to take the kids away.

Several times this woman considered putting her children in foster care, but her little girl told her she would kill herself if she were taken away from her mother.

Another woman said she considered placing her children in foster homes for a while. As with the other two women, she experienced enormous ambivalence and guilt, in spite of the fact that she faced monumental struggles with housing, finances, jobs, and college. She resolved her ambivalence about her children quite soon after leaving the shelter. Her story also illustrates the complexity of the issue of non-violent discipline at the shelter. Early in the research during a discussion of 'power, discipline, and violence', this woman made her values clear and also revealed her own distinction between discipline and child abuse:

> Power is influence over a majority of people. Women have power over children. Men are supposed to be out there to protect us, but we have to protect against them. Discipline is showing children right from wrong, teaching them values appreciation ... physical things to an extent – if they're crossing the street, burning them-selves. Violence disrupts someone's peacefulness. [At this point this woman became reflective and looked troubled. Then she went on.] It's hard to talk about this 'cuz I've been violent with my kids lately. It makes them unstable in their whole life – makes them fear you and fear themselves to the point of being afraid to be who they are or were. By bringing this out it will help me realize how I've been violent with my kids, what I've done to them. I some-times look at my kids and compare them ... like the other day I would hit them with a belt and threaten them with it too so they fear me – their eyes, I really don't like that, the way they're reacting is the way I did when my husband came home screaming. I should write about this ... Sometimes I'm so impatient with them they're

not gonna learn that way. I really do believe children learn better with love, to reinforce what they do right. I have so many things to straighten out, doing what I want to do. [She then spoke about her disappointment with a man she had been seeing, and said she noticed herself being harsh or violent with her children every time she experienced a new disappointment with men.]

This woman resolved her ambivalence about foster care, and her concern about her disciplining practices, by seeing a therapist once a week. Several times during the months of the research, I observed her verbal and sometimes physical outbursts against her children. Her involvement in the research apparently served as a catalyst for reflection on her interaction with her children. She made numerous references to her concerns about growth and development for herself and her children. Also, I had ethical concerns about whether to limit the discussion about the children's father, based on this remark: 'Whenever I talk about their father it stirs up lots of mixed emotions, a lot of feelings of hurt and anger ... I think I spank them because I never know how to do any better – that's all I was worth.'

The other ethical question was whether or not to assist this woman directly with alternative approaches to her children. Certain behaviours suggested that she desired assistance, for example, openly displaying her behaviour with the children and verbally expressing her distress about it. I decided it was unethical to continue observing the woman's behaviour toward her children without offering her explicit help in changing it. Therefore, I made a conscious separation of this activity from my research role, incorporating assistance when the situation called for it, as illustrated by the following examples:[2]

This woman, her two children and I had spent an afternoon winter outing first with two other women in the study, then with her brother and sister-in-law and their four children, followed by supper. During the quite noisy meal with the six children, the woman study participant explained, then demonstrated a technique she had learned from her children's day care centre for getting children to calm down without physical force: that is, turn the lights very low and speak to the children in a very soft voice. As she demonstrated the technique, the children's voices were audibly lowered by several decibels. Later the woman was asked if she had tried this at home [she had been heard a number of times yelling at her children]. Somehow she had never thought of using the technique in her usual attempts to discipline her children.

On another occasion when she was expressing her frustration in disciplining the children, she was asked if she had considered using the hotline of Parents Anonymous. She said she had called them once and found the peer counsellor very helpful, but found it difficult to ask for help because 'my pride gets in the way', that is, she somehow feels responsible for managing her problems alone without having to ask for help. After discussion she saw that the burdens she currently felt the need to shoulder alone may have been a residual effect of the sense of failure she felt as a teenager with heavy responsibility for the care of younger siblings. I suggested that she post the Parents Anonymous hotline number on her telephone and that when she felt the urge to strike her children, to substitute that urge with a telephone call to a peer counsellor. She accepted and implemented this suggestion.

During another conversation this woman said that one of her greatest frustrations was in getting the children to sleep at night, so that she could have at least a few hours to herself. She lacked separate beds for them and so they just continued to play with each other after being put to bed. I suggested that she put one child to sleep in her own bed, the other in the children's bed, and transfer the first child to the children's bed after he or she is asleep. This she did, with a dramatic reduction in parental stress at the children's bedtime. This woman was also given a copy of a book entitled, *Without Spanking or Spoiling* (Crary 1979), a manual for parents containing non-violent approaches to child rearing and discipline.

These examples support two observations: first, there is sometimes a fine line between physical discipline and child abuse; second, while most parents believe in the necessity of corporal punishment in certain instances, some of those who use it in excess do so because they lack knowledge and skill in alternative approaches to parenting. While this woman's participation in the research was an avenue for obtaining assistance, such help is widely available through parent support groups. Her situation also suggests the need for services to battered women for months after leaving the shelter. During the course of the research, this woman's interaction with her children was noticeably more gentle and patient. The following account illustrates this change. She had called late one night to express her anger over having had her monthly welfare check reduced, requiring her to borrow money from her father in order to pay the bills. She said:

I feel really violent, like smashing the windows ... and I came home and the outside door was locked by the tenants upstairs. I felt like breaking the door down. I said to the kids 'Go in the other room ... I don't care what you do ... Mommy's upset but it's nothing you did.' I didn't take it out on the kids ... there's a time when I might have.

This woman's story of her interaction with her children underscores several issues that have received little attention until very recently: (1) the need to acknowledge and deal with the potential and actual violence of women; (2) the need to reinforce the concept that violent behaviour is learned, rather than innately determined, and that it therefore can be replaced by other behaviours that can also be learned; (3) the need to realize that women's violence toward children resembles men's violence toward women since both are expressions of power over another.[3]

Women's violence toward children, however, also seems to be connected to their own powerlessness in the larger sociocultural milieu, and their absorption of feelings of worthlessness that some men reinforce. Cloward and Piven (1979) suggest that women's deviant tendencies are directed primarily toward themselves, a theory reinforced by the prevalence of suicidal tendencies among battered women. But, as we saw in Chapter 3, all the women in this study also reported feeling homicidal toward their mates, and even children may become the objects of their anger and rejections. Newberger (1980) and Gil (1987) make a strong case for de-emphasizing the child abuse 'syndrome' (a medical approach implying parental psychopathology (Kempe and Helfer 1980)) and redirecting our attention to the social sources of child abuse: sexism, racism, and classism. Since child care is considered women's major responsibility and it is widely believed that physical discipline is necessary, what is notable is not that women are sometimes abusive of children, but that men are equally or more abusive of children even though they spend proportionately much less time with them.

Three of the women had no ambivalence toward their children. One of these women had her first child several months after leaving the shelter. Her husband actively supported her during a difficult labour and afterwards was quite attentive to her and the baby. The woman's long-desired baby, however, appeared to play a central role in her final decision to leave, as discussed in Chapter 4, pp. 59–60. Although she and her husband were considering reconciliation, she resisted his sexual overtures, stating she had 'no time or inclination' since the baby came. This woman's intense attachment to her baby tended to magnify the husband's irresponsible behaviour of 'borrowing' (which she interpreted as 'stealing') $35 from the baby's bank. This incident symbolized her husband's devaluation of the baby's importance and became the 'last straw' in a chain of events that presaged her final decision to divorce her husband. This woman's child was also central in her final break from her in-laws who heckled her about how she was caring for the baby, and urged her to reconsider the divorce as they believed their grandson 'had changed'.

The effects of child custody conflicts

The children of two other women who had moved out and were in process of divorce both suffered significant harm. An excerpt from one woman's interview reveals how children may be caught in custody arrangements. Both parents in this relationship have graduate degrees.

> When Robert came here one day to try to get me to come back, David [her son] and Jane [her daughter] were here and he started crying and he got down on his hands and knees. And David came running up – David's only 3 years old – pushed him away, and said, 'Don't hurt Mommy. Don't hurt Mommy. Don't you dare touch Mommy.' And Robert said: 'See what you've done to them? You've got them believing that I beat you.' Oh, God, I felt like killing him ... The oldest one [Jane] blocks it out. David's very protective of me, extremely protective, to the point of when I go out on a date – I'm dating someone now – he's very clingy. He wants to know if I have enough money. He wants me to call him if I have a problem. And he also watches at the window as we walk away. It's really sad.
>
> *What about the custody arrangement?* I want my children with me full time. I was feeling sorry for Robert. He wanted the children halftime, so we originally started a week apiece. One week my house, one week his. We were in the same school district, same bus. The kids have the same class. So I thought that was OK. But then he wanted them at his house because his house was bigger so he said he could provide more for them than I could. And I said 'Bullshit, I can provide just as much as you can.[4] What makes you think that you're any better than I am? And what makes you think that you're a better parent than I am?' I gave him this big struggle. Now it's a month apiece. I must say that David calls me at least five times a day, at least, when he's at his father's. And it's very hard for me. I think, I'm just waiting for the right time. His girlfriend is moving in. She's in Washington in another PhD programme. And I think once she moves in for good, she's not going to want to have those kids around.

This woman's child David expressed his feelings through art. The message that this mother gets from her child's art is sorrow over a broken family. She said about one drawing: 'David says I'm the one in red. Interesting – I'm the only one without a smile, and note the position of the hand [reaching out to strike] on the gentleman with the tie!' The evidence from this affluent family supports what every social worker and child health worker knows from clinical experience: that education, financial security, and social status are weak hedges against the damage that can be done to children if violence between the parents is observed and children are used as bartering points.

The evidence is similar in a poorer family. In this case the woman was almost beaten to death during her seventh month of pregnancy. When the father came to the hospital during her confinement to see the newborn infant, this woman was understandably reluctant to allow visitation. The husband's lawyer made a case for the father's affection for his child. The woman's lawyer advised her that she could jeopardize her case for child custody if she refused him visitation rights with the newborn. However, as the woman said: 'What do you mean he cares about the baby? He just about killed both of us.' Finally after several weeks of legal negotiations, a visitation agreement was worked out for all the children. Each visit, however, was fraught with tension for mother as well as children. The mother complained that the father did not feed the children or change the infant's diapers. The oldest child, age 5, said simply: 'He makes me cry.' Also, in a most blatant display of using a child in parental battles, he said to the child:

Tell your mother I don't want her anymore ... I want her to die [although he continued to test every avenue through relatives and a pastor to persuade his wife to come back]. Say to your mother 'I don't love you.' Tell your mother she's got money and I don't have any, to give me some. [This mother was being supported on Aid to Families with Dependent Children – AFDC.]

This father may have been more desperate than most since he was prevented from contacting her by a Restraining Order (relatives served as intermediates when he came to visit the children). Yet, although he had abused the older child, he was still legally entitled to visit the children. This woman's situation was even more complicated because of a legal entanglement concerning her marriage certificate. This case suggests that the efforts of child advocates to influence divorce and custody decisions to assure the welfare of children are by no means sufficient. This father's treatment of the children suggests that he might not have visited them at all if he had not entertained the hope of getting his wife back through this mechanism. While he did not openly express hostility about the mother to the children at the beginning of the separation, as his hope for her return dwindled, his visits became increasingly irregular and his barbs at the mother through the children more pointed and vicious.

The mother's options, however, were limited legally. Unless the father was physically abusive toward the children – even though he had a history of such abuse – the mother could not prevent him from seeing the children. To do so would damage her legal chances of obtaining exclusive custody at the final divorce hearing. Meanwhile, as the legal wheels slowly turned, the children were slowly but surely exposed to the effects of continuing venom passed back and forth between the parents. The mother was explicitly advised by her lawyer and by the researcher when appropriate not to discuss negative things about the children's father in their presence, nor to question them in a way that would leave the child in a conflicted position, except to ascertain discreetly if any physical abuse had occurred.[5] This was another of those instances where I felt an ethical obligation to depart from the research role and intervene for the sake of the children. After this man's divorce from his previous wife he never visited the three children of that marriage, although they were not far away. His former wife and the woman in this study met periodically in order to provide the half-siblings from these two marriages an opportunity to visit one another. The two women were also friendly and exchanged stories about the similar pattern of abuse in each of their marriages.

These examples illustrate some of the most explicit ways in which the children of battered women suffer. In this, they resemble millions of other children whose divorcing parents conduct their marital affairs in a manner that suggests they are abandoning their role as responsible parents as well. The great personal stress experienced during these transition states suggests the need for contemporary rites of passage to assist a battered woman in redefining her new role in the community as a divorced person and single parent. Currently, this process is accomplished largely as an individual matter between her, her husband, and the respective lawyers whose tendency is to handle these cases in the general adversarial framework of law practice. Through contemporary rites of passage, this process would be extended to include other concerned members of the community. Thus the parents' changed roles and responsibilities could be redefined and publicly supported to reduce the possibilities of parents and children alike becoming scapegoats for a problem that extends beyond the immediate family concerned.

Even when divorce and custody issues are resolved and children have been spared the direct impact of violence against their mothers, observation of the women in this study suggests that the indirect effects are everywhere visible. There is, of course, no question that to be free of actual abuse or its constant threat is a great boon to both mother and child. But as one woman said after months of homelessness with two young children: 'It's the pits – today I'm number 11 on the emergency housing list. Here I am scrunched in one room, the baby's clothes in a bag, no room for a crib, and there's rats here. I've lost hope in the housing authority.' The effect of such housing crises on children is bound to endure, though its full dimension may only be revealed in the next generation (Kozol 1988).

Because of the life-threatening nature of the crises it deals with, the battered women's movement has, of necessity, focused on refuges to protect women and children from immediate danger. As an unintended consequence, less attention has been given to what happens after resolution of the immediate crisis. Follow-up programmes for women and children after they leave shelters are rare or their services quite limited. This situation presents a sober reminder of how very new the battered women's movement is and of how much work remains to be done. It also underscores the irony of the fact that women and their children – the victims of violence – must struggle to re-stabilize their lives in home and school, while their assailants enjoy the comforts of the marital dwelling.

The experience of these women strongly suggests a need to re-examine the societal approach to victims and perpetrators of violence. Thus, some of the women had left their violent mates several times before their final departure. Either they found the struggles of parenting alone simply too much, or they perceived the difficulties of single parenthood as too insurmountable to even try it. If these factors are combined with the women's powerful socialization toward responsibility for making a marriage work, it is not difficult to understand why battered women stay as long as they do. In fact, the women's fears and anticipation of the struggles of single parenthood and establishing a new household are well founded. Their sharing of these struggles is not intended to suggest in the least that they would prefer the horrors of living in a violent relationship. Still, the price some women pay for freeing themselves of such violence is very high. The experience of some battered women and their children for months after leaving a violent mate presents poignant evidence of how little the women's movement has touched the lives of many battered women. More importantly, the long-term effects of violence on the children is yet to be revealed.

The women's ideals regarding womanhood and women's work

The harsh realities of violence for the women's children clash dramatically with the women's ideals regarding marriage and the family. Besides their general disappointment with failed marriages, none of the women anticipated how much 'work' their mothering role would entail, especially as single parents. To address the issue of the contrast between their ideals of womanhood and women's work and the reality of their experience, the women were asked: 'What did "becoming a woman" mean to you?'

> My fantasies were of getting married, having children and a house and garden ... being strong, having freedom, being myself and being good at it. *Being a woman?* It means being free, accomplishing my goals, being a mother to my kids, understanding myself and life. A woman can be 20 people in one which is what my ex-husband wanted me to be.

> Becoming a woman meant being a homemaker, becoming a wife and mother, nurturing and caring, loving. I thought all other aspects of life – art, music, babysitting, taking care of others – would enhance these two roles. *Being a woman?* It means caring, nurturing, being emotionally available, sharing, loving, being a positive element in the lives around me ... caring for myself as well as others. [This woman's family history included two generations of professionals and community elites, yet her emphasis is on traditional roles of women.]

> Becoming a woman meant independence, being an adult. Biological sex should not determine what a person becomes ... To me it means being in charge of myself. I should not have standards set for me based only on my femininity. It's my intelligence that it should be based on ... I don't buy: 'If it's a little boy, I'll get him a truck, if it's a girl I'll get a doll.' I go by how smart the kid is ...

> I guess becoming a woman maybe meant having a kid ... I don't know really – being able to do a lot of things you couldn't before, a lot more responsibility, having a baby.

> Having a career, being on my own, doing things by myself and being able to say 'Wow! I did it! It was hard, but fun!' *Being a woman?* The same thing – a career, helping others. I like motherhood, but the most important thing is a career and learning how to deal with people, doing something that's satisfying to me.

> When I started my period I became a woman. I was always compet-

ing with my girlfriend. I wanted to be like a woman, but not so much physically. *Being a woman?* I'm still trying to find that out.

Most of these responses reveal a dual vision of what it means to be a woman: taking on the role of mothering and caring for others, and the ability to do things on one's own, to be independent. The women talked about freedom in concert with responsibility as wives and mothers, and for some, success in a career. Three women chose careers that complemented the spousal and maternal roles. The understanding of womanhood for some of these women encompasses traditional and contemporary ideals, and a process of changing role expectations. These shifting role expectations might constitute in part a context for battering to occur; i.e. the rates of battering increased in States where equality of women is publicly supported but traditional values prevail in couple interaction (Yllo and Straus 1981).[6]

When asked about 'women's work' and how it differs from 'men's work' the general response was that there *should* be no difference, that it *should* be 'anything she can do, anything he can do'.

It should be equal but it isn't ... the [men] wouldn't stoop to things like a nurse's aide. There's no such thing as 'man's work'. Both should take care of the kids. I can't think of anything a man can do that a woman can't. But women are better parents because they're more understanding and patient ... It's the way society has put it.

Woman's work, man's work ... That's a sore point with me. It depends on who's more qualified. If he can cook better, he should cook. I don't think a man should necessarily have to take out the garbage.

One woman stated that woman's work is in the house with the kids and a man's is outside the home. But she went on to note that her mother works outside the home and her father does most of the cooking and housework because of disability-related unemployment. The woman gave examples of how childcare responsibilities nevertheless fell to her mother, noting that her younger siblings seemed 'spoiled' while in their father's charge. Finally she concluded: 'Women's work is taking responsibility for everything.'

Another woman said 'Women must carry the pregnancies and deliver the babies and nurse. Otherwise, I don't believe that any task is the function of one sex or the other.' Another woman said:

Women's work ... the old messages ... women's work was in the

Social life without violence

home. You cook and clean and you wait on other people and you make them happy doing whatever they want. You become socially defined, you know, all the little things that women know such as etiquette ... And women are more geared towards reading, but nothing important, all the soft stuff, because women are soft. These old messages, calling housework women's work. It's, I tell you, it's drudgery. Because I've done it for years, and it's unfulfilling and it's a damn shame. [This woman holds a graduate degree and works full time in a professional position as well as the housework she describes.] *Men's work?* Well, a man goes out in the world, making deals with people and he earns a whole lot of money because men are more suited to that – the old message, you know, and you're not supposed to question this if you're a woman. *How do they differ?* Women's work was delicate things like, well, take clerical positions, that was traditionally women's work ... nursing – women's work, caring for other people was supposed to be women's work. Man's work required more strength of some kind, it was implied, thereby making them more valuable as human beings, and women were weak, which is absolutely nuts. It's oppression again for women. Today, I think women are coming out of that a little bit ... Women are accepting themselves as human beings. I don't think they [men's and women's work] really do differ.

These responses reveal the women's clear ideas of what the division of labour should be, but their equally clear recognition of societal failure to uphold that ideal. Evidently, the women also absorbed traditional ideology as part of their consciousness about themselves, e.g. 'men are strong, women are weak'. Most of them are also explicit in their valuation of the traditional roles of wife and mother along *with* the opportunity for a career, independence, etc. In this they do not differ greatly from the majority of American women.

Their accounts of values regarding work suggest that the influence of the women's movement has filtered down from the body politic to the consciousness of individual women. The women's responses strongly support Chodorow's (1978) claims regarding the 'reproduction of mothering'. They are highly aware of the tension between the 'domestic' and 'public' spheres of work (MacCormack and Strathern 1980; Merchant 1980; Elshtain 1981; Smith 1987). But they are aware that this division is a socially constructed one, e.g. 'It's the way society has put it', 'you become socially defined'. In short, the women espoused both traditional and feminist values, although none of them defined themselves as 'feminists' in the formal sense.

Responses to the question: 'How would you describe the life of women (for example, in comparison to the life of men)?' supports this interpretation:

Women are subordinate.

Women have to fight for their rights from day one. Men have it easy. Women have the responsibility of being pregnant, being a mother, providing home.

I had to pretend I was weak. Men have a better deal than women because they can come and go as they please. They can fool around and never lose out. We lose ... We're not supposed to be human and have desires.

Outside of the work setting, that is, the home, women are more in tune with the emotional needs of the people. They pay more – probably too much – attention to the needs of others, put others first.

Now, women are coming into their own. It's not as hard as it was. Women are barely beginning to be recognized as people, but we have a long, long way to go. There are a lot more men now who are ready to accept the fact that we're not just gonna sit home and raise little ones and them. Women are finally being able to be 'men'. *Able to be men?* It's now accepted that we're intelligent enough ... Anything most men can do we can – all along we've been the strength. We are not the weaker sex. I never could figure out how this could be ... In a broken home the woman ended up with the children and going to work. She became the 'man' of the house and mother besides, doing all the things that two parents should provide. We're beginning to come into our own as far as strength is concerned. Most people when they think of strength think of men. Relationships are [now] more 50–50 versus 90–10 or 100–0. There are still a lot of macho men. Women are 'allowed' to do more than sit home, clean, take care of kids, and cry all day long over soap operas.

Women are put down about a lot of things. Men are talked up to and women are talked down at. They [women] have a worse deal, they're home with the kids. Men work and do what they want when they come home. The father gets involved sometimes, but it's not like it should be.

Women are worse off financially. People put women down ... Women even seem to put women down. I worked in a hospital part of the time I was being battered ... The nurses were so un-understanding. Men can get things moving more than women. If they [men] were in this [battering] situation they'd get something done about it. Society *thinks* men can do and women can't, that they're so stupid and weak.

Contrary to many popular images and myths of battered women as socioeconomically, culturally, and intellectually deprived, these women demonstrated keen insight into their disadvantaged position in society. Their expressions also point to awareness of the social construction of reality, e.g. 'I had to pretend I was weak ... ', 'We're not supposed to be human and have desires.' The women also have a tendency to reify society (i.e. to treat it as a thing or person with feelings, etc.): e.g. 'Society thinks men can do and women can't.'

Besides comparing their situations with that of men, the women were asked how satisfied they were with achieving their life goals.

I had an unhappy marriage, no children, and hadn't finished my education. I did buy a house the last year and owned a summer cottage in the mountains, but this was not important to me – a family was.

I had no real goals, just dreams – of going to school, having a home. Then a year before I left [my husband] religion became important to me ... All things seemed possible through Jesus Christ.

I just survived ... I was suicidal but didn't know how. I didn't even care if he beat on me anymore. Going to work helped ... I was active in a union battle.

I didn't know where I was going. I figured I'd never get anywhere so I might as well go with him.

I wanted to be a court stenographer. I know the marriage was falling apart but other things were falling in place ... I was off drugs and in school.

Besides highlighting the women's disappointment in their failed marriages, these accounts suggest the beginning of burnout, despair, giving up. Ironically, the woman with the most obvious career success in this group is also the one who expressed most strongly that career is secondary to success as a wife and mother. Also, while others in the group dreamed about a house, etc., she owned two homes but discounted their importance compared to desire for a family. It is almost as though she took her career success for granted; or, if she *had* failed in it, the failure would have been less significant than failure as a wife and mother.

Women, work, child care, and leisure

Aspirations for marriage and motherhood notwithstanding, none of the women anticipated how much 'work' was entailed in their mothering role – especially as single parents. Recent research reveals that women, whether married or single, in or out of the wage market, spend significantly more hours per week working than men do (Hartmann 1981; Burden and Googins 1984). This is particularly interesting in view of common language used about women and work: 'Working women' are those who earn money in the wage market where, as a group, they still earn only 59 cents (five years later it is only 65 cents) to every $1 earned by men, regardless of the Equal Pay Act passed decades ago. Everyday language and economic institutions thus blatantly reveal the devaluation of women as well as the work of rearing children and other domestic tasks (Spender 1980; Oakley 1981b; Smith 1987; Sommers and Shields 1987). Regardless of such public discounting of what women do, however, all countries which report labour statistics find that women simply work more than men do (Boserup 1970; Hartmann 1981; Leghorn and Parker 1981). As reported at the UN-sponsored International Women's Conference, Forum '85, in Nairobi, Kenya: women do two-thirds of the world's work, earn only one-tenth of the world's income, and own less than one-hundredth of the world's property.

It is not surprising, then, that throughout the months of this research, a recurring theme was that the women had little or no leisure time. This was true of the two women who were not going to college and/or working for pay as well as all the others, though to a lesser degree. One woman kept a diary of her activities during a 'typical week'.[7] A glimpse into a typical week of this woman – single parent, college student, homemaker, and low-paid housecleaner – revealed that her 'cleaning up' jobs extended even to her college work-study programme. Her advertisement for housecleaning jobs depicted a woman with six hands surrounded by billows of dirt. The woman's diary highlights the fact that a woman this busy and this poor has to work extra for the meagre student aid she receives, and that her leisure consists of a few hours of TV. The picture her typical week presents is a constant cycle of cleaning, cooking, child care, trips to the laundromat, racing to class, paying bills, studying, worrying about her children, and wondering whether she will ever get off welfare and have a decent house. Her diary provides the subjective side of the statistical studies documenting women's work (e.g. Hartmann 1981). So pressing were the women's child care responsibilities that if a woman wanted to go to a social gathering, attend a special class at college, or go out for an evening, child care was her first concern.

221

This problem was compounded by the fact that most of the women could not afford to pay for child care, which also affected the women's ability to go to support groups.

It could be argued that concerns about child care, money, and leisure time are not unique to battered women. However, battered women's similarity to other women is precisely the point. Their problems arising from violence cannot be fully understood apart from the socioeconomic deprivations and problems most women experience. As noted in Chapter 10, battered women clearly have something in common with other women supported on public welfare. But there is also continuity between their situations and those of affluent women. During the course of this research, a consultant of the researcher was struggling with medical complications during her pregnancy, while at the same time fulfilling university tenure requirements. She was faced with choosing between taking health precautions to protect her unborn infant and advancing her career. Her decision process around this issue was remarkably similar to that faced by the battered women in this study.

Men's roles in child care

Women of all socioeconomic levels often find themselves in a Catch-22. While a woman is encouraged to develop her talents and interests through a career, if she combines this choice with motherhood, society's response to her choice suggests that the procreation of babies is something that women do all by themselves, in that they are usually entirely responsible for the results of procreation for the duration of a child's dependent years. LaFontaine (1981: 338, 340–2) underscores this point by noting the lack of studies on the relation between definitions of men and their paternal role – as though their only 'work' in society was in the public sphere. Such neglect is also observed routinely, for example, in media stories. That is, if a house burns down and young children perish, an absent mother will be highlighted with no mention of absent fathers. It is these kinds of approaches that perpetuate centuries-old notions of strict dichotomies between the domestic and public spheres, notions implying – among other things – that a father's only role is to impregnate women, a notion supported by the fact that after divorce the majority of fathers contribute no material or social support to their children.[8]

In the case of intact marriages, fathers usually provide financial support, while some are assuming a larger role in direct child care than they did traditionally. Increasingly, however, it is necessary for a mother to contribute to household income by paid work as well. Often this will be part-time or after the children are older. Her career, therefore, unlike that of most fathers, often suffers from the break in paid employment. If a divorce occurs, her income is dramatically reduced (by 73 per cent) in most cases, while the husband's is increased (by 42 per cent), since the majority of divorced women either support themselves and their children, or receive public assistance. As one feminist slogan puts it: 'every woman is a man or a divorce away from welfare.'

If a woman decides on the traditional role of working only as a wife and mother, she may be regarded after a while as less interesting and attractive than many 'career' women and therefore is at risk of being discarded after she has sacrificed earlier opportunities for career development. One woman's puzzlement over this issue is expressed in her two essays cited earlier: 'The Advantages and Disadvantages of the Single Life' and 'What Do Marriage and Slavery Have in Common?' When considering the complexity of this issue and the enormous pressures these women experience as single parents it is not surprising that many women give up and simply settle for dealing with daily survival. In spite of the obstacles similar to those many other women face, the participants in this study strove for considerably more than merely daily survival: homemaker, college student, single parent, paid worker.

Their struggles to fulfil several roles with minimal financial advantage were so prevalent throughout this research that it became the focus of one of the group discussions. The discussion was intended to elicit the women's ideas about how the battered women's movement might become more involved with women once they left the shelters. A central theme that emerged from this discussion was the women's need for assistance with child care. Significantly, the other was their reliance on 'God' to assist them with their numerous problems. If a child care programme were made available to battered women, it should not lose sight of the underlying social values which reinforce a woman's role as primarily – and often the *only* – caretaker of children. As Jean Baker Miller (1976: 128) puts it:

If we *as a human community want* [emphasis in original] children, how does the total society propose to provide for them? How can it provide for them in such a way that women do not have to suffer or forfeit other forms of participation and power? How does society propose to organize so that men can benefit from equal participation in child care?

Egalitarian parenting has become more central in feminist discourse and practice (e.g. Dinnerstein 1977; Chodorow 1978; Elshtain 1981; Gross and Averill 1983). Nevertheless, women's continuing burden of child rearing in female-dominated childrearing patterns blames women for all sorts of psychological and social ills. Traditional child-psychiatric literature cites numerous child-related problems which psychotherapists trace to the mother–child relationship. As unfair as it is to assign the major responsibility of child rearing to women, the injustice is compounded by blaming them for not doing a perfect job of a nearly impossible task.[9]

Feminist theory is way ahead of social practice regarding child care (see, for example, Harding and Hintikka 1983; Segal 1987; Ruddick 1989). An interview with a male network member of one of the study participants, however, uncovered some evidence of changing practice along these lines. In the metropolitan area of this research a group of men have formed a Men's Child Care Collective. This action supplements the changes occurring in individual parenting practice. Here are excerpts from the men's description of their organization:

> We are a group of men (gay and straight) who ... want to support women who are breaking away from the limiting and male domi-nated relationships of the family and the larger society.

> We live in a society in which child rearing and nurturing have been defined as 'women's work', as unproductive and therefore unpaid. Men have been forced to compete for paying jobs outside the home which often exclude them from supportive, loving interac-tion with children, other men, and of course women. In reality, many Third World and poor women must earn money at low paying jobs, do the housework, and also take care of their children (and their husbands). This sexual division of labour serves to maintain the power of the capitalist class and divides and op-presses everyone else ...

> We want to do child care support for women who are in transition from a nuclear family or those already in an alternative lifestyle, such as lesbian mothers, battered women, and welfare mothers. We would also like to support women's political and cultural space by doing child care for feminist events, freeing more women to participate actively. Through doing these things we will be help-ing to relieve women's oppression. By showing children that men can be gentle and supportive of them and each other, we will be creating free and confident people who will be able to topple an inhuman system that depends on male privilege to exist.

> For men working against sexism, doing child care is a way we can come together and do something that has an immediate, positive

effect. It also ... involves us in a supportive and nurturing way with each other ...

In describing the frustrations and joys of working with the children of battered women, one man wrote:

One woman who stayed at the shelter reported that, prior to that time, her son was afraid of men – perhaps due to his violent father. After being at the House for five weeks, the woman saw her son opening up to men again. His time spent with the Childcare Collective had allowed him to reach out again. It is this kind of positive feedback that keeps the men in the Collective going.

Even a single example of men's participation in child care is significant, for it makes an important symbolic statement that it is neither impossible nor unnatural for men to involve themselves in child care and assume non-traditional roles.[10] While the Collective's emphasis is to assist women in alternative life styles, the greater challenge perhaps lies in the full participation of men in routine child care in mainstream families and in day care facilities where usually no males are found and where the low wages for this necessary social task typify society's devaluation of 'women's work'. Currently the norm is that men sometimes 'babysit' their children, a linguistic indication of the notion that men are more related to their children as hired worker than as parent. When men, like women, 'take care of' their children rather than 'babysit', an era of greater mutuality in child care will have dawned. Such changes in parental roles, such re-definitions between appropriate 'public' and 'private' work may help reduce the incidence of violence against women.

Part IV

Conclusions, implications, follow-up

Chapter twelve

Summary and conclusions

Summary of findings

This study uncovered complex relationships between individual women, their social networks, and the larger society. Their life histories revealed that some had suffered sexual abuse from fathers during childhood, and nearly all experienced some form of violence even before being battered by their husbands. Both the source and age at which these traumatic events occurred influenced the effect of such violence on these women. No evidence supported the popular notion that mothers collude in fathers' sexual abuse of daughters. Rather, just as alcohol is used as an 'excuse' to batter, so some fathers seem to use a mother's absence as an 'excuse' to abuse their daughters with impunity. Nor was there evidence to support an 'intergenerational cycle of violence'. Most importantly, the women's histories contradict the common assumption that women's own psychopathology constitutes a cause of violence.

During the battering phase, traditional values regarding women formed a powerful foundation for both victim blaming and self-blame. In spite of the apparent influence such values played in these women's lives, there was little evidence to support the popular concept of the 'cycle of battering' and even less to justify the notion of 'learned helplessness'. Instead, the women were knowledgeable, capable people who developed strategies for coping within the violent relationship, as well as for eventually leaving it. Their ability to cope with life-threatening crises in spite of self-blame and intimations from others that they were somehow responsible for their plight, reveals them more as survivors than as helpless victims. While their progression through the life cycle was dramatically disrupted, they demonstrated a capacity for mastery and growth in response to traumatic events and crises.

Their ability to manage the crises battering entails was evident in spite of the limited help they received, especially from agency representatives. Natural network members, however, particularly close kin, strongly disapproved of the violence, and were generally supportive of battered daughters and sisters. This finding contradicts the stereotype that family members are indifferent toward battered women. Some family members were dismayed to learn that an abused woman had deliberately kept the knowledge of violence from them, which underscores the extent to which women have absorbed the value of their personal responsibility for their victimization. In spite of family members' disapproval of violence and willingness to help, however, they often were not able to do so for complex reasons. Thus, while battering occurs in the domestic sphere, it is clearly a complex public problem beyond the ability of the family alone to manage.

Formal network members for the most part were either negative or indifferent to the women. Their attitudes suggest how health and human service professionals collude in defining violence as a private matter. Most network members, like the women themselves, believed that violence is primarily a medical problem, something demanding treatment. But when the women did interact with health and human service professionals, they sensed that institutional representatives regarded battering as 'taboo', and that they were shunned rather than helped. In striking contrast, the women spoke very positively about the assistance they received while in an emergency shelter.

Analysis of the post-battering phase of the women's lives revealed poverty and homelessness, complicated by the stress of single parenthood and social isolation during a major life transition. These problems served as powerful reminders that violence has far-reaching effects, and thus a crisis approach alone is not sufficient for assisting victims of violence. Housing authorities and political figures were particularly indifferent to the plight of homelessness that some women suffered for months after leaving emergency shelters. The criterion 'homeless through no fault of one's own' and the deliberate exclusion of battering as a qualifier for emergency housing assistance, suggest that 'victim blaming' and implicit social approval of male violence are embedded in public policies. Also significant was the relative absence of support groups and child care assistance for the women leaving the shelter. If such services existed, they were either inconveniently scheduled or too expensive. Barriers such as these allow the women little or no leisure time or social outlets.

The prolonged after-effects of violence for women and children were traced to a traditional ideology which defines women primarily as bearers and nurturers of children, and to attendant social arrange-

230

ments that support this ideology and eventually come to be seen as 'natural'. The irony that battered women and their children had to live virtually as fugitives in a secret refuge or on the street, while their assailants enjoyed the comforts of the marital dwelling, was especially striking when juxtaposed with women's conventional socialization to think of the home as their 'proper' place.

Conclusions and implications

This study has implications for theory, methodology, human service practice, and public policy.

Theoretical significance

This research focused on how network members, societal norms, and values about women, marriage, the family, and violence, influence battered women. Social network members influenced the women in their attempts to cope with battering and its long-term after-effects: family members generally were positive, but agency representatives (except for shelter staff) generally were not supportive. Poverty complicates the results of violence, but alone does not explain why women remain in, leave, or return to violent relationships.

Besides addressing the specific questions the study defined, this research also suggests that the most frequent question, 'Why do battered women stay?', is probably the wrong question to ask, since it emerges from traditional ideology about women, marriage, the family, and violence. Thus, the prevalence of this question underscores a major conclusion: that the problem of violence against women can be attributed in part to traditional ideologies which serve only to justify and maintain the status quo. Such customary ideas include male dominance and beliefs and practices regarding women's primary responsibility for the family. In short, the study revealed processes by which micro-factors (the trouble of the individual woman) are linked to macro-factors (values and norms that are institutionalized), as expressed through social network interaction.

The complex interactional process between these personal, cultural, and political-economic factors is powerfully tenacious, creating a climate that entraps women and one in which violence flourishes. Indicative of this process is the traditional knowledge system that has guided research about women. In this male-dominated system women have been associated symbolically with the private, domestic sphere of life, an ideology supporting a view of violence in marriage as a private matter between the couple.

Once begun, violence occurs in spite of both the victim's and the assailant's shock and expectations that it won't be repeated. Violence continues, however, not because women reinforce it, or are helpless, or have provoked it. Its repetition is evidence that, for complex reasons, violent men repeatedly break their promises not to beat their wives. Significantly, little attention has been paid to violence as social action for which men should be held accountable. Instead, researchers and the general public ask: 'Why do battered women stay?' From this premiss follows the blaming of women for their 'stupidity' or collusion. Human service practice and public policy conspire to imply that the victims are responsible for their assailants' action.

Battered women themselves have absorbed this ideology. They blame themselves for the violence and accept primary responsibility for preserving the marriage, even at the price of their own brutalization. On the other hand, should they themselves become violent, women are typically judged more harshly than men, since they have deviated from the traditional feminine norm of non-aggression. The women's repeated forgiveness of their violent husbands reflects their socialization, the cumulative product of what they are taught about relatedness and caring for others. Conversely, men's socialization to be aggressive, distant, and objective in relationships, seems to lay the foundation for a pattern of male dominance in sexual relations. Such interaction flourishes in a cultural milieu and political economy that supports male dominance and provides fewer opportunities for women in general, and for battered women in particular.

In such a context violent mates of battered women are practically impervious to protests by concerned individuals and families. Violent men *know* from experience that they can usually get by with violence against their wives; while women absorb traditional values and come to 'know' themselves as somehow deserving of and responsible for the violence. Thus, violent men face little prospect of homelessness or restriction of their personal freedoms. Their victimized wives and children, however, live as fugitives in fear of further brutalization or death, all the while wondering what *they* did to deserve their fate.

These dynamics may lead to battered women remaining in violent relationships for reasons that may not make sense to outsiders who interpret such problems in a social-cultural vacuum. This research reveals that these women are indeed victims, but they are also knowledgeable, capable agents who may be aware of the perversion of justice and ask themselves: 'Why should *I* leave? *He* is the one who forfeited his right to be here.' Indeed, except for the deeply embedded social acceptance of victim-blaming, it is remarkable that people should still ask 'Why does she stay?' when more appropriate questions are: 'Why is *he*, the assailant, *allowed* to stay?'; 'Why should *she*, the victim, be *expected* to leave?'; and 'Why have we as a society for so long expected victims to be accountable for the violent action of their assailants?'

A battered woman's reasoning about whether and when to leave must include plans for her children, money, housing, security from being found, overcoming shame, etc. Her decision is influenced by her reluctance to disrupt her marriage, her children, and her progression through the life cycle. Violence forces her, in effect, to start over. Thus, a woman may indeed decide to stay, but her decision depends on a multitude of complex factors, including the strength of social and material factors beyond her control.

Methodological issues

The methodological issues that emerged from this research concern the problem of access to a research population, and the therapeutic effects the research had for the participants.

Methodological problems were exacerbated by the gap found between feminist activists and academic researchers and professionals like nurses. The lack of health and mental health professionals in shelters underscores this gap. Access to this population could not have been resolved through traditional research methods such as surveys or even single interviews. Instead, I developed a methodology that convinced both the women participants and their radical feminist advocates of the ethical grounds of the research. The methodology explicitly recognized the principle that 'Research is intervention'. From this acceptance followed a delicate juggling of overlapping ways of relating with the women as research collaborators, friends, and women in need. The women were engaged actively in the research process, and were promised a share of the benefits of the research well beyond a one-line acknowledgement. They were never referred to as 'informants', but rather as 'study participants' or 'collaborators'. They were also offered explicit assistance with crises involving children, housing, and related problems. In short, extraordinary effort was made to ensure not only that the research participants would not be harmed in any way, but also that the research results would be presented in a way that allowed examination of their usefulness in the women's movement.

Distinguishing between potential effects of the research and all the other factors that had an impact on the participants was a significant part of the research process. It touched on the political aspect of studying this sensitive topic and the antagonism between some feminist activists and researchers. Various measures were pursued throughout the months of the research process to document and clarify these interacting factors. Without exception, the study participants spoke of the beneficial effect of collaborating in the research. The women's responses to the research process, along with the support they received in the shelter, suggest that the shelter staff and the researcher functioned to some extent as 'ritual experts' during 'contemporary rites of passage' for these women's difficult transition from a violent marriage to a life free of violence.

However, the women's needs for assistance with housing, child care, legal and other problems extended well beyond what was available through shelter staff or the researcher. Society's failure to provide formal help after battering coincides with the general indifference of institutional representatives to the women during battering, and is yet another result of the traditional definition of violence against women as a private rather than public issue.

The long-term damage of battering and the secondary positive effects of the research process were apparent because of the women's active collaboration during the extended months of field work in a naturalistic setting. In addition to their ability to cope with the trauma of battering, the women revealed themselves as capable research collaborators. Their testimony also supports the contention that research with disadvantaged groups not only need not be exploitative, but also can help close the gap between feminist academics and activists. In short, the unique approach used in this study contributes to its credibility among activists, and suggests to social analysts a fresh, non-exploitative approach to old problems.

Human service practice and public policy

The implications of this research cross public policy and human service domains. The findings present a powerful case for preventing violence. They also support the position that violence against women goes much deeper than personal psychopathology or family trouble. Terms such as the 'battered wife syndrome' and 'domestic violence' reveal an interpretation of wife battering as only a 'family' or medical problem and tend to mask the political and broader social ramifications of the more explicit term 'violence against women'. This research shows that while most family members were supportive of the women, this was not enough. Nor was emergency shelter enough. Besides political awareness, health and human service professionals need to incorporate formal crisis and follow-up strategies into their repertoire of skills in order to help battered women rebuild their lives with less stress and secondary victimization than many now experience.

This research also supports feminists and critical theorists who argue that too much is expected of families as the only support for troubled members. Renewed efforts are necessary to raise awareness and implement widespread social action on behalf of disempowered groups such as battered women and their children. What is implied from the research is the necessity for serious consideration of the feminist ideal of equality between women and men in the pivotal social task of parenting. While the unequal responsibility for child care affects most women world-wide, battered women who are poor and homeless suffer a disproportionate burden of parenting alone. Re-examining traditional social arrangements for the reproduction of society implies recognizing that these arrangements are not biologically determined or divinely ordained. Therefore we can change them so that they are more just and fruitful for women, men, and children.

While working to eliminate the roots of violence against women through socio-economic equality between the sexes and egalitarian child rearing, an intermediate goal is envisioned from this research. While progressive Abuse Prevention Acts exist in most industrialized societies, women victims will be forced to leave their homes to avoid further brutality or death so long as such laws are not vigorously enforced and violent men continue to assume they may be violent toward their wives with impunity. In the US, such laws generally do not work actually to protect women. As this study was being completed, a bill was introduced in the State legislature of the study setting that would further reduce the law's effectiveness by charging a battered woman, already usually economically disadvantaged, a fee to activate a restraining order on a violent husband.

Such examples of oppression of women should be replaced by policies that establish holding/counselling centres for violent persons as an alternative to current arrangements whereby *victims* are required to live as fugitives from their violent mates. Combined with condemnation of violence by the churches and other powerful social institutions, such a move would serve to put violent men (and women) on notice that they, rather than their victims, will be held accountable for their violence. Over time, abused women could thus be assured of safety while remaining in their homes, secure that when they call on network members such as police for help, their assailants, not they, will be expected to leave the marital dwelling. The time required in the holding/counselling centre would be based on a violent person's progress toward learning non-violent responses to his/her problems, plus consciousness-raising around public non-tolerance of violence.

This recommendation holds promise if several conditions are met: (1) that widespread public education regarding violence against

235

women be instituted in order to reverse what has generally characterized public response to it; (2) that human service professionals and policy makers re-examine the current tendency to medicalize and excuse violence, and move beyond crisis and family aspects of treating the problems; (3) that all women working in shelters for battered women combine the crisis work of sheltering abused women with activism around the political aspects of the problem, as was the case at the shelter described in this study. While shelters for abused women are currently a life-saving necessity, they should eventually become unnecessary (or be converted to holding centres for assailants), as the community develops more just and reasonable methods to deal with its violent members.

To conclude, this study demonstrates an inextricable link between our ideology and practice in the human service and political arenas concerning violence. Theory, research, and practice are not value-free as has long been claimed. Rather, theoretical assumptions, approaches to research, and practice with victims and assailants all reveal either our commitment to the status quo regarding women, marriage, the family, and violence; or our desire to initiate broad social change on an issue of vital concern to women, children, men, and all of society.

Epilogue

Five years later

These women are not merely victims; they are survivors. Several years after participating in this study, their resilience prevails despite continued hardships, some springing directly from the violent relationships they endured, and some from gender and class issues in American society. For several women the violence and its aftermath spans more than 15 years, including the years before they became involved in the study. Follow-up interviews with seven of the women (two could not be contacted) reveal their experiences since the study was completed in 1983. The picture that emerged, together with interpretive analysis and implications for policy and human service practice on behalf of battered women and their children, conclude the study.

With one exception, the women's daily struggles present a constant challenge to their survival skills. While none of the women currently lives with a violent mate, other problems have kept some of them in virtual bondage. To assess the meaning of the battering experience over time, I asked the women: 'Now, as you look back, what is the most significant thing for you about the fact that you were battered?' Two themes emerged from the women's responses. On the one hand, they still find it shocking that the violence occurred; that the man they loved actually beat them up. As one woman said: 'To think that I stayed around and took it for 13 years!' Two of the women said they found it scary to recall that they had allowed another person to exercise such power over them. The continued shock of their battering, however, was joined to a sense of victory, self-mastery, and recognition that they somehow survived and are here today to tell the story. The very fact that they have avoided another violent relationship is clear evidence that they learned something from the experience. As one woman said: 'I learned to rely on myself.'

In discussing what their greatest struggle now is the women said that learning to be self-reliant is tinged with continual striving for self-acceptance and the right to assistance. New relationships with men constituted the greatest challenge for three of the women. These relations are troubling because they seem to repeat previous patterns even though physical abuse is absent. One of the women has remarried, given birth to a second child, and lost a child through miscarriage. Her second husband earns a substantial income in his own business, but squanders much of it on alcohol. Just as she excused her first husband's violence and drug abuse, this woman excuses her second husband's alcohol abuse while berating herself for violently attacking him over one of his drinking bouts. She feels housebound with two small children, depressed, and lonely, is less involved with her nearby family, and abuses alcohol herself as a flight from her problems.

Another woman feels similarly isolated, and struggles financially after an unsuccessful attempt at reconciliation with her husband. She also mourns the loss of an infant by crib death and her oldest son who chose to live with his father when the parents separated again. This woman also abuses alcohol now, though she expresses confidence in her ability to stop drinking as soon as she finds a job again or returns to college. She poignantly revealed her social isolation and near desperation by repeatedly expressing relief and gratitude when I contacted her for the follow-up interview. When she received my letter she said she could not think of a single other person to confide in about her current troubles.

Another woman is similarly isolated and has repeated a past pattern of excessive dependency on a male partner. Though she has ample financial means, she agreed to live in a geographically isolated setting with a man who is often away on professional business and who is emotionally and verbally abusive, though he has not hit her. This woman does, however, recognize the pattern of accepting abuse and is working on the issue with a therapist. Two other women have had regular individual counselling sessions over the past five years and also have used support groups such as Overeaters Anonymous and a local church.

One of the women traces her continued struggles with men to her incest experience. She describes her unhappy liaisons with men as an addiction. But she also sees it as a quest for the love of her father. Her inattention to the danger of AIDS from unprotected sex also reveals a self-destructive impulse. This woman is the only one who has been seriously suicidal during the past five years, which she traces to unresolved issues around sexual abuse from her father. Gradually, however, she is growing in her ability to confront men who let her down, and has recently acted to protect herself from unnecessary AIDS exposure. Despite her continued struggle with relationships, she has graduated from junior college and has been accepted into a prestigious women's college for language and international studies. To supplement her public assistance income, she runs a small housekeeping business.[1]

Only two of the women have developed satisfactory relationships with men. Coincidentally, these are the same two women who were most seriously suicidal during and immediately after their battering experience. Today they are not suicidal at all. But even these women are avoiding re-marriage for the time being as they try to rebuild their trust in men. What coping strategies did these two women employ to avoid self-defeating patterns or suicide as a response to stress? The woman who nearly died six years ago from a lethal overdose of aspirin, says that the love of her children combined with the sheer relief of just getting away from her husband and 'not being bossed around by him anymore' eliminates suicide as an option. She says, 'If I killed myself there would be no one for them [the kids] ... I'm glad I was saved from suicide.' On the other hand, this woman had thought about killing her husband during her attempt at reconciliation, but was 'scared to go to jail'. She also had occasional sessions with a social service worker, and receives much emotional support and some financial assistance from a lover.

The other previously suicidal woman presents another coping pattern. She feels strength simply from the realization that she started over and survived. She also sought counselling and says that her relationship with the man she has lived with for six years 'is different in every way'. This man truly loves her, but also, after divorcing her violent husband, she had insisted in her own mind that there would never be violence in another relationship. Both she and her companion actively work on avoiding violent language and resolving differences calmly. Although childless, she has re-ordered her priorities regarding children. Instead of spending elaborate sums to become pregnant (because medical problems had thus far prevented pregnancy), she fixed up her house and devoted her maternal energies to nurturing her partner's children. Once she decided not to kill herself, she focused on the quality of life she wanted, and gradually experienced satisfaction in combining career development with a happy life at home. When she feels depressed for some time, she returns to a counsellor.

Four of the women said that their children and setting an example for them is their most important motivation now. Learning to accept themselves and getting to know themselves better is also important. Their involvement in the study over time constitutes an avenue for continued self-reflection and a healthy means of sharing their experience. All of the women maintain the hope that others will benefit from their experience. One of the professional women in health care counselling cites her greater empathy and ability now to help anyone caught up in self-destructive behaviour.

This rather grim picture of struggle and unhappiness for all but two of the women underscores the emotional scars left by battering. Indeed, when asked directly whether they felt healed from victimization by violence, only one woman replied 'yes' without qualification. Some of the women said 'yes' because they feel confident they would never let a man beat them again. But one woman said that she still gets overwhelmed sometimes with anger and hurt, but not hate anymore: 'I'm 41 and most of my life has been tainted, and the effect is still there on my children [she cries].' This woman's greatest pain arises from the loss of her children to foster care during the years she was battered. Thus, her greatest sense of victory lies in the return of her children to her care, even though she still sees a counsellor about continuing problems with them. For three of the other women the major current struggles are also on issues of children: being strapped alone with their care; feeling conflicted about continuing as a single parent or placing the children in foster care; shortfalls in financial support; the need to protect daughters (in three instances) from sexual advances and physical abuse of fathers; repeated questions from boy children about their absent father.

As already noted, four of the women have had either regular or periodic assistance from social workers or therapists. Only one of them cited a case worker as the main source of her emotional and social support. The two women with the most stable relationships with men cited the men as their main sources of support. Other sources are a church group, Overeaters Anonymous, and a priest. One woman said apologetically that her teenage children were her greatest support. Only one woman cited several women friends as sources of support, while another noted that a neighbouring woman was helpful. Not a single woman was in regular contact with women's support groups or special groups such as those for incest survivors.

What is the meaning of this rather stark picture of the women's continuing struggles and social isolation five years after freeing themselves from a violent relationship? I had originally intended to contact battered women who might want to participate in the study through follow-up programmes for battered women leaving emergency refuges. But I discovered that such programmes did not exist. Although collaboration in the study provided an avenue for follow-up and emotional support, the women's on-going struggles reveal that much more than research collaboration is needed for women and children victimized by domestic violence, incest, and problems rooted in gender bias. It is already well known among human service and mental health professionals that follow-up care is perhaps the weakest link in the chain of services necessary for victims and those with deep-seated family problems. One result of the system's weakness is that a minority of clients with chronic problems consume a major portion of mental health service budgets. Advocates of battered women's shelters are also keenly aware of the need for follow-up service for battered women and their children, but financial constraints generally have prevented them from realizing their vision of a broad-based service. (An exception to this pattern was cited in Chapter 10, note 3.)

Battered women's complex needs attest that woman abuse is more than a personal crisis. It is a public health problem which arises from traditional values that regard women as appropriate objects of violence and male control; from the chronic problem of women's continued economic disparity in a wealthy industrialized society; and from the gender-based division of labour regarding child care. Thus, while these women may no longer be in crisis from life-threatening violence, little has changed for most of them regarding traditional values of dependency on men in unhealthy, intimate relationships. While widespread societal change might some day render men less prone to abuse women, there is still here and now the need for more extensive support than crisis intervention for the legions of women who suffer violence from their intimate partners. The women's stories debunk the common myth that battered women 'always return to their batterer' or that they find another violent partner. Five years later none of the women interviewed have put up with physical abuse from a man after leaving a violent relationship. Furthermore, they all made explicit statements affirming their determination never to tolerate physical abuse again. Even the two who attempted reconciliations with their husbands took the lead in finally ending the relationship when these reconciliations failed.

Although the women are survivors, the fact that they continued to suffer and struggle with a myriad of issues and problems affirms the view that their struggles are rooted in issues and values beyond themselves as individuals. Their individual strength is necessary to maintain their lives free of abuse. But it is not sufficient to deal with problems of gender violence that are so deeply rooted in our society's value system. As one woman suggested (Chapter 8, p. 152), shelter staff should offer group sessions on how to develop constructive relationships with men and 'how to let them go'. The life-saving role of shelters and the importance of the feminist approach to empowering battered women have already been noted, as have contemporary 'rites of passage' to assist women in building a life free of violence.

Conclusions, implications, follow-up

But in addition, these women's experiences reveal the need to develop more integrated services, such as:

>more systematic links with support and consciousness-raising groups – and in some instances psychotherapy – during the crisis phase to address some women's dependency arising from traditional gender roles in society;

>a programme in which social service or mental health personnel sensitive to battered women's issues initiate follow-up calls every six months or so for two or three years, to assess the women's needs, and make appropriate services available;

>material assistance for adequate housing and child care support to alleviate much of the stress and social isolation these women experience, and to make it possible for them to attend programmes such as women's support groups.

Thus far there has been no systematic longitudinal study of a large sample of women to determine the long-term results of wife-battering on the women and their children. The in-depth accounts of these women and the aftermath of violence they suffered affirms the view that many battered women are crisis managers and survivors against great odds. But the study also suggests the urgent need to implement comprehensive services for battered women and their children, while continuing work on the political agenda to change the social climate that encourages violence against women.

Appendix

Theoretical and methodological issues

Theoretical framework

A sociocultural rather than a psychopathological framework guided my analysis and interpretations of data. In Chapter 1 I noted that theory and research are not value-free, and the methodology used has powerful implications for human service practitioners who serve battered women. Victim-blaming theories do not advance the mental health and welfare of battered women. Table 1.1 summarizes the implications of the psychiatric labelling process of battered women; Table 1.2 schematically depicts the major concepts that guided this research.

Methodological issues

The interrelationship between the researcher, topic, theory, and method are particularly evident when research is undertaken on a value-laden topic like violence against women. Issues discussed here include the different purposes of research designs in relation to feminist politics; how power issues emerged in this study; and how research may be conducted in a way that does not exploit those researched nor compromise the principles of scientific enquiry. The section concludes with a description of how the research engaged the women as active collaborators, not merely victims and passive 'subjects' whose stories need 'validation' by a researcher claiming objectivity.

Previous research in critical perspective

Chapter 1 noted some major differences between mainstream and feminist approaches to violence against women. While feminists and other critics claim that traditional researchers fail to make their

Table 1.1 Concepts, assumptions, and practice implications related to labelling theory*

Key concepts and propositions	Assumptions	Practice implications
Victim-blaming: holds victims responsible for their victimization. Psychiatric labels contribute as ideology to justify this practice.	To hold victims, rather than assailants, responsible for the behaviour of assailants, represents a reversal of the moral order.	Consciousness-raising and public education. Examination and reform of health and human service practice that supports victim-blaming and misplaced self-blame.
Misplaced self-blame: battered women's assumption of responsibility for others' actions is rooted in victim-blaming and functionalist definitions of women that define them primarily *for* reproducing and nurturing others.	Humans are rational, conscious moral beings who are accountable for social action they engage in, for example, violence.	Establishment of holding/counselling centres to which violent assailants rather than their victims are required to go. Education and political action to enforce Abuse Prevention Laws so that victims are not forced out of their homes.
Medicalization of violence: follows from medicalization of life and other social problems, and may conveniently serve as ideology to excuse assailants from accountability for social actions.	Violence is a form of social action, though under certain circumstances such action may be excused, e.g. insanity or self-defence.	Examination of practice regarding violent persons whose behaviour crosses over between the mental health and criminal justice systems.

*These concepts are prevalent in theoretical discourse as well as in the commonsense reasoning revealed in everyday language.

Table 1.2 Schematic representation of conceptual framework of this research

Key concepts and propositions	Assumptions	Practice implications
Sex-role tendencies (e.g. women inclined toward relatedness and subjectivity, and men toward separation and objectivity) are rooted in parenting practices during early childhood which lay the foundation for later conflict between the sexes: nurturant/cooperative (female) and dominant/competitive (male).	Parenting practices and sex-role differences are rooted in values and social structure, and in the sexual division of labour which come to be seen as natural or biologically determined, an ideology serving to maintain traditional practice.	Consciousness-raising for men and women. Social and political action to change current social arrangements around parenting.
Beliefs and power structures may be revealed empirically through language and other interaction, ritual, and symbols.	Unless claims about 'patriarchy', 'sexism', and the oppression of women are grounded in the language and other realities of everyday life, they represent reification and the political process, not social analysis.	Examine the language of everyday life, of social theory, and the practice of research for their relevance to the topic of violence against women.
Violence against women occurs in a climate of social-structural inequalities; these are supported by ideologies about women which implicitly approve of such violence. Violence against women can be contextually situated with the political and economic structures and complementary values of a particular society. 'Patriarchy' and 'sexism' are two concepts that describe such *contexts* in which violence against women flourishes.	An appropriate analysis of violence against women assumes the dual basis of class and gender, and the critique of a knowledge system in which women's subordination is defined as 'natural' and/or 'divinely' ordained.	Formation of individual consciousness toward egalitarian ideology about nature and role of women as a prelude to social and political action to redefine and change oppressive social arrangements.

Table 1.2   (continued)

Key concepts and propositions	Assumptions	Practice implications
Traumatic events and life passages are points of danger and opportunity; they are not illnesses to be treated, but problems to be solved and life tasks to be achieved.	Persons experiencing these events are knowledgeable agents, capable of choice, growth, and development.	Training for health and human service professionals to increase skills in assisting women in crisis around battering.
Stress, crisis, and illness around battering are interactionally, not causally related: stress usually precedes and follows battering; crisis and illness may or may not accompany battering episodes. Crises around battering are rooted in more than personal or family issues, and therefore demand responses beyond the personal and familial: natural *and* formal crisis management.	Battered women, while needing assistance during crisis, are not helpless victims, but survivors. Personal coping alone is inadequate not because the women are helpless, but because their crisis originates in the social structure, cultural values, and the deviant action of another.	Development of education programmes, peer support groups, and 'contemporary rites of passage' for battered women.
Appropriate crisis management strategies are tailored to the differential origins of crisis: individual approaches to social problems can lead to victim-blaming.		

ideological interests explicit, mainstream researchers fault their critics both for their subjectivity and lack of empirical evidence in analysing patriarchy. Feminists and critical scholars assume a relationship between the personal and political. One of the earliest contributors to this debate was C. Wright Mills who wrote: 'It is the political task of the social scientist – as of any liberal educator – continually to translate personal troubles into public issues, and public issues into the terms of their human meaning for a variety of individuals' (1959: 187).

Before research can be conducted on either personal or social problems, one must define the issue and ascertain the *extent* of the problem. For this purpose, survey research is undoubtedly the most efficient method available. Examples of such survey data are the studies of crime by Wolfgang (1958) and statistical reports of government agencies such as the Uniform Crime Report and annual FBI reports. Although scholars are becoming increasingly aware of the flaws and inadequacies of such survey data (e.g. Cicourel 1964), statistical data nevertheless are used liberally by protagonists and antagonists in the political process of dealing with violence against women. Feminist activists, for example, cite FBI and other reports to inform legislators and the general public that nearly two million women are severely beaten each year in the US (Martin 1976; Browne 1987). On the other hand, activists take serious issue with statistics that report equal violence by men and women (Hilberman and Munson 1977/78: 527). These arguments underscore the political relevance of purportedly objective research methods.

Such survey analysis does increase our understanding of the *incidence* of violence in relationship to other factors such as alcoholism and unemployment. Yllo and Straus (1981), for example, using multivariate analysis of survey data, studied the relationship between the social-structural and ideological elements of sexual inequality and the comparative rates of violence against wives in American states. This study demonstrates that questions raised by feminists can be answered by a range of research designs. Its findings also support the work of Rubenstein (1982) who found that men whose wives earned more than they did were more likely to be violent toward their wives.

Such statistical associations between wife-beating and public policy issues regarding women are significant. But it is important not to impute causality to concepts such as 'patriarchy' and 'sexism'. This implies specifying that, as Rubenstein suggests, 'real men' who are knowledgeable about their culture and capable of doing otherwise (Giddens 1900: 9, 29–39), behave violently toward wives who threaten the traditional societal norm of male superiority. In short,

247

survey research contributes important general knowledge about the problem when carefully selected samples are studied and causal claims are avoided.

Frequently, studies such as Pagelow's (1981), Hilberman and Munson's (1977/78), Roy's (1977), and LaBell's (1977) are limited in another way. Like most researchers, they draw samples largely from psychiatric, social service, and shelter caseloads, resulting in an over-representation of poor women who are more likely to use public sources of aid in crisis. A few studies provide an exception to this general pattern. Walker's (1979) and Browne's (1987) studies draw on women not only from caseloads, but also from indigenous sources, and the interviews were not pre-structured. Other exceptions are sociological studies by Gelles (1974), *The Violent Home*, and Steinmetz (1977b), both of whom studied samples of 'normal' families. Though they avoid some problems, these studies are nevertheless limited by the small percentage of men in the samples.

In general, survey methods and case studies alone seemed ill-suited to examine the questions raised by this research. The challenge, then, was to devise a research protocol that would correct or mitigate the gaps uncovered in previous research. In this process, the context-specific work of Dobash and Dobash (1979) was most influential in developing the study's methodological framework. Through in-depth interviews, they focused extensively on the relationship between patriarchy, sexism, traditional beliefs, and woman-battering. Pagelow (1981) drew similar conclusions from her research using an extensive questionnaire with an interview option. None of the research reviewed, however, used a naturalistic field method of inquiry in which battered women participated in the study as active research collaborators over time *after* their shelter experience.

Field research, of the type used in anthropological studies for decades, seemed particularly appropriate for examining the sociocultural values and historical beliefs relevant to my research questions (Geertz 1973; Agar 1980).[1] An in-depth processual approach, therefore, appeared appropriate to examine the influence of societal values and related political-economic factors on battered women in a comparative life-history framework before, during, and after their experience of battering and emergency shelter.

The politics and ethics of researching violence against women

The choice of a naturalistic field approach emerged from analysing the multi-faceted issues this topic involves. Seeking a natural setting in which to proceed yielded valuable insights about the methodology of research with disadvantaged groups. Finding an appropriate setting was a major process which lasted several months. The descriptive analysis of this process supports my contention concerning the inextricable relationship between the problem, theory and method, and the researcher. It also reveals strikingly the political and ethical implications of researching any value-laden topic.

A major issue of conducting a field study in an urban setting took shape as the 'problem of access'. Initial efforts to gain access to a research population included police patrol settings, neighbourhood associations, a community-based shelter for battered women, a neighbourhood parish with an activist pastor, and a counselling service for violent men. Additionally, I considered, but eventually rejected, hospital casualty units and professional agency caseloads. These sources were not used because of safety issues, time limitations, and factional conflict between activists and researchers which were beyond my study purposes.[2]

All remaining efforts to gain access were devoted to the shelter in which I had trained as a volunteer. I became fully acquainted with this setting, and the research possibilities it afforded, through the shelter's work with the women, staff meetings, and exploring my research ideas with three former battered women who acted as 'methodological consultants' to the project.

The next step was to develop a letter inviting women to participate in the study. Normally a simple step, here it revealed a major conflict between feminist activists and academics. Residents of the shelter provided feedback about the letter and the study as a whole; without exception they expressed interest in taking part in the project. When the letter and the aims of the study were presented to the shelter Collective's decision-making Committee, however, clear antagonism between activist and academic goals was revealed.

During the many months spent researching theoretical issues, I had asked myself more than once: 'Why are feminists so angry at mainstream social scientists who acknowledge that "sexism", a "culture of violence", and "patriarchy" are responsible for much of the violence against women?' After pondering and critically examining the literature, I thought I understood some of the reasons. What I discovered was that the arguments between 'mainstream' (e.g. Straus, Gelles, and Steinmetz (1980) and minority (feminist) academics (e.g. Dobash and Dobash 1979) had filtered down to the political practice arena. (These arguments were still evident at the 1987 domestic violence research conference in New Hampshire.)

The lay-person's scepticism about traditional research (especially 'one-shot questionnaires') paled next to the almost militant resistance encountered from some members of the shelter Collective.

These women wanted to know in detail how I considered myself different from all of my predecessors. They made strenuous efforts to protect shelter residents from being 'used'. I had to explain the specifics of university-required consent forms, procedures for guaranteeing privacy, etc. Paradoxically, I was asked to furnish details of my research which were not yet formulated because of the participatory, processual approach I envisioned. To have supplied such pre-structured details would have meant engaging in the very impositional-type research I had so painstakingly tried to avoid. Three of the older, more experienced women in the Collective sensed that my approach was indeed different from those of earlier studies they had rejected as being exploitative. But the Collective's precedent for refusing collaboration in research had somehow to be weighed against the 'different' proposal I presented. Throughout the entire discussion I felt very intimidated and powerless, while at the same time convinced of the value of the project and the appropriateness of the research methods chosen.

This meeting led to another one with a long-time member of the Collective and a resident participant in this discussion. We were to explore further the issue of a collaborative approach to the research. In two weeks, the results of this mini-session led finally to the Collective's support of the research, though some members remained reluctant.[3]

What is the meaning of such resistance to research by a group of feminist activists? Was this 'problem of access' symptomatic of the relationship between the theory, problem, and method of the research (Reinharz 1979) plus the person of the researcher? In historical perspective, the Collective members' scepticism is entirely understandable. Frequently, allegedly neutral 'scientific' studies omit contextual elements and thus tend to distort and confuse popular views on the subject (Roberts 1981; Wardell, Gillespie, and Leffler 1981). For example, feminist activists struggling for a political stand on the issue of woman abuse showed how a national survey of 'domestic' violence illustrated the exploitative uses of research. This survey revealed that women were 'equally as violent' as men (Straus, Gelles, and Steinmetz 1980), a finding which contradicted practically everyone's subjective knowledge of this topic. It also defied local County hospital statistics citing 70 per cent of assault victims as battered women, not men. But, as noted in the discussion of context in Chapter 1, when these surprising findings were analysed further, it was found that women engage in violence just about as often as men when merely *counting* physically violent acts (from pushing or a slap, to use of lethal force and weapons). However, women's acts of violence are *usually* in self-defence and are much less physically damaging than men's. But by this time the damage had already been done as far as feminist activists were concerned. Various 'professionals' had quoted the survey findings *out of context* to support their argument of 'equality' of violence between men and women.

Mills' (1982) research underscores this point. Her re-analysis of the national survey data on domestic violence clarifies why the Collective members were extremely cautious about any academic association. When I explained that my research was 'different', the response was 'That's what they all say.' Also, I was suspect because of my association with academia. The importance of reconciling the concerns of feminist activists and academics is underlined by the power of the knowledge system in the traditional oppression of women (Okin 1979; Elshtain 1981; Harding and Hintikka 1983).

If I was suspect because I was an academic, my background as a mental health professional did not help either. In this Collective, professional credentials were in no way sought, and for the most part, were ignored if the staff person did not qualify in the ways that counted there: 'politically correct', empathetic with battered women, appreciation of violence as a possibility in the lives of *all* women in current social arrangements. While I did not deliberately hide my professional credentials, I was very careful not to flaunt them. Overtly, my credentials were a clear liability in establishing trust and rapport; covertly, they were an asset in helping me understand the dynamic process and regulate my behaviour accordingly.

The Collective's staff shared both an anti-academic bias, and an anti-professional bias. It was, after all, well documented (as in the case of research) that mental health and social service professionals, for the most part, were part of the problem for battered women (Dexter 1958; Martin 1976; Stark, Flitcraft, and Frazier 1979; Hilberman 1980). Therefore, without evidence based on more extensive experience with me, their suspicions of me as an 'infiltrating professional' were not surprising. The general attitude was something like this: after centuries of collusion by society's major institutions – including more recently researchers and human service professionals – to define the issue of violence against women as a 'private' matter (Dobash and Dobash 1979), feminists nevertheless managed to bring the matter to public attention as a social/political problem. Now that the issue was exposed as something more complex than a matter of the individual psychology of battered women, professionals and academics were perceived as wanting to jump on the bandwagon of a popular issue and exploit it for their own individual gain or ideological purposes (Ahrens 1980; Schechter 1982). For example, if surveys reveal that the numerical incidence of male/female violence is approximately equal, and the *context* of violence is de-emphasized, it is not difficult to redefine the problem of violence against women as 'domestic' or 'family' violence. Collective members therefore resisted data-collection that might compromise political goals or misrepresent shelter residents, especially poor women and women of colour.

At first glance such a defensive posture by the shelter Collective may appear unfounded. After all, many sincere and sympathetic persons – professional and lay – have contributed to the service of sheltering battered women and their children (Schechter 1982). Yet the caution of these feminists – based solely on their practical, political experience – corresponds to the academic minority critique of mainstream social science which, for all its claims of objectivity, has often functioned as a powerful tool to support ideological agendas (Wardell, Gillespie, and Leffler 1981; Bleier 1984).

The politicized women working in the women's movement in this urban American setting seemed remarkably similar to citizens of politically awakened developing countries that had thrown off the shackles of colonialism. People being researched, having observed some anthropologists who were used as tools of colonial administrators (albeit disguised in the purportedly 'neutral' language of science), and having embarked on a path of self-determination, now required researchers to pass a test based on their needs and values (duToit 1980; Adams 1981: 155–60).[4] The standard term 'subjects of research' now took on a different meaning: in this traditional mould those being researched seemed more like 'objects' who were 'subject' to the researcher's pre-determined designs. Even the term 'informants', traditionally used by anthropologists, is inadequate to describe the researcher's role in working with politically sensitized members of society, since it too implies a superordinate/subordinate relationship.

It is one thing, however, to acknowledge and another to incorporate the needs of those being researched into the research design. How does one accomplish this integration without compromising the researcher's 'objective' knowledge goals to the political objectives of the researched? In this research that problem was resolved by declaring my basic assumption from the outset: research with disempowered groups on a value-laden topic such as violence against women is not *only* a scientific endeavour; it is also an ethical and political act. Failure to acknowledge the intertwined connection between the political and scientific aspects of research is a major factor in polarizing academics and social activists concerned with women's problems.

Yet I still faced the practical problem of bridging the gap between feminist theory and practice. This meant gaining the Collective's co-operation in my research aims. It seemed especially important to challenge on its own terms the traditional knowledge system that informs social and political practice oppressive to women. Collaborating with a researcher who is ready and willing to correct sexist bias and exploitation through research would seem beneficial to the political movement directed toward stopping violence against women. I shared this and other thoughts with a few members of the Collective who explicitly supported the project.

Engaging the research participants

A few weeks later the Collective reached a consensus to support my project. The project also gained support from the State Coalition of shelter service groups. The foundation was laid to invite shelter residents to participate in the research. Invitation letters were given only if the women manifested some interest in the study through my informal interaction with them during the normal course of my staffing shift. Other than introducing the topic and signing the Consent Form, the women did not participate formally in the research until after leaving the shelter. Approximately six months were spent in this introductory getting-acquainted phase. My volunteer staffing and active involvement in Collective meetings served several purposes. (1) I gained much general knowledge and experience about how a non-traditional shelter operates and what it was like for the women and children living there and for those working there. This constituted vital information for placing the women's pre- and post-shelter experience in comparative perspective. (2) It provided a necessary and trusting context in which I could inform residents about the study and provide the basis for a truly informed consent. (3) It provided vitality to my claim that I planned to do a collaborative study with only the broad objectives outlined at this preliminary stage, while the details were to be developed with the participants as we proceeded.

During these six months in the field, participant-observation remained general and unfocused for two reasons. First, women in the shelter were usually quite preoccupied with the stressful activities of finding housing, dealing with financial and legal problems, and managing the problems of learning to live with six or seven other women and ten to twenty children – all strangers to each other before coming to the shelter (Chapter 8 contains a fuller discussion of this issue). Asking them to become actively involved in the research at this point would have imposed an additional burden on an already complex struggle for survival. Second, even though a few of the women seemed willing and ready to get into more focused discussion, I refrained out of my concern for keeping my word to the Collective members who did *not* want research pursued in the house. The extensive field notes I took during my time at the shelter might provide material for future analysis, if the Collective decided that additional research could benefit all the women concerned.

As I waited for women participants to leave the shelter, I began to consider how I would focus my participant-observation with them once they were in their own homes, using the sensitizing concepts noted above to guide my approach. However, I was faced with this dilemma within the research time limits: How does one structure observation and in-depth interviews without imposing pre-defined categories on the people whose knowledge and values are sought (Oakley 1981a)? How does one avoid on the one hand a mere journalistic account, and on the other hand becoming engulfed in reams of unstructured data with no basis of comparison between the study participants? To resolve this dilemma, after consulting the three women who assisted with methodology, I decided to combine structured and unstructured data-gathering techniques. What evolved was the data-gathering plan described in Chapter 1 – with the caveat that this was subject to change depending on input from the women and the outcomes of my actual involvement with them after leaving the shelter.

Study participants

The nature and extent of the involvement of the twelve participants in the study was of two types. (1) Three of the women assisted with the 'problem of access' and provided input and feedback about the methods suggested for gathering information and involving the women in the study. The focus of participation for this group was *process*. (2) Nine women comprised the participants who examined over time the questions identified for this study. The focus for this group was on *content*, although they were also involved in the on-going evaluation of process and methodology. The ethnic identities of these twelve women included: one black, two Italian-American (one with English language barrier), one Indian-West Indian, one Canadian Indian-white, six caucasian. The number of children ranged from zero to six. The ages of the women ranged from 19 to 49. Four of the twelve women received full AFDC (Aid to Families with Dependent Children), two received public housing assistance in addition after battering. Three received partial AFDC support and worked outside the home to supplement this public assistance. Their jobs included teaching English, legal secretary, word processing, housecleaning, human service professionals. All but one woman had at least a high school diploma. Two were taking additional technical training during the study period, one was in regular college classes, one was in graduate school (social science), three already held graduate degrees (masters). One high school graduate (trained as a medical assistant) has a goal of eventually becoming a nurse; three have goals to become lawyers or CPAs. These women constitute a 'convenience sample'. They were contacted through state shelter and health networks.

Notes

Chapter one

1   The term 'feminist' does not imply a monolithic viewpoint on gender issues. Feminist perspectives are broadly classified as liberal, socialist, radical, and psychoanalytic. While all feminists are concerned about women's equality, they differ – sometimes widely – about how such equality is to be achieved and about their vision of an egalitarian society (see Segal 1987; Reiter 1975; Eisenstein 1979; Smith 1981/82); see also Stacey (1986) regarding pro-family feminists such as Elshtain (1981). This book favours non-separatist, socialist feminism as elaborated later in this chapter and the Appendix.

2   The recent movie *Nuts* highlights the struggle of a woman for a trial based on 'self-defence' rather than 'insanity' after she killed the man who abused her.

3   See, for example, the following sources: epidemiology (Berkman and Syme 1979); sociology (Granovetter 1973; Lopata 1973; McKinlay 1973, 1981; Kaplan, Cassel, and Gore 1977); anthropology (Bott 1957; Mitchell 1969; Robinson 1971; Barnes 1972; Boissevain 1979); nursing (Norbeck, Lindsey, and Carrieri 1981; Maxwell 1982); medicine (Cobb 1976); social psychology (Antonovsky 1987); social psychiatry (Caplan 1964, 1974; Polak 1971; Speck and Attneave 1973; Garrison 1974; Hansell 1976; Gottlieb 1981).

4   The gap between social network concepts and their application in practice is highlighted by the research of Stark, Flitcraft, and Frazier (1979). These researchers, in a study of 489 battered women, uncovered the social construction of a public issue (i.e. violence against women by their mates) into a private event through the process of psychiatric labelling of the woman victim, especially in emergency facilities and through psychiatric referrals. Such labelling implies that a woman is personally responsible for her victimization and thereby lays the foundation for excusing the action of her attacker. For further discussion of the hazards of labelling in crisis and health care practice, see Hagey and McDonough (1984) and Hoff (1989: Ch. 3).

5. See Shupe, Stacey, and Hazlewood (1987) for a more recent study of

256

women's violence as uncovered in a sample of 45 couples in a counselling programme for violent partners. These researchers affirm the active
role of women during violent episodes. They also report the futility of
women's attempts to defend themselves through violence and that
revenge is often a key motive for their violence.

6   See Breines and Gordon (1983: 509, 519) for a critique.

7   See Oakley (1981a), esp. pp. 46–58, Geertz (1973), esp. pp. 3–30, and
Keller (1985), esp. Ch. 9.

8   The ideological function of 'theory' and 'scientific methodology' as
agents of social control is not new to social science, nor is it limited to issues concerning women (Blau 1981; Spelman 1983: 18). Moynihan
(1965) presented 'evidence' from correlational analysis of data to support his racist/sexist conclusion that causal relationships existed between
juvenile delinquency and black households headed by women, and between black women wage-earners and emasculated black men.

9   In addition to the 12 women and 131 social network members in the formal aspect of this study, several other women participated in one
formal interview after leaving the shelter and discontinued because of
continual problems with housing, childcare, or family objection to research.
   Another participant in this research was one man, Bob, who had
beaten his wife. Bob was referred through the pastor of the neighbourhood parish discussed around the 'access' process (see Appendix).
Contact with Bob was infrequent though it extended over eight months.
It included six hours of in-depth interviewing and occasional phone contacts in the parish house or his home. There was also one interview with
Bob's wife before they finally parted ways.

10 The framework for the life-history interviewing was a 17-item Self
Evaluation Guide adapted from a record system of a community mental health service that incorporated routine crisis assessment and social
network factors into every intake interview. See the original work in
Hoff (1984b) and Hoff (1984a) for details regarding this instrument
and the practice-research-practice links influencing its use in this research. Hoff (1989) in future references is a revised edition of the
1984a work.
   Additional interview guides included a 47-item Values Index and a
25-item Social Network Questionnaire constructed for this research.
The Values Index was designed to reveal feminist and/or traditional
values regarding women, marriage, the family, and violence. The Social
Network Questionnaire – adapted from Norbeck, Lindsey, and Carrieri
(1981) – was used to identify and compare the following aspects of a
woman's social network: reachability, density, range, content, directedness, intensity, frequency, durability.

11 Sayers (1982) and Elshtain (1981) provide comprehensive feminist
critiques of the social uses of theory. Segal (1987) offers a critique of 'es-
sentialist' feminist theories that argue for women's 'naturally' greater
humanity for saving the world from disaster.

Notes

Chapter two

1   Items in the Self Evaluation Guide include: *Life Functions*: physical health; self-acceptance/self-esteem; vocational/occupational; immediate family; intimate relationships; residential; financial; decision-making/cognitive functions; life philosophy/goals; leisure time/community involvement; *Signals of Distress*: violence experienced; lethality-self; lethality-other; substance use; legal; agency use.

2   In this study *stress* is defined as the discomfort, pain, or troubled feeling arising from emotional, social, or physical sources and resulting in the need to relax, be treated, or otherwise seek relief. I also distinguished between *acute* stress, which is brief and can result in crisis, but differs from *insidious* or chronic stress, which arises from diverse sources, is less obvious to the person experiencing it, and usually has cumulative effects such as burnout and/or disease.

3   *Emotional breakdown* describes an individual's inability to manage feelings to the point of chronic interference in normal functioning. Its signs are manifested by depression, anger, fear, etc., and is often referred to as a 'nervous breakdown'. *Mental breakdown* describes a disturbance in a person's cognitive functioning where one is not able to think and act normally, ultimately interfering in the expression of feelings, interaction with others, and the conduct of daily behaviour.

4   To interpret these self-evaluations, an ascending scale of 1 to 5 signified the degree of stress they experienced. Put another way, if a woman stated that she was 'always very satisfied' regarding leisure time/community involvement, or was 'always successful' in obtaining help from agencies, her functioning was interpreted as adequate, and stress levels low. On the other hand, if she reported that there was a 'very high risk of suicide or assault' her stress level was interpreted as very high. For individual women, therefore, a cumulative score of 17 signified the lowest possible stress score, while 85 signified the highest possible score, and 52 represented a moderate degree of stress.

5   In mental health settings, moderate to high scores on the SEG Items indicate acute crisis, serious risk of suicide, and/or emotional/mental breakdown.

6   Though physical discipline does not necessarily constitute abuse, research and popular opinion suggest that physical discipline of children and violence between siblings is so widespread as to be considered 'normal' (Steinmetz 1977b; Straus, Gelles, and Steinmetz 1980).

7   For a recent random survey of incest and its effects, see Russell (1986).

Chapter three

1   Just how this relates to the 'therapeutic' side effects of the research process will be discussed in Chapter 9.

2   Pitkin (1972: 76–9) cites the problem of conceptual confusion regarding 'power', 'authority', and 'influence' which is related to the debate regarding cross-cultural variations in women's domestic and public

involvement. Raphael (1975) states that 'the power intrinsic in determining the outcome of each new generation is unparalleled' (p. 111). Thus, if power is seen as limited to the public sphere, men dominate in western societies and in the majority of traditional societies. Whereas, if power is defined as 'the ability to bear, educate, and determine the personality, the values, beliefs, hates and loves of each new member of a society, in fact, to control the decisions of who will or will not survive then females are certainly dominant' (p. 111). See also Chodorow (1978) for women's great influence in the parenting process. Tiffany (1979: 430, 436–7) cites the vague and contradictory use of terms like power, influence, and authority, and notes 'spirit possession' (Lewis 1971) in Africa and the British and American 'cult of female invalidism' as examples of informal political behaviour employed by those deprived of access to formal power. In this vein, Gordon (1988) refers to women's power in their successful efforts to obtain assistance during victimization, a view that accords with a vision of battered women as capable managers.

I suggest it is debatable whether these are forms of 'power', simply learned coping devices, or at most, 'influences'. In this study, is it really 'power' we are talking about if a woman is actively violent but does not succeed in asserting her will over another in the case of most male/female conflict situations? On the other hand, a man with usually greater physical strength, plus knowledge that external authority figures such as police will not intervene to stop his threats of physical force, could be said to have 'power' over his wife.

3 See last section of this chapter and Shupe, Stacey, and Hazlewood (1987).
4 The expression 'female sexual slavery' is used here in the popular derogatory sense, i.e. the assumption by some that battered women who stay do so because of an insatiable craving for sex. Technically, 'female sexual slavery' refers to the use and abuse of women who are bought and sold for services world-wide. See Barry (1979).
5 I am grateful to Sol Levine for his ideas about this association.
6 See also a later study (Kurz and Stark 1988) that supports these findings regarding the medical response to battering.
7 As moral agents, women are accountable as men are for their own violence that cannot be excused on grounds of self-defence or insanity. Acknowledging this is different from spurious arguments about the 'equal' violence of women. The controversial 'battered woman syndrome' may compound the tendency to medicalize victimization and violence rather than treating them contextually.
8 See also Counts (1987) and Stephens (1985).
9 See Hoff (1985) for a detailed critique of the Neuringer and Lettieri (1982) work.
10 See note 6 above.
11 This is one manifestation of the 'biology is destiny' theory.
12 In an opposite vein, Steinmetz (1977a) proposes that the most serious domestic violence problem is husband battering and that the reason it is not yet in the public eye is because men are too ashamed to acknow-

ledge being beaten by a woman. This claim is hotly repudiated by feminists (e.g. Hilberman and Munson 1977/78; Mills 1982) who interpret it as a theoretical smokescreen to obscure the political aspect of violence against women. The depths of shame and stigmatization expressed by the women in this study suggest that shame also figured in their decision to reveal or conceal their abuse.

Chapter four

1 See Chapter 3, note 4.
2 One of the women in this study, after leaving her partner, wrote an essay for a college class with the following title: 'What Marriage and Slavery Have in Common'. Some excerpts follow.

> Conformity ... means harmony, agreement, compliance, and obedience. Conformity is created in a marriage, in the first place, by conditioning ... In the second place, women conform as a result of being stereotyped which means repeating – or carrying on – the same customs and attitudes without originality or individuality ... In the third place, she is intimidated to conform. For instance, because a woman's reputation is as fragile as an eggshell, should she ever be aggressive and act on her own decisions, people would degrade her with a bad reputation. If a woman does anything outside the norms set by society, she becomes an outcast. Also, because she knows how cruel society can be to a woman on her own, she is deterred from getting out of a bad marriage and from bettering herself. After all, at least she has some kind of security for shelter, food, and clothes for herself and her children ... Finally, discrimination is another reason for causing women to conform to their husband's will. For example, because she gives up her last name and assumes that of her husband, she feels she must also become like her husband and conform to his ways, leaving her ways behind ... Another thing that marriage and slavery have in common is dependency ... intellectual and emotional dependency ... I see how women are treated by society today; I've experienced some of their brutal punches. I have also noticed that even though slavery is supposed to be ancient, it still exists with women and people from low incomes and poor backgrounds.

For further discussion of this issue see Chapman and Gates (1977).
3 See Chapter 1, especially pp. 3–10, and note 8.
4 According to this concept (Walker 1979), a period of tension (stage 1) is released by a violent episode (stage 2). The reconciliation and sweetness that follow (stage 3) are eventually displaced by rising tension, a repeat of the violence, and so on in a repetitious cycle.
5 See Breines and Gordon (1983) and Wallston (1981).
6 Complementing this view are concepts of stress and life-span development (Danish, Smyer, and Nowak 1980; Gergen 1982). Considered in relation to violence, persons in acute or chronic stress ordinarily would not by that fact also be automatically judged mentally incompetent and

therefore excusable from responsibility for behaviour. Maslow (1970), in his research on normal people experiencing traumatic life events, underscores the apparent growth-promoting influence of high stress situations for achieving self-actualization, not self-destruction or assault on others.

7   For a critique of Caplan's theory see Hoff (1989: 11–14).

8   People in crisis are not necessarily ill. Traumatic events, possibly resulting in crisis, are endemic to life. Psychopathology, which implies treatment, is not. For further discussion of these distinctions see Hoff (1989), especially Chapters 1 and 4.

9   See Chapter 3, note 6.

10 Controversy over battered women's culpability is dramatized by the highly publicized trial (in New York 1989) of a man convicted of killing his illegally adopted daughter. In this trial, the child's mother, a battered woman, testified that she was unable to save her daughter, presumably because of her own traumatized state. Feminists are divided about whether this woman should also have been indicted and tried for the child's death.

11 Thanks go to Sol Levine for his ideas about this concept. For further discussion of crisis management principles, see Hoff (1989: Ch. 4).

12 For a fuller description of these crises, see Hoff (1989: 37–46, and Part III: Crises Related to Situational and Transition States).

13 See Hoff (1989) for clinical application of this broader interpretation of emotional crisis.

14 As Bloch (1977: 287) states: 'people may be extensively mystified by the static imaginary models of their society which gain a phenomenological reality in ritual communication'.

Chapter five

1   One of the directions network analysis has taken is toward mathematical graph theory. Boissevain (1979: 392–3) notes that the 'arsenal of concepts, terms, and mathematical manipulations' has resulted in overkill by social scientists and minimal increase in understanding of social relations: 'Flies are killed with dynamite.' This is decidedly not the direction taken in this study.

2   See Chapter 1, note 3.

3   Adapted from Norbeck, Lindsey and Carrieri (1981)

Chapter six

1   Five years later (1988) in this State, three judges were publicly censured for their indifferent attitudes toward battered women's requests for restraining orders against violent husbands. One of the women, age 23 and five months pregnant, was killed by her husband after a judge publicly reprimanded her for 'wasting the court's time' with her domestic squabbles.

2 The women's reasoning process concerning rights and responsibilities around help for troubled people resemble those Watson (1978) and Sacks (1967) describe of callers to suicide prevention hotlines.

3 Kurz and Stark (1988: 249–66), citing studies from New Haven and Philadelphia, trace the medical response to battered women to three factors: misinformation, sexist attitudes, and the medicalization of victimization which locates the problem in the woman's behaviour rather than social inequality. See also Rieker and Carmen (Hilberman) (1986).

4 See Reverby (1987); also Hoff (1990, in press) for a feminist analysis that locates nurses' slow response to battered women in the historical oppression of nurses on gender and class grounds.

5 See Hoff (1989: Ch. 4) for criteria regarding drug prescription for people in crisis.

6 See notes 3 and 4 above.

7 This situation appears to be changing. Several feminist nurses, for example, have formed a Nursing Research Consortium on Violence and Abuse. Contact author for more information.

8 Since completing this study, some progress on this point is evident in the United States. See the Report of the Surgeon General's Workshop on Violence and Public Health (1986) for specific recommendations regarding preparation of health professionals in the care of victims.

Chapter seven

1 The interview with this woman's parents suggests many features of the traditional bourgeois family. It also points to the current feminist/mainstream debate about the role of the family in contemporary American society. Central figures in this debate are Lasch (1977) and Berger and Berger (1983) arguing explicitly in *favour* of the bourgeois model of the family characteristic of nineteenth-century capitalism. Barrett and McIntosh (1982) and Poster (1978), on the other hand, are vocal critics of the bourgeois family model, arguing that too much has been asked of the traditional family, and that many problems can be traced to the age and gender divisions in the bourgeois family. This interview and later analysis suggest support for such a critical theory of the family.

2 For example, in Miller and Challas' (1981) 25-year longitudinal study, 29 parents were abused as children and 89 parents were not abused as children. They found that '45 per cent of the persons abused as children were rated as *not* abusive to their own children, while 47 per cent of persons who were *not* abused as children do have some potential for child abuse' (emphasis in original). These researchers conclude: 'While child abuse casts a long shadow, it does not determine the next generation's fate, but poverty, ignorance, and unstable parental careers may' (p. 8). I would add that all parents, as rational, indeterminate creatures, have the *potential* for abuse of their children; but social and cultural factors influence most parents in not acting on this potential.

3 See Chapter 3, pp. 53–5.

4   No attempt is made here to resolve the debate over substance or food
    abuse as 'illness' versus a behavioural problem.
5   In spite of the economic and other factors this woman cited, her firm
    commitment to interpreting overeating and alcoholism as 'illness' is
    completely consistent with the philosophy of organizations that have
    been more successful in helping people with these problems: Alcoholics
    Anonymous, Al-Anon, Overeaters Anonymous. She was active in these
    peer support groups which substituted for her non-supportive biological
    family. For her, rejecting the group's definition of the problem as 'ill-
    ness' would be tantamount to rejecting the basic tenets of the
    programme which she found so supportive after leaving her violent hus-
    band. Even though these groups' 'treatments' focus heavily on
    abstinence and ritualistic behaviours such as weighing and measuring
    food, the fact of defining these behaviours in a medical rather than
    social paradigm attests to the widespread tendency toward medicaliza-
    tion of various life problems.
        However, it is possible that the success of these programmes can be
    traced more accurately to a new experience of support and healthy in-
    terdependency, rather than to attachment of an illness label to such
    problems. While the illness metaphor apparently has been useful in re-
    spect to problems like alcoholism, it presents serious questions when
    applied to violence against women. It also has profound implications for
    the values guiding the development and operation of shelters, as dis-
    cussed in Chapter 8.
6   The widely publicized Carol DiMaiti Stuart case in Boston (1989–90)
    underscores (in hindsight) the public's unawareness of everyday signs of
    domestic trouble, and that one-third of all women murdered are killed
    by a husband or boyfriend. That a whole city and country were willing
    to believe Charles Stuart's (white, upper-middle class) claim, that a
    Black man had killed his wife, reveals the complex interplay of class and
    race with gender issues around domestic violence. Once it was clear,
    however, that Stuart himself was the killer, the tendency was to medi-
    calize the event by associating Stuart's violence with his 'sociopathic
    personality'.

Chapter eight

1   This view is supported by follow-up studies comparing women who at-
    tended coeducation colleges with those who attended women's colleges.
    Those graduates from women's colleges have records of greater success
    in leadership and other roles.
2   The fact that until very recently most women preferred male therapists –
    and one of the women in this study wanted male shelter staff – can be
    traced to the widespread belief that only men were competent (Kaplan
    1984: 10).
3   See Chapter 4, note 8, regarding crisis counselling and treatment for psy-
    chopathology.
4   Most suicide prevention centres have broadened their function to in-

clude assistance to people in a variety of crisis situations besides suicide (Hoff and Miller 1987).

5   These differences are highlighted in the toilet regulations in shelters. In a traditionally-run shelter, the toilet had this sign on the door: STAFF ONLY. At Woman House, the toilet is shared by residents and staff.

6   This staffing pattern is integrally related to the mental health/illness issues that accompany society-wide responses to suicidal people. While there are on-going debates about the 'right to commit suicide' (Szasz 1970; Battin and Mayo 1981), there is also wide consensus that *most* people who are suicidal are in crisis, while many are seriously depressed and in need of therapy.

7   See Kurz and Stark (1988) and Hoff (1989: esp. Chs 2 and 8), for elaboration of this point.

8   The classist issue is also reminiscent of traditional practice in psychiatric settings. There the professional staff, predominantly white, can and will discuss the psychodynamics of patients for hours, while poorly paid and poorly trained aides or technicians (often people of colour) are left to attend the patients.

9   The visions and struggles of the battered women's movement and its relationship to mainstream social structures can be understood further by drawing on the concept of 'Cargo Cults', also known as 'chiliasm' and 'millennialism'. These terms describe certain social movements, notably of the oppressed peasant strata during the middle ages, various islanders in Melanesia during colonial rule, and the Sioux Indian Ghost Dance at Wounded Knee (Cohn 1957; Burridge 1960, 1969; Worsley 1968). Briefly, a 'cargo cult' involves an oppressed group's dream for a new and better world, a desire for a share in the cargo of the privileged, and repeated frustration because the cargo never arrives (Burridge 1960) – in short, a belief that the millennium is at hand, or a medium for the social aspirations of the poor. Central to a millennial movement is the adoption of new assumptions, a new redemptive process, a new political-economic framework, a new integrity, a new community (Burridge 1969: 13). The most significant cargo theme, Burridge says, is 'moral regeneration' (1960: 247). Cargo movements occur in three phases: (1) the creation of a myth-dream which can take weeks, months, or years; (2) attempts to realize the myth-dream; (3) the aftermath and recommencement of the cycles. In this phase there is either a revolution, or the desires of the dispossessed are accommodated within the existing social order (some would say 'co-opted'); or the oppressed are put down even further through the brute force of those in power.

It is not difficult to detect in this description some themes from the feminist movement(s), as well as the different approaches to feminism discussed in Chapter 1 and the Appendix. The liberal feminist approach to change through the existing establishment corresponds to the cargo theme of looking to the 'moral European' for more humane and fair treatment of the disadvantaged. The 'myth-dream', revolutionary objectives and cynicism of some feminists are evident in the writings of radical feminists like Mary Daly (1973, 1978). Only history can tell us the eventual outcomes of the current feminist movement(s), and how the struggles within the movement itself and with powerful mainstream institutions will be resolved: by accommodation, radical change in traditional social arrangements, co-option, or defeat and a strengthening of the status quo. See also Segal (1987) regarding the potential future influence of feminism.

Chapter nine

1   Because of delays in preparing the work for publication, I have since paid the women at the rate of $5 per hour for the total number of hours they spent with the researcher.
2   An example of this is presented in Chapter 11 in which I assisted a woman in changing her harsh behaviour toward her children.
3   The 1987 conference for researchers on domestic violence at the University of New Hampshire revealed that such tensions are still rampant.
4   Ritual can also serve a negative function (Spencer 1965, 1973). For example, women's traditional subordination to men is symbolized in the contemporary marriage rituals in which the father 'gives away the bride', symbolizing the transfer of 'ownership' from father to husband. This custom, along with the woman giving up her name (in most western societies), is in process of change among couples espousing a more egalitarian marriage relationship. See Hoff (1989: Ch. 11) for a fuller discussion of contemporary rites of passage in relation to life crises.
5   In developing countries, some battered women appear caught in changing social systems in which they have neither the support that was sometimes available through extended family networks, nor contemporary assistance such as shelters offer in most industrialized societies. During a workshop on violence against women which I conducted at the UN International Congress on Women, Forum '85, in Nairobi, this problem and the tendency to medicalize violence were highly visible. But it was also clear that western style shelters are not necessarily the answer for battered women in other cultures. World-wide, women are developing culturally-specific approaches to assisting abused women, while campaigning for greater national and international attention to the issue. See *Isis International*, 1988.
6   As men who counsel battering men have observed, many violent men seem to realize the enormous price of violence only after they have lost their spouse. See Adams (1988).
7   Durkheim (1951) noted nearly a century ago that marriage is less advantageous for women than it is for men (see also Chapman and Gates 1977; Turner and Avison 1987). Still, as Chodorow (1978) and others note, most women are more emotionally invested in marriage than men are.
8   See Campbell (1986), NiCarthy (1986), and Hoff (1989: Chs 5 and 8) for contemporary approaches to such support groups for battered women.

9   See Surgeon General's Report on Violence and Public Health (1986) re-
    garding professionals' responsibilities toward victims of violence.
10 The lag in implementing these recommendations is dramatized by a
    Massachusets legislator's effort legally to require assesment for batter-
    ing in all pre-natal health protocols. This initiative was inspired by
    Charles Stuart's brutal murder of his seven-months pregnant wife, and
    the high incidence of battering among pregnant women (about 20–
    25 per cent).

Chapter ten

1   This and other figures in this chapter represent 1983 housing and income
    values in the US.
2   Five years after this study, this housing picture is essentially unchanged
    except for greater numbers of homeless – now in the thousands – of
    which nearly half are families with children. See Kozol (1988) for a poig-
    nant description of this escalating problem in the United States that is
    associated largely with federal housing and welfare policies; also Hirsch
    (1989) which cites homelessness as a symbol of community failure.
3   Staff from the Elizabeth Stone House in Boston have partially alleviated
    this housing problem with a transitional housing facility for fifty women
    and children leaving their 'Therapeutic Community' and the Battered
    Women's Program. Public and private benefactors made possible this
    innovative programme which opened in 1987. In a metropolitan area of
    four million, however, much more is needed.
4   The dismal failure of this punitive policy was finally recognized and the
    policy changed to one which maintained a woman's public benefits and
    provided child care while women completed training programmes
    which would lead to eventual self-sufficiency. This welfare reform suc-
    cess is now touted as a national example.
5   See Chapter 6, note 1, regarding current inattention to the Abuse Pre-
    vention Act.

Chapter eleven

1   See Chapter 7, note 2, regarding the 'Intergenerational cycle of violence'
    concept; also Chapter 2.
2   See Oakley 1981a for a description of a similar approach used during
    field research with post-partum mothers who asked the researcher for
    advice on various topics. This same process has been the experience of
    anthropologists in the field for years: trusting relationships develop be-
    tween the researcher and participants which leads to the give and take
    common in other relationships of trust. In research, my prior training as
    a therapist was helpful in keeping clear the distinction between this and
    therapy processes.
3   See Ruddick (1989) for an in-depth analysis of the work of mothering,
    'preservative love', and its relationship to violence and the politics of

peace. Ruddick's work supports that of other feminists (e.g. Segal 1987) who contest the sociobiological view that the lower incidence of violence by women can be traced to innate rather than social factors.

4   See Chesler (1986) for the growing trend of awarding custody on grounds of most fathers' *economic* advantages, regardless of their prior or current role in parenting.

5   Conflict over visitation rights continued for four more years and was finally resolved in the mother's favour when the father sexually molested the oldest child.

6   This finding evokes a classic debate regarding law and values: whether laws should be passed to affirm and uphold the values of the majority, as laws will be empty if people do not believe in what they represent; or whether laws should be passed to represent an *ideal* not yet achieved and thus assist in the process of changing people's beliefs and practices in the direction of the ideal (Maine 1870). The relevance of this law-values debate for this research is exemplified in the class action suits brought against police departments for failing to enforce the legal rights of domestic violence victims. Recent rulings in favour of battered women in several US city jurisdictions have led some departments to voluntarily change their policies without litigation (Gee 1983: 554–67). One can assume that some individual police officers still espouse traditional beliefs about woman battering, but in this instance the law is a vehicle for changing practice to conform to a new ideal.

7   See the original work (Hoff 1984b) for a detailed description of this 'typical week'.

8   There are, of course, some exceptions to this general pattern, in which fathers are left with little or nothing for self-support. That this is an exception, however, is attested by the efforts of the Federal government to enforce court ordered child support, and statistical evidence that the majority of poor people in this country – and world-wide – are women and children in female headed households. This is sometimes referred to as the 'feminization of poverty'. The Federal government's recent concern with enforcement of child support obligations should not be construed as pro-woman activity. Rather, it reflects the government's concern in being less responsible for various entitlement programmes.

9   Research is needed to explore the relationship between men's need to control and dominate women and their primary rearing by mothers (Hartsock 1983: 299–301). If such a relationship exists, it would not imply that mothers are to be blamed, but rather, it suggests further examination of a social custom that is so entrenched it is assumed to be 'natural', but which may have far-reaching damaging effects for the entire society (Flax 1983; Hubbard 1983).

10 The work of this Collective is also important in undoing the stereotype of gay men as child abusers, when the reality is that most sexual abuse of children is committed by fathers against daughters (Herman 1981).

Notes

Epilogue

1　Three months after this interview, this woman told me she was engaged to marry, and feels more confident that she is now avoiding some of her previous self-defeating behaviours in relationships with men.

Appendix

1　Such studies have been done by feminist anthropologists examining other issues pertaining to women; none of these, however, have focused on violence in the marital relationship. Since completing this study, anthropologist Dorothy Counts (1987) has reported case studies on the relationship between suicide and wife-abuse in the West New Britain Province of Papua New Guinea.

2　Readers are referred to the original research report (Hoff 1984b: Appendix A) for details and process analysis concerning the 'problem of access' to these potential sources. While experienced field researchers will find familiar themes in this account, the material may particularly interest those examining the 'research process' as a topic in itself.

3　Recent (1988) conversation with a member of the shelter Collective revealed that, while still very cautious about researchers, the Collective's attitude toward them has relaxed somewhat.

4　Chatwin (1988) elaborates on this issue as 'First, Second and Third Degree Ethics in Anthropology'.

References

Adams, D. (1988) 'Counseling men who batter: a pro-feminist analysis of five treatment models', in *Feminist Perspectives on Wife Abuse*, K. Yllo and M. Bograd (eds), Newbury Park, CA: Sage.

Adams, R.N. (1981) 'Ethical principles in anthropological research: one or many?' *Human Organization: Journal of the Society for Applied Anthropology*, 2: 155–60.

Agar, M. (1980) 'Stories, background knowledge and themes: problems in the analysis of life history narrative', *American Ethnologist*, 7: 223–36.

Ahrens, L. (1987) 'Battered women's refuges: feminist cooperatives vs. social service institutions', *Radical America*, 14: 41–7.

Antonovsky, A. (1987) *Health, Stress and Coping*, San Francisco: Jossey-Bass.

Atkinson, J.M. (1978) *Discovering Suicide: Studies in the Social Organization of Sudden Death*, Pittsburgh: University of Pittsburgh Press.

Barnes, J.A. (1972) *Social Networks*, Reading, MA: Addison-Wesley.

Barrett, M. and McIntosh, M. (1982) *The Anti-social Family*, London: Verso Editions/NLB.

Barry, K. (1979) *Female Sexual Slavery*, New York: Avon Books.

Bateson, M.C. and Goldsby, R. (1988) *Thinking AIDS: The Social Response to the Biological Threat*, Reading, MA: Addison-Wesley.

Battin, M.P. and Mayo, D.J. (eds) (1980) *Suicide: The Philosophical Issues*, New York: St Martin's Press.

Becker, H. (1963) *Outsiders*, New York: Free Press.

Benson, D. and Hughes, J.A. (1983) *The Perspective of Ethnomethodology*, London: Longman.

Berger, B. and Berger, P.L. (1983) *The War over the Family: Capturing the Middle Ground*, Garden City: Anchor Press/Doubleday.

Berger, P.L. and Kellner, H. (1981) *Sociology Reinterpreted*, New York: Anchor Books.

Berger, P.L. and Luckmann, T. (1967) *The Social Construction of Reality*, New York: Anchor/Doubleday.

Berkman, L.F. and Syme, S.L. (1979) 'Social networks, host resistance, and

mortality: a nine-year follow-up study of Alemeda County residents',
American Journal of Epidemiology, 109: 186–204.

Berman, L. (1983) 'Survey of professional schools', Committee Report to
American Association of Suicidology Board of Directors, Central Office, Denver.

Bernstein, R.J. (1978) *The Restructuring of Social and Political Theory*, Philadelphia: University of Pennsylvania Press.

Blau, F.D. (1981) 'On the role of values in feminist scholarship', *Signs: Journal of Women in Culture and Society*, 6: 538–40.

Bleier, R. (1984) *Science and Gender: A Critique of Biology and Its Theories on Women*, New York: Pergamon Press.

Bloch, M. (1977) 'The past and the present in the present', *Man*, 12: 278–92.

Bograd, M. (1984) 'Family systems approaches to wife battering: a feminist critique', *American Journal of Orthopsychiatry*, 54(4): 558–68.

Boissevain, J. (1979) 'Network analysis: a reappraisal', *Current Anthropology*, 20(2): 392–4.

Borkowski, M., Murch, M., and Walker, V. (1983) *Marital Violence: The Community Response*, London: Tavistock.

Boserup, E. (1970) *Women's Role in Economic Development*, New York: St Martin's Press.

Bott, E. (1957) *Family and Social Networks*, London: Tavistock.

Breines, W. and Gordon, L. (1983) 'The new scholarship on family violence', *Signs: Journal of Women in Culture and Society*, 8: 490–531.

Brim, O.G. and Ryff, C.D. (1980) 'On the properties of life events', *Life-Span Development and Behavior*, 3: 367–88.

Brosnan, J.A. (1976)'A proposed diabetic educational program for Puerto Ricans in New York City', in: *Transcultural Nursing*, P.J. Brink (ed.), Englewood Cliffs, NJ: Prentice-Hall.

Brown, G.W. and Harris, T. (1978) *The Social Origins of Depression*, London: Tavistock.

Browne, A. (1987) *When Battered Women Kill*, New York: Free Press.

Burden, D. and Googins, B. (1984) Preliminary Research Findings reported in 'The World'. Boston: Boston University School of Social Work.

Burridge, K. (1960) *Mambu*, Great Britain: Camelot Press.

Burridge, K. (1969) *New Heaven, New Earth*, Oxford: Basil Blackwell.

Campbell, J. (1986) 'A survivor group for battered women', *Advances in Nursing Science*, 8(2): 13–20.

Caplan, G. (1964) *Principles of Preventive Psychiatry*, New York: Basic Books.

Caplan, G. (1974) *Support Systems and Community Mental Health*, New York: Behavioral Publications.

Caplan, G. (1981) 'Mastery of stress: psychosocial aspects', *American Journal of Psychiatry*, 138: 413–20.

Caplan, G. and Grunebaum, H. (1967) 'Perspectives on primary prevention: a review', *Archives of General Psychiatry*, 17: 331–46.

Chapman, J.R. and Gates, M. (1977) *Women into Wives: The Legal and Economic Impact of Marriage*, Beverly Hills, CA: Sage.

Chapple, E.D. and Coon, C.S. (1942) *Principles of Anthropology*, New York: Henry Holt & Co.
Chatwin, M.E. (1988) 'Subtle interaction: first, second and third degree ethics in anthropology', *Human Organization: Journal of the Society for Applied Anthropology*, 47(2): 176–80.
Chesler, P. (1972) *Women and Madness*, New York: Doubleday.
Chesler, P. (1986) *Mothers on Trial: The Battle for Children and Custody*, Seattle: Seal Press.
Chodorow, N. (1978) *The Reproduction of Mothering: Psychoanalysis and the Sociology of Gender*, Berkeley: University of California Press.
Cicourel, A.V. (1964) *Method and Measurement in Sociology*, New York: Free Press.
Cicourel, A.V. (1981) 'Notes on the integration of micro- and macro-levels of analysis', in: *Advances in Social Theory and Methodology*, K. Knorr-Cetina and A.V. Cicourel (eds), London and Boston: Routledge & Kegan Paul.
Cloward, R.A. and Piven, F.F. (1979) 'Hidden protest: the channeling of female innovation and resistance', *Signs: Journal of Women in Culture and Society*, 4: 651–69.
Cobb, S. (1976) 'Social support as a moderator of life stress', *Psychosomatic Medicine*, 38: 300–14.
Cohn, N. (1957) *Pursuit of the Millennium*, London: Secker & Warburg.
Coulter, J. (1979a) 'Beliefs and practical understanding', in: *Everyday Language: Studies in Ethnomethodology*, G. Psathas (ed.), New York: Irvington Publishers.
Coulter, J. (1979b) *The Social Construction of Mind*, Totowa, N.J.: Rowman & Littlefield.
Counts, D. (1987) 'Female suicide and wife abuse: a cross-cultural perspective', *Suicide and Life-threatening Behavior*, 17(3): 194–204.
Crary, E. (1979) *Without Spanking or Spoiling*, Seattle: Parenting Press.
Daly, M. (1973) *Beyond God the Father*, Boston: Beacon Press.
Daly, M. (1978) *Gyn/Ecology: The Metaethics of Radical Feminism*, Boston: Beacon Press.
Daniels, A.K. (1978) 'The social construction of military psychiatric diagnosis', in: *Symbolic Interaction* (3rd edn), Jerome G. Manis and Bernard N. Meltzer (eds), Boston: Allyn & Bacon.
Danish, S.J., Smyer, M.A., and Nowak, C.A. (1980) 'Developmental intervention: enhancing life-event processes', *Life-Span Development and Behavior*, 3: 339–66.
Davidson, T. (1977) 'Wifebeating: a recurring phenomenon throughout history', in: *Battered Women: A Psychosociological Study of Domestic Violence*, M. Roy (ed.), New York: Van Nostrand Reinhold Co.
Dexter, L.A. (1958) 'A note on selective inattention in social science', *Social Problems*, 6: 176–82.
Dinnerstein, D. (1977) *The Mermaid and the Minotaur: Sexual Arrangements and Human Malaise*, New York: Harper Colophon Books.
Dobash, R.P. and Dobash, R.E. (1979) *Violence Against Wives: A Case Against the Patriarchy*, New York: Free Press.

271

References

Douglas, J.D. (ed.) (1970) *Understanding Everyday Life*, Chicago: Aldine.

Douglas, M. (1966) *Purity and Danger*, London: Routledge & Kegan Paul.

Durkheim, E. (1951) *Suicide*, New York: Free Press.

duToit, B.M. (1980) 'Ethics, informed consent, and fieldwork', *Journal of Anthropological Research*, 36: 274–86.

Ehrenreich, B. and Ehrenreich, J. (1970) *The American Health Empire: Power, Profits, and Politics*, New York: Random House.

Ehrenreich, B. and English, D. (1979) *For Her Own Good: 150 Years of the Experts' Advice to Women*, New York: Anchor Books.

Ehrenreich, J. (ed.) (1978) *The Cultural Crisis of Modern Medicine*, New York: Monthly Review Press.

Eisenstein, Z.R. (ed.) (1979) *Capitalist Patriarchy and the Case for Socialist Feminism*, New York: Monthly Review Press.

Elshtain, J.B. (1981) *Public Man, Private Woman: Women in Social and Political Thought*, Princeton, N.J.: Princeton University Press.

Erikson, E. (1963) *Childhood and Society* (2nd edn), New York: W.W. Norton.

Farberow, N. (1981) 'Suicide prevention in hospitals', *Hospital and Community Psychiatry*, 32: 99–104.

Federal Bureau of Investigation (1982) *Crime in the United States*, Washington DC: US Dept. of Justice.

Flax, J. (1983) 'Political philosophy and the patriarchal unconscious: a psychoanalytic perspective on epistemology and metaphysics', in: *Discovering Reality*, S. Harding and M.B. Hintikka (eds), Dordrecht, Holland and Boston, US: D. Reidel.

Freidson, E. (1970) *Profession of Medicine*, New York: Harper & Row.

Freud, S. (1950) *Totem and Taboo*, London: Routledge & Kegan Paul.

Frieze, I.H. (1983) 'Investigating the causes and consequences of marital rape', *Signs: Journal of Women in Culture and Society*, 8: 532–53.

Fromm-Reichmann, F. and Gunst, V.K. (1973) 'On the denial of women's sexual pleasure', in: *Psychoanalysis and Women*, J.B. Miller (ed.), New York: Brunner/Mazel.

Garrison, J. (1974) 'Network techniques: case studies in the screening-linking-planning conference method', *Family Process*, 13: 337–53.

Gee, P.W. (1983) 'Ensuring police protection for battered women: the Scott v. Hart suit', *Signs: Journal of Women in Culture and Society*, 8: 554–67.

Geertz, C. (1973) *The Interpretation of Cultures: Selected Essays by Clifford Geertz*, New York: Basic Books.

Gelles, R.J. (1974) *The Violent Home*, Beverly Hills, CA: Sage.

Gelles, R.J. and Cornell, C.P. (1985) *Intimate Violence in Families*, Beverly Hills: Sage.

Gelles, R.J. and Straus, M.A. (1979) 'Determinants of violence in the family: toward a theoretical integration', in: *Contemporary Theories about the Family*, Vol.2, W.R. Burr *et al.* (eds), New York: Free Press.

Gergen, K.J. (1982) *Toward Transformation in Social Knowledge*, New York: Springer-Verlag.

Gerhardt, U. (1979) 'Coping and social action: theoretical reconstruction of the life-event approach', *Sociology of Health and Illness*, 1: 195–225.

272

Gibbs, L. (1982) *Love Canal – My Story*, Albany: State University of New York Press.

Giddens, A. (1979) *Central Problems in Social Theory*, Berkeley: University of California Press.

Giddens, A. (1983) *Profiles and Critiques in Social Theory*, Berkeley: University of California Press.

Gil, D.G. (1987) 'Sociocultural aspects of domestic violence', in: *Violence in the Home: Interdisciplinary Perspectives*, M. Lystad (ed.), New York: Brunner/Mazel.

Giles-Sims, J. (1983) *Wife Battering: A Systems Theory Approach*, New York: Guilford Press.

Gilligan, C. (1982) *In a Different Voice*, Boston: Harvard University Press.

Giovannini, M.J. (1983) Personal communication.

Goffman, E. (1961) *Asylums*, New York: Anchor Books.

Goffman, E. (1963) *Stigma: Notes on the Management of Spoiled Identity*, Englewood Cliffs, N.J.: Prentice-Hall.

Golan, N. (1969) 'When is a client in crisis?' *Social Casework*, 50: 389–94.

Goldberg, S. (1973/74) *The Inevitability of Patriarchy*, New York: William Morrow.

Goode, W. (1971) 'Force and violence in the family', *Journal of Marriage and the Family*, 33: 624–36.

Goody, J. (1962) *Death, Property and the Ancestors*, London: Tavistock.

Gordon, L. (1988) *Heroes of Their Own Lives: The Politics and History of Family Violence*, New York: Viking Press.

Gottlieb, B.H. (ed.) (1981) *Social Networks and Social Support*, Beverly Hills, CA: Sage.

Gove, W. (1978) 'Sex differences in mental illness among adult men and women: an examination of four questions raised regarding whether or not women actually have higher rates', *Social Science and Medicine*, 12: 187–98.

Granovetter, M.S. (1973) 'The strength of weak ties', *American Journal of Sociology*. 78: 1360–80.

Gross, M. and Averill, M.B. (1983) 'Evolution and patriarchal myths of scarcity and competition', in: *Discovering Reality*, S. Harding and M.B. Hintikka (eds), Dordrecht, Holland and Boston, US: D. Reidel.

Hagey, R. and McDonough, P. (1984) 'The problem of professional labeling', *Nursing Outlook*, 32(3): 151–7.

Halleck, S.L. (1987) *The Mentally Disordered Offender*, Washington DC: American Psychiatric Press.

Hansell, N. (1976) *The Person in Distress*, New York: Human Sciences Press.

Harding, S. and Hintikka, M.B. (eds) (1983) *Discovering Reality*, Dordrecht, Holland and Boston, US: D. Reidel.

Hart, B.J. (1983) 'Memorandum regarding Attorney General's Task Force Recommendations', Harrisburg, PA: Pennsylvania Coalition against Domestic Violence, 14 December.

Hart, H.L.A. (1951) 'The ascription of responsibility and rights', in: *Essays on Logic and Language*, A. Flew (ed.), New York: Philosophical Library.

Hartmann, H.I. (1981) 'The family as the locus of gender, class and political struggle: the example of housework', *Signs: Journal of Women in Culture and Society*, 6: 366–94.

Hartsock, N.C.M. (1983) 'The feminist standpoint: developing the grounds for a specifically feminist historical materialism', in: *Discovering Reality*, S. Harding and M.B. Hintikka (eds), Dordrecht, Holland and Boston, US: D. Reidel.

Hayden, D. (1981) *The Grand Domestic Revolution*, Cambridge, MA and London: MIT Press.

Hedin, B.A. (1986) 'A case study of oppressed group behavior in nurses', *Image*, 18(2): 53–7.

Helm, D.T. (1981) *Conferring Membership: Interacting with 'Incompetents'*, PhD dissertation, Boston: Boston University.

Herman, J. (1981) *Father-Daughter Incest*, Cambridge, MA: Harvard University Press.

Hilberman, E. (Carmen) (1980) 'Overview: the "wife beater's wife" reconsidered', *American Journal of Psychiatry*, 137: 1336–47.

Hilberman, E. and Munson, K. (1977/78) 'Sixty battered women', *Victimology*, 2: 460–70.

Hirsch, K. (1989) *Songs from the Alley*, New York: Ticknor & Fields.

Hoff, L.A. (1984a, 3rd edn 1989) *People in Crisis*, Menlo Park, CA: Addison-Wesley.

Hoff, L.A. (1984b) *Violence against Women: A Social-cultural Network Analysis*, PhD dissertation, Boston: Boston University (No. 8422380, Ann Arbor, MI: University Microfilms International).

Hoff, L.A. (1985) 'Book review: *Suicidal Women: Their Thinking and Feeling Patterns*', by C. Neuringer and D. Lettieri (1982), New York: Gardner Press. *Suicide and Life-Threatening Behavior*, 15(1): 69–73.

Hoff, L.A. (1990) 'History of human abuse and nursing's response', in: *Anthropology and Nursing*, P. Holden and J. Littlewood (eds), London: Routledge.

Hoff, L.A. and Miller, N. (1987) *Programs for People in Crisis: A Guide for Educators, Administrators, and Clinical Trainers*, Boston: Northeastern University Custom Book Service.

Holmes, T.H. and Rahe, R.H. (1967) 'The social readjustment rating scale', *Psychosomatic Medicine*, 11: 213–18.

Holmstrom, L.L. and Burgess, A.W. (1978) *The Victim of Rape: Institutional Reactions*, New York: John Wiley & Sons.

Howell, M.C. (1978) 'Pediatricians and mothers', in: *The Cultural Crisis of Modern Medicine*, J. Ehrenreich (ed.), New York: Monthly Review Press.

Hubbard, R. (1983) 'Have only men evolved?' in: *Discovering Reality*, S. Harding and M.B. Hintikka (eds), Dordrecht, Holland and Boston, US: D. Reidel.

Illich, I. (1976) *Limits to Medicine: Medical Nemesis – The Expropriation of Health*, Middlesex, England: Penguin Books.

Isis International (1988) 'Campaigns: putting an end to domestic violence', *Women's Health Journal*, March–June: 26–37.

Jones, A. (1980) *Women Who Kill*, New York: Holt, Rinehart & Winston.

Kaplan, A.G. (1984) 'Female or male psychotherapists for women: new formulations', in: *Work in Progress*, Stone Center for Developmental Services and Studies, Wellesley, MA: Wellesley College.

Kaplan, B.H., Cassel, J., and Gore, S. (1977) 'Social support', *Medical Care*, 15: 47–58.

Keller, E.F. (1983) 'Gender and science', in: *Discovering Reality*, S. Harding and M.B. Hintikka (eds), Dordrecht, Holland and Boston, US: D. Reidel.

Keller, E.F. (1985) *Reflections on Gender and Science*, New Haven and London: Yale University Press.

Kelly, M.P.F. (1981) 'The sexual division of labor, development, and women's status', *Current Anthropology*, 22: 414–19.

Kempe, H. and Heffer, R.E. (1980) *The Battered Child* (3rd edn), Chicago: University of Chicago Press.

Kepferer, B. (1969) 'Norms and the manipulation of relationships in a work context', in: *Social Networks in Urban Situations*, J.C. Mitchell (ed.), Manchester: University of Manchester Press.

Kimball, S.T. (1960) 'Introduction to *Rites of Passage* (1909) by A. van Gennep, Chicago: University of Chicago Press.

Knorr-Cetina, K. and Cicourel, A.V. (eds) (1981) *Advances in Social Theory and Methodology*, London and Boston: Routledge & Kegan Paul.

Kozol, J. (1988) *Rachel and Her Children: Homeless Families in America*, New York: Crown Publishers.

Kurz, D. and Stark, E. (1988) 'Not-so-benign neglect: the medical response to battering', in: *Feminist Perspectives on Wife Abuse*, K. Yllo and M. Bograd (eds), Newbury Park, CA: Sage.

LaBell, L.S. (1977) 'Wife abuse: a sociological study of battered women and their mates', *Victimology*, 4: 258–67.

LaFontaine, J.S. (1981) 'The domestication of the savage male', *Man*, 16/3: 333–49.

Lasch, C. (1977) *Haven in a Heartless World: The Family Besieged*, New York: Norton.

Leach, E. (1976) *Culture and Communication*, Cambridge: Cambridge University Press.

Leghorn, L. and Parker, K. (1981) *Woman's Worth: Sexual Economics and the World of Women*, London and Boston: Routledge & Kegan Paul.

Lemert, E. (1962) 'Paranoia and the dynamics of exclusion', *Sociometry*, 25: 2–20.

Levine, D.N. (1971) *Georg Simmel: On Individuality and Social Forms*, Chicago and London: University of Chicago Press.

Lewis, I.M. (1971) *Ecstatic Religion*, Middlesex, England: Penguin Books.

Lindemann, E. (1944) 'Symptomatology and management of acute grief', *American Journal of Psychiatry*, 101: 101–48 (reprinted (1965) in *Crisis Intervention: Selected Readings*, H.J. Parad (ed.), New York: Family Service Association of America).

Lindsey, K. (1981) *Friends as Family*, Boston: Beacon Press.

Lopata, H.Z. (1973) *Widowhood in an American City*, Cambridge, MA: Schenkman Publishing Co.

Maine, H. (1870) *Ancient Law*, London: John Murray.

MacCormack, C. and Strathern, M. (eds) (1980) *Nature, Culture and Gender*, Cambridge: Cambridge University Press.

Martin, D. (1976) *Battered Wives*, San Francisco: Glide Publications.

Maslow, A. (1970) *Motivation and Personality* (2nd edn), New York: Harper & Row.

Maxwell, M.B. (1982) 'The use of social networks to help cancer patients maximize support', *Cancer Nursing*, 5: 275–81.

McGee, R. (1974) *Crisis Intervention in the Community*, Baltimore: University Park Press.

McKinlay, J.B. (1973) 'Social networks, lay consultation and help-seeking behavior', *Social Forces*, 51: 275–92.

McKinlay, J.B. (1979) 'A case for refocusing upstream: The political economy of illness', in *Patients, Physicians and Illness* (3rd edn.), E.G. Jaco, (ed.), New York: Free Press.

McKinlay, J.B. (1981) 'Social network influences on morbid episodes and the career of help-seeking', in: *The Relevance of Social Science for Medicine*, D.Eisenberg and A. Kleinman (eds), The Hague: Reidel.

Melick, M.E., Steadman, H.J., and Cocozza, J.J. (1979) 'The medicalization of criminal behavior among mental patients', *Journal of Health and Social Behavior*, 20: 228–37.

Merchant, C. (1980) *The Death of Nature: Women, Ecology and the Scientific Revolution*, New York: Harper & Row.

Miller, D. and Challas, G. (1981) 'Abused children as adult parents: a twenty-five year longitudinal study', paper presented at the National Conference for Family Violence Researchers (21–24 July), Durham, N.H.: University of New Hampshire.

Miller, J.B. (1976) *Toward a New Psychology of Women*, Boston: Beacon Press.

Millet, K. (1970) *Sexual Politics*, New York: Doubleday.

Mills, C.W. (1959) *The Sociological Imagination*, London: Oxford University Press.

Mills, T.L. (1982) *Violence and the Self*, unpublished PhD dissertation, Chapel Hill: University of North Carolina.

Mitchell, J. Clyde (ed.) (1969) *Social Networks in Urban Situations*, Manchester: Manchester University Press.

Mitchell, J. and Oakley, A. (eds) (1986) *What is Feminism?: A Re-examination*, New York: Pantheon.

Mogul, K.M. (1982) 'Overview: the sex of the therapist', *American Journal of Psychiatry*, 139: 1–11.

Monahan, J. (1981) *The Clinical Prediction of Violent Behavior*, Rockville, Md.: The National Institute of Mental Health.

Moulton, J. (1983) 'A paradigm of philosophy: the adversary method', in: *Discovering Reality*, S. Harding and M.B. Hintikka (eds), Dordrecht, Holland and Boston, US: D. Reidel.

Mousnier, R. (1969) *Social Hierarchies*, London: Croom Helm (trans.).

Moynihan, D.P. (1965) *The Negro Family: A Case for National Action*, Washington DC: US Government Printing Office.

Neuringer, C. and Lettieri, D.J. (1982) *Suicidal Women: Their Thinking and Feeling Patterns*, New York: Gardner Press.

Newberger, E. (1980) 'New approaches needed to control child abuse', paper presented before the Subcommittee on Select Education of the Committee on Education and Labor, Washington DC: United States House of Representatives.

NiCarthy, G. (1986) *Getting Free: A Handbook for Women in Abusive Relationships*, Seattle: Seal Press.

Norbeck, J.S., Lindsey, A.M., and Carrieri, V.L. (1981) 'The development of an instrument to measure social support', *Nursing Research*, 30(5): 264–9.

Oakley, A. (1981a) 'Interviewing women: a contradiction in terms', in: *Doing Feminist Research*, H. Roberts (ed.), London: Routledge & Kegan Paul.

Oakley, A. (1981b) *Subject Women: Where Women Stand Today – Politically, Economically, Socially, Emotionally*, New York: Pantheon Books.

Okin, S.M. (1979) *Women in Western Political Thought*, Princeton, N.J.: Princeton University Press.

O'Neill, N. and O'Neill, G. (1972) *Open Marriage*, New York: M. Evans.

Orlinsky, D.E. and Howard, K.I. (1978) 'The relation of process to outcome in psychotherapy', in: *Handbook of Psychotherapy and Behavior Change: An Empirical Analysis* (2nd edn), S.L. Garfield and A.E. Gergin (eds), New York: Wiley.

Ortner, S.B. (1974) 'Is female to male as nature is to culture?' in: *Woman, Culture and Society*, M.Z. Rosaldo and L. Lamphere (eds), Stanford: Stanford University Press.

Pagelow, M.D. (1981) *Woman-Battering: Victims and Their Experiences*, Beverly Hills: Sage.

Parkes, C.M. (1975) *Bereavement*, Middlesex, England: Penguin Books.

Pearlin, L.I. and Schooler, C. (1978) 'The structure of coping', *Journal of Health and Social Behavior*, 19: 2–21.

Phillips, D.L. (1973) *Abandoning Method*, San Francisco: Jossey-Bass.

Pitkin, H. (1972) *Wittgenstein and Justice*, Berkeley: University of California Press.

Pizzey, E. (1977) *Scream Quietly or the Neighbors Will Hear*, Short Hills, N.J.: Ridley Enslow Publishers. (First published by Penguin Books, 1974.)

Polak, P.R. (1967) 'The crisis of admission', *Social Psychiatry*, 2: 150–7.

Polak, P.R. (1971) 'Social systems intervention', *Archives of General Psychiatry*, 25: 110–17.

Poster, M. (1978) *Critical Theory of the Family*, New York: Seabury Press.

Raphael, D. (1975) 'Women and power: introductory notes', in: *Being Female: Reproduction, Power and Change*, Dana Raphael (ed.), The Hague: Mouton.

Rapp, R. (1978) 'Family and class in contemporary America: notes toward an understanding of ideology', *Science and Society*, 42: 278–300.

Rapp, R. (1979) 'Anthropology: review essay', *Signs: Journal of Women in Culture and Society*, 4: 497–513.

Reinharz, S. (1979) *On Becoming a Social Scientist*, San Francisco: Jossey-Bass.

Reiter, R.R. (ed.) (1975) *Toward an Anthropology of Women*, New York: Monthly Review Press.

Reverby, S. (1987) *Ordered to Care*, Cambridge: Cambridge University Press.

Riddle, D. (1974/75) 'New visions of spiritual power', *Quest*, 1: 7–16.

Rieker, P. and Carmen (Hilberman), E. (1984) *The Gender Gap in Psychotherapy: Social Realities and Psychological Processes*, New York: Plenum.

Rieker, P. and Carmen (Hilberman), E. (1986) 'The victim-to-patient process: the disconfirmation and transformation of abuse', *American Journal of Orthopsychiatry*, 56: 360–71.

Roberts, H. (ed.) (1981) *Doing Feminist Research*, London: Routledge & Kegan Paul.

Robinson, D. (1971) *The Process of Becoming Ill*, London: Routledge & Kegan Paul.

Rounsaville, B.J. (1978) 'Theories on marital violence: evidence from a study of battered women', *Victimology*, 3: 11–31.

Rowbotham, S. (1973) *Woman's Consciousness, Man's World*, Middlesex, England: Penguin Books.

Roy, M. (ed.) (1977) *Battered Women: A Psychosociological Study of Domestic Violence*, New York: Van Nostrand Reinhold.

Rubenstein, C. (1982) 'Real men don't earn less than their wives', *Psychology Today*, 16: 36–41.

Ruddick, S. (1989) *Maternal Thinking: Toward a Politics of Peace*, Boston: Beacon Press.

Russell, D. (1982) *Rape in Marriage*, New York: Collier Books.

Russell, D. (1986) *The Secret Trauma: Incest in the Lives of Girls and Women*, New York: Basic Books.

Ryan, W. (1971) *Blaming the Victim*, New York: Vintage Books.

Sacks, H. (1967) 'The search for help: no one to turn to', in: *Essays in Self-destruction*, E. Shneidman (ed.), New York: Aronson.

Sacks, H. (1974) 'On the analysability of stories by children', in: *Ethnomethodology*, R. Turner (ed.), Harmondsworth, England: Penguin.

Sayers, J. (1982) *Biological Politics*, London and New York: Tavistock.

Schechter, S. (1982) *Women and Male Violence*, Boston: South End Press.

Schwartz, H. and Jacobs, J. (1979) *Qualitative Sociology*, New York: Free Press.

Segal, L. (1987) *Is the Future Female? Troubled Thoughts on Contemporary Feminism*, London: Virago Press.

Sherman, L.W. and Berk, R.A. (1983) 'Police responses to domestic assault: preliminary findings', Santa Barbara, CA: University of California.

Shupe, A., Stacey, W.A., and Hazlewood, L.R. (1987) *Violent Men, Violent Couples*, Lexington, MA: Lexington Books.

Sidel, R. (1986) *Women and Children Last: The Plight of Poor Women in Affluent America*, New York: Penguin.

Smith, D.E. (1978) '"K is mentally ill": the anatomy of a factual account', *Sociology*, 12: 23–53.

Smith, D.E. (1987) *The Everyday World as Problematic: A Feminist Sociology*, Boston: Northeastern University Press.

Smith, J. (1981/82) 'Sociobiology and feminism: the very strange courtship of competing paradigms', *Philosophical Forum*, 13: 226–43.

Sommers, T. and Shields, L. (1987) *Women Take Care*, Gainsville, FL: Triad.

Sontag, S. (1979) *Illness as Metaphor*, New York: Vintage Books.

Sontag, S. (1989) *AIDS and Its Metaphors*, New York: Farrar, Straus & Giroux.

Speck, R. and Attneave, C. (1973) *Family Networks*, New York: Pantheon.

Spelman, E.V. (1983) 'Aristotle and the politicization of the soul', in: *Discovering Reality*, S. Harding and M.B. Hintikka (eds), Dordrecht, Holland and Boston, US: D. Reidel.

Spencer, P. (1965) *The Samburu*, London: Routledge & Kegan Paul.

Spencer, P. (1973) *Nomads in Alliance*, Oxford: Oxford University Press.

Spender, D. (1980) *Man Made Language*, London: Routledge & Kegan Paul.

Spiro, M.E. (1967) *Burmese Supernaturalism*, Englewood Cliffs, N.J.: Prentice-Hall.

Stacey, J. (1986) 'Are feminists afraid to leave home? The challenge of conservative pro-family feminism', in *What is Feminism?: A Re-examination*, J. Mitchell and A. Oakley (eds), New York: Pantheon.

Stack, C.B. (1974) *All Our Kin*, New York: Harper & Row.

Stark, E., Flitcraft, A., and Frazier, W. (1979) 'Medicine and patriarchal violence: the social construction of a "private" event', *International Journal of Health Services*, 9: 461–93.

Steinmetz, S.K. (1977a) 'The battered husband syndrome', *Victimology*, 2: 499–509.

Steinmetz, S.K. (1977b) *The Cycle of Violence: Assertive, Aggressive, and Abusive Family Interaction*, New York: Praeger.

Stephens, B.J. (1985) 'Suicidal women and their relationships with husbands, boyfriends, and lovers', *Suicide and Life-Threatening Behavior*, 15(2): 77–90.

Straus, M.A. (1973) 'A general systems theory approach to a theory of violence between family members', *Social Science Information*, 12: 105–25.

Straus, M.A., Gelles, R.J., and Steinmetz, S.K. (1980) *Behind Closed Doors: Violence in the American Family*, New York: Anchor Books.

Surgeon General's Workshop on Violence and Public Health. (1986) *Report*, Washington DC: Health Resources and Services Administration.

Szasz, T. (1970) *The Manufacture of Madness*, New York: Harper & Row.

Therborn, G. (1980) *The Ideology of Power and the Power of Ideology*, London: Verso.

Thomas, W.I. (1931) 'The definition of the situation', in: *Symbolic*

Interaction (3rd edn) J.J. Manis and B.N. Meltzer (eds), (1979) Boston: Allyn & Bacon.

Tiffany, S.W. (1979) 'Women, power, and the anthropology of politics: a review', *International Journal of Women's Studies*, 2: 430–9.

Tolsdorf, C.C. (1976) 'Social networks, support, and coping: an exploratory study', *Family Process*, 15(4): 407–17.

Truax, C.B. and Carkhuff, R.R. (1967) *Toward Effective Counseling and Psychotherapy*, Chicago: Aldine.

Truzzi, M. (ed.) (1974) *Verstehen: Subjective Understanding in the Social Sciences*, Reading, MA: Addison-Wesley.

Turner, R.J. and Avison, W.R. (1987) 'Gender and depression: assessing exposure and vulnerability to life events in a chronically strained population', paper presented at Annual Meeting of American Public Health Association, New Orleans, LA.

Turner, V. (1968) *The Drums of Affliction*, Oxford: Clarendon Press.

US Department of Labor (1983) *Federal Register* (17 February), Washington DC: US Government Printing Office.

van Gennep, A. (1960) *The Rites of Passage*, London: Routledge & Kegan Paul.

Vetterling-Braggin, M., Elliston, F.A., and English, J. (eds) (1972) *Feminism and Philosophy*, Totowa, N.J.: Littlefield, Adams.

Wald, B. (1983) 'Letter to Barbara Hart', 29 Dec., Boston: Emerge.

Walker, L.E. (1979) *The Battered Woman*, New York: Harper Colophon Books.

Wallston, B.S. (1981) 'What are the questions in psychology of women? A feminist approach to research', *Psychology of Women Quarterly*, 5(4): 597–617.

Wardell, L., Gillespie, D.L., and Leffler, A. (1981) 'Science and violence against wives', paper presented at the National Conference for Family Violence Researchers, Durham, N.H.

Warrior, B. (1978) *Working on Wife Abuse* (7th edn), Cambridge, MA.

Warshaw, R. (1988) *I Never Called It Rape*, New York: Harper & Row.

Watson, D.R. (1978) 'Categorization, authorization and blame – negotiation in conversation', *Sociology*, 12: 105–13.

Watson-Franke, M.R. (1980) 'Bias, male and female', *Man*, 15: 377–9.

Weber, M. (1964) *The Theory of Social and Economic Organization*, New York: Free Press.

Williams, B. (1969) 'The idea of equality', in: *Philosophy, Politics and Society*, P. Laslett and W.G. Runciman (eds), Oxford: Basil Blackwell.

Winch, P. (1958) *The Idea of a Social Science and its Relation to Philosophy*, London: Routledge & Kegan Paul.

Withorn, A. (1980) 'Helping ourselves', *Radical America*, 14: 25–39.

Wolfgang, M. (1958) *Patterns in Criminal Homicide*, Philadelphia: University of Pennsylvania Press.

Wolfgang, M. (1986) 'Interpersonal violence and public health: new direction, new challenges', in: Surgeon General's Workshop on Violence and Public Health: *Report*, Washington DC: Health Resources and Services Administration.

Wolfgang, M. and Ferracuti, F. (1967) 'Subculture of violence: a socio-psychological theory', in: *Studies in Homicide*, M. Wolfgang (ed.), New York: Harper & Row.

Woodburn, J. (1982) 'Egalitarian societies', *Man*, 17: 431–51.

Worsley, P. (1968) *The Trumpet Shall Sound* (2nd edn), London: MacGibbon & Kee.

Yllo, K. and Bograd, M. (eds) (1988) *Feminist Perspectives on Wife Abuse*, Beverly Hills: Sage.

Yllo, K. and Straus, M.A. (1981) 'Patriarchy and violence against wives: the impact of structural and normative factors', paper presented at the National Conference for Family Violence Researchers, Durham, N.H.

Name index

Adams, D. 265n
Adams, R.N. 252
Agar, M. 248
Ahrens, L. 157, 251
Antonovsky, A. 23, 66–7, 73, 133, 256n
Atkinson, J.M. 48
Attneave, C. 82, 256n
Averill, M.B. 223
Avison, W.R. 51, 265n

Barnes, J.A. 82–3, 93, 256n
Barrett, M. 10, 98, 115, 126, 262n
Barry, K. 259n
Bateson, M.C. 113
Battin, M.P. 264n
Becker, H. 48, 51
Benson, D. 92, 94, 123, 199
Berger, B, 262n
Berger, P.L. 5, 14, 51, 262n
Berk, R.A. 143
Berkman, L.F. 23, 67, 256n
Berman, L. 105
Bernstein, R.J. 5
Blau, F.D. 257n
Bleier, R. 252
Bloch, M. 261n
Bograd, M. 5, 48, 115
Boissevain, J. 81, 256n, 261n
Boserup, E. 221
Bott, E. 82, 88, 256n
Breines, W. 257n, 260n
Brim, O.G. 67
Brosnan, J.A. 150
Brown, G.W. 28, 51

Browne, A. 54, 69, 247–8
Burden, D. 135, 221
Burgess, A.W. 28
Burridge, K. 264n

Campbell, J. 265n
Caplan, G. 68–9, 71–3, 82, 152, 173, 256n, 261n
Carkhuff, R.R. 105, 112, 159
Carmen (Hilberman), E. 112, 262n
Carrieri, V.L. 256n, 257n, 261n
Cassel, J. 23, 82, 256n
Challas, G. 262n
Chapman, J.R. 43, 260n, 265n
Chapple, E.D. 67
Chatwin, M.E. 268n
Chesler, P. 51, 267n
Chodorow, N. 6, 42, 46, 51, 57, 59, 61, 125, 136, 218, 223, 259n, 265n
Cicourel, A.V. 5, 9, 136, 247
Cloward, R.A. 10, 28, 52, 211
Cobb, S. 23, 256n
Cocozza, J.J. 48
Cohn, N. 264n
Coon, C.S. 67
Cornell, C.P. 126
Coulter, J. 95, 97, 122–3, 136, 192
Counts, D. 259n, 268n
Crary, E. 210

Daly, M. 264n
Daniels, A.K. 48
Danish, S.J. 260n
Davidson, T. 43
Dexter, L.A. 8, 105, 251

Dinnerstein, D. 125, 223
Dobash, R.P. and R.E. 5, 8, 10, 33,
    42–3, 58, 95, 113, 128, 138, 156,
    248–9, 251
Douglas, J.D. 48
Douglas, M. 113
Durkheim, E. 265n
duToit, B.M. 252

Ehrenreich, B. 14, 48, 159
Ehrenreich, J. 14, 48
Eisenstein, Z.R. 256n
Elshtain, J.B. 5, 10, 14, 52, 61, 136,
    199, 218, 223, 251, 256n, 257n
English, D. 48, 159
Erikson, E. 67

Farberow, N. 152
Federal Bureau of Investigation
    (FBI) 7, 200, 247
Ferracuti, F. 138
Flax, J. 169, 267n
Flitcraft, A. 5, 8, 48, 101, 113, 156,
    159, 251, 256n
Frazier, W. 5, 8, 48, 101, 113, 156,
    159, 251, 256n
Freidson, E. 14, 48
Freud, S. 58, 67
Frieze, I.H. 58
Fromm-Reichmann, F. 58

Garrison, J. 82, 256n
Gates, M. 43, 260n, 265n
Gee, P.W. 267n
Geertz, C. 68, 248, 257n
Gelles, R.J. 8–9, 69, 126–7, 132,
    138, 248–50, 258n
Gergen, K.J. 7, 14, 68, 260n
Gerhardt, U. 10, 28, 52, 67, 75, 77
Gibbs, L. 173
Giddens, A. 5, 247
Gil, D.G. 211
Giles-Sims, J. 32, 65
Gillespie, D.L. 6, 250, 252
Gilligan, C. 6, 28, 112
Giovanni, M.J. 67
Goffman, E. 113, 156
Golan, N. 46

Goldberg, S. 130
Goldsby, R. 113
Goode, W. 9
Goody, J. 170
Googins, B. 135, 221
Gordon, L. 257n, 259n, 260n
Gore, S. 23, 82, 256n
Gottlieb, B.H. 256n
Gove, W. 28, 51
Granovetter, M.S. 96, 256n
Gross, M. 223
Grunebaum, H. 73
Gunst, V.K. 58

Hagey, R. 256n
Halleck, S.L. 48
Hansell, N. 23, 69, 82, 114, 152,
    161, 256n
Harding, S. 10, 43, 224, 251
Harris, T. 28, 51
Hart, B.J. 143, 202
Hart, H.L.A. 95
Hartmann, H.I. 135, 221
Hartsock, N.C.M. 267n
Hayden, D. 154, 184
Hazlewood, L.R. 256–7n, 259n
Hedin, B.A. 105
Heffer, R.E. 211
Helm, D.T. 48, 199
Herman, J. 28, 267n
Hilberman (Carmen), E. 30, 48, 73,
    158, 247–8, 251, 260n
Hintikka, M.B. 10, 43, 224, 251
Hirsch, K. 266n
Holmes, T.H. 173
Holmstrom, L.L. 28
Howard, K.I. 112
Howell, M.C. 28
Hubbard, R. 267n
Hughes, J.A. 92, 94, 123, 199

Illich, 48

Jacobs, J. 136
Jones, A. 54, 69

Kaplan, A.G. 112, 155, 263n
Kaplan, B.H. 23, 82, 256n

Subject index

abuse: childhood 24–31, 262n; psychological 128
academics, and activists 4, 6, 169, 233
'access problem' 5–6, 148, 249–50
alcohol 132–3
authority 41–2

bereavement 173–83
biological determinism 128–31
blame 7, 22; self- 38, 46–9, 52–3, 232, 244; victim 7, 22, 46–9, 229, 230, 232, 243, 244
breakdown 258n
burnout 22–3

cargo cults 264–5n
'causes', of violence 5–6
children: abuse of 24–31, 262n; care of 136, 221–5; custody conflicts 136, 205, 212–15; effects of woman-battering 204–6; fostered 205–6; and men 222–5; physical punishment of 126–7, 203, 208–10; in shelters and beyond 206–12
class 134–9; and shelters 151, 162–3
'coherence', sense of 66–73
collaborative research 10, 12–14, 166–9, 233–4
competition, economic 134–5
context, of violence 8–9, 11–12
crime statistics 7, 200, 247
crisis 22, 67–72; definition 67–8; development phases 71–2; origins and resolution 75–8; and shelters 159–60; women as crisis managers 72–5

cultural/social-structural origins of crisis 76–7
culture of violence 126–8
custody of children, conflicts 136, 205, 212–15
'cycle' of violence 24–31, 229

decision-making 63–4; shelter 150–2
depression 32, 51
determinism, biological 128–31
developmental, *vs.* medical paradigms 69–71

'Eileen' 19–20, 187–8, 194
Emerge 143
equality, economic 134–9, 247
ethics, of researching violence against women 248–53
explanation, social 5–6

'Family violence' 115
fathers 222–5; of battered women 118–25
feminism 256n; and academics 4, 6, 169, 243, 247–9; and cargo cults 264–5n; and crime statistics 247; and parenting 223–4; research 4–6, 8, 9–10, 14, 249–53; and shelters 148, 159
follow-up 237–42
formal networks 4, 83, 85–6, 100–15, 230
fostering 205–6

gender and 'innate' aggression 128–31; and stress 52; *see also* men; women

DATE DUE

OCT 23 '96			
OCT 13 '97			
AR 01 05			
Oc 23 07			
GAYLORD			PRINTED IN U.S.A.